Saving The Beautiful Lake

A Quest For Hope

by

Susan Peterson Gateley

Saving The Beautiful Lake

Copyright 2015 by Susan Peterson Gateley
published by Ariel Associates/Whiskey Hill Press
12025 Delling Road Wolcott NY 14590
printed in the United States of America

All rights reserved. No part of this book may be reproduced scanned or distributed in printed or electronic form without permission from the publisher except by a reviewer who may quote brief passages in a review

Acknowledgments
My thanks to all who contributed to our Kickstarter campaign for the video project
Saving The Beautiful Lake

Many individuals, activists, concerned citizens, scientists and sailors assisted in the production of this book. They include Sherri Mason, John Casselman, Ed Mills, Robert O Gorman, Joseph Gardella, Connie Patterson, Ray Stiefel, Jeff and Jodi Andrysick ,Joanne Hameister, Jean Siracusa, Doug and Lois Collins, Bruce Milan, Paul Baines, Emma Lui, the members of the *Sara B* co-op and the quiet man who made this and my other lake related projects possible-Chris Gateley.

note to the reader

This book was the basis for the educational video *Lake Ontario, A Love Story And A Quest for Hope.*
For more information on this work visit my website www.susanpgateley.com and or contact me.

French philosopher Jean Vanier once wrote "Love is not to do things for people. It is not to tell people what to do. It is to reveal." That is the goal of both the video as well as this work. To show the lake's beauty, gifts, our thoughtless use of it, and to reveal an alternate way and possible new relationship with our water.

Table of Contents

How Did Lake Ontario Become So Polluted?..1
1. Adventures In Gasland...11
2. Some Sustainable Solutions..32
3. Dead Birds and Cheap Food..50
4. Cow Power And Other Clean Water Solutions.........................67
5. Water And Power...81
6. Pipelines, Unconventional Oil Plays and the Lake...................100
7. Plastic Is Fantastic But Not In Food and Water......................128
8. The Great Atomic Lake Down In The Dumps.........................150
9. Great Atomic Lake Power and Light and Heavy Water..........171
10. Reweaving The Lake's Web of Life..189
11. The Lake and Climate Change..215
12. Commons Comeback Could It Be Our Last Chance?............237
13. Last word; what can we all do to save our Great Lakes?......257
Notes on Sources Of Information..261

How Did Lake Ontario Become So Polluted?

Near my home the land rises to terminate at the edge of Lake Ontario in a 90 foot bluff. I have spent many hours here seated on a wooden bench with a forest at my back and an inland sea before me. Gazing out over a seemingly limitless expanse of water, I have watched December snow squalls and August thunderstorms move down the lake. I have joined other family members to savor sunsets that closed long lovely summer days. Flocks of mergansers geese and bufflehead ducks sometimes sprinkled winter gray waters before me, and on breezy July afternoons I've been entertained by as many as eight newly fledged eagles as they practice their soaring skills and maneuvers during summer flying school.

"Ontario" is said to mean great or beautiful lake in the language of those who lived here before me. This place of infinite variations on water and skyscapes still remains beautiful to look upon. Yet I also see signs of change, some of them disturbing.

I've been a lake watcher for sixty years. As a toddler taken to the neighbors' beach for picnics and summer swimming, I stumbled over a cobbled shore littered with dried dead sardine-like mooneyes and delighted in flinging wads of soggy seaweed at my long suffering big sister. She usually returned fire with a decisive pelting. In the 1950s even a seagull sighting was worthy of note. The shoreline eagles I see each summer now were long gone, recalled only by an occasional place name like Eagle Creek or Eagle Cliff Farm.

At that time Lake Ontario, like all the other Great Lakes, was feeling the effects of over fishing invasive species and far too much untreated sewage from shoreline towns and cities. Masses of putrid algae a foot thick mixed with rotting alewives that swarmed with hordes of flies covered our neighbor's swim beach after a summer storm churned things up and blew the whole mess ashore. A hundred miles upstream the Niagara River was being enhanced by a stew of toxic chemicals and heavy metals from factory pipes and unregulated dump sites. A little further west Lake Erie had been declared dead.

Back then the summer skies over Buffalo and Hamilton were as often gray as they were blue thanks to pervasive clouds of smog. During occasional family road trips to visit my aunt and uncle in Chicago, I marveled at all the pretty colors of smoke- orange, black, gray, and white coming from the tall chimneys that marked the Buffalo skyline. And in the apple orchards around my house the ever present drone of spring time sprayers pumping out DDT Dieldrin and other persistent killer chemicals was never given a second thought.

I got my hands on a copy of *Silent Spring* when I was in seventh grade. That was in 1964. A few years later Cleveland's Cuyahoga River caught fire. It wasn't the first fire to occur on that sadly polluted river of sludge, oil, tar, and sewage, but this particular blaze did catch the public's attention. Mine had already been caught by Rachael Carson's precise haunting descriptions of convulsing robins and withered roadside flowers. The events on and by Lake Erie along with her book were partly responsible for a surge of legislation and funding for some seriously overdue environmental clean up including the Clean Water Act and the Great Lakes Water Quality Agreement between the U.S.

and Canada.

Gradually Lake Ontario became cleaner. Birds that had been rare or non-existent when I was a kid began coming back. A considerable amount of money and manpower went into re-establishing bald eagle populations in New York State, while other birds like the osprey, the double crested cormorant, and the Caspian tern began returning to the lake's shores without direct human assistance. And the lake's open water recreational fishery got a boost from stocking programs for several species of hatchery raised salmon.

New York's Department of Environmental Conservation (DEC) obtained federal funding to control sea lamprey populations in the 1960s. The DEC shortly thereafter followed Michigan's lead and began stocking various nonnative species of west coast salmon. The theory was that the hungry salmon would gobble up all the excess "mooneyes" as the little alewives that fouled the lake's beaches so badly in the 1950s and 60s were generally called. The salmon did a pretty good clean up job. Today a dead mooneye is a rare sight.

By the 1980s many new and upgraded sewage plants were on line, some of the worst factory discharges has stopped, and clean up of some really ugly Superfund sites was well underway. Anglers were driving from Pennsylvania and New Jersey to fish for Lake Ontario salmon supporting a lake based sport fishing industry worth over 50 million dollars a year in New York State alone, and I saw my first osprey flying over Sodus Bay. Thanks to another invasive species, the filter feeding zebra mussel, the water was looking as clean and clear as I had ever seen it. It appeared that the lake was making a comeback.

But in 2006 I saw my first major outbreak of botulism poisoning among the lake's fish eating birds. Hundreds of dead loons washed up on my area's shoreline. That same year I also began seeing unfamiliar species of dead fish on the neighborhood beach. Some were fish that I had never seen before. Walleyes, freshwater drum, round gobies, and even a burbot showed up along with numerous carp and some bass. Most of the fish were victims of a disease new to the lake called viral hemorrhagic septicemia, a sort of Ebola for fish, that causes them to die from internal bleeding. This particular pathogen hit the lake's fishes pretty hard as they had never before been exposed to it. They had little resistance to the strain of virus that first was documented in the lake's waters around 2005.

That summer it seemed to me that the lake's web of life was being rewoven in new and as yet little understood ways. Thankfully, the botulism and the VHS appeared to fade away. But notice had been served that all was not quite as well with the lake as I had thought.

In early 2013 a group of Michigan University researchers released a stunning graphic of the five Great Lakes, each colored according to the levels of 34 environmental stressors. They published this "threat assessment map" hoping that it would help direct the latest surge of federal funding called the Great Lakes Restoration Initiative for repairs and remediation on the lakes to best effect. The map showed Lakes Superior and Huron colored cobalt blue, still predominantly "unstressed" while Michigan was shaded with intermediate pale blue, green, and cautionary yellow with a few spots of highly stressed red. Even Lake Erie, once declared dead, was only about half "highly stressed". But Lake Ontario was almost solid blood red.

The Beautiful Lake I live and sail on is now the most polluted and impaired of the five magnificent water bodies that together represent a fifth of earth's entire surface fresh water supply. How did this happen? We have spent vast sums of money on research and clean up projects since 1972 when the Great Lakes Water Quality Agreement, an environmental treaty between the U.S. and Canada that attempted to identify and remediate the worst areas of pollution, was signed. Yet, we are losing our lake.

Even before I saw the map, I knew the lake was in trouble. I had seen increasingly frequent toxic blue green algae blooms in both protected bays and the open lake itself, along with those dead fish littering the beach. More outbreaks of botulism had killed more fish eating birds. I had seen a five legged frog near Chimney Bluffs and had swatted one winged blowflies hopping and spinning around the dead fish on two of my neighborhood beaches and on the shores of Canada's Main Duck Island. But the map took me aback. The Great Lakes Restoration Initiative launched in 2010, is the latest of a long list of efforts to clean up the lakes, and has received over a billion dollars so far. Will it help the lake this time? Or is it too late?

You probably suspect that I don't think it's too late since I wrote this book after an exploratory 'fact finding' cruise with our elderly schooner yacht around the lake in 2013. But I do think it's getting very close to 'midnight' on Lake Ontario's ecological doomsday clock. I believe we could be nearing a tipping point as far as the ecosystem goes. I will describe in the following chapters what we saw and what actions and efforts have been taken that have begun to win our lost lake back. But we face a big complex problem as we attempt this restoration. These waters span two nations, eight states, and a Province, plus dozens of towns cities and First Nation jurisdictions all of which are part of the problem and have their own priorities procedures and decision making processes. The piecemeal approach employed so far is progressing slowly. I believe a few fairly simple actions on the part of our two federal governments could go a long ways towards restoration of the Beautiful Lake. But time is short.

Second chance stories of redemption and renewal have great appeal. Some very old and famous tales are still told today on these themes. We like to think we can find our way back home. That we can heal and repair and restore. And working with the amazing resilience of nature, sometimes we can. It's been done in a number of places on a small scale in our Great Lakes watershed. But it's not enough. Our waters are still troubled as I learned during that recent tour aboard the good ship *Sara B*.

We need to embrace a broader approach. The present strategy of remediation is too slow. We continue to lose ground lake wide even as small areas improve. I believe we need to consider a radically different way of doing business, one that elevates renews and empowers an ancient concept, that of the Commons to embrace the entire watershed.

The notion of the Great Lakes as a Commons shared by all and managed for the benefit of its entire living ecosystem, humans included, was first put forth a few years ago. It's a grassroots effort with both American and Canadian participants, and it fits right in with the growing global open source movement. Water is a relationship and a connection that belongs to no one and is essential to everyone's life. Because all people must be involved in the care and responsibility of a common resource, the movement for a Great Lakes Commons is both appropriate and powerful. Water is a public trust and, as the Commons movement says, water also has rights. Our laws must be compatible with those of nature. We violate the 'rights' of water to remain pure and life giving at our own peril.

By applying these principles we can give the lake another chance to re-create itself. At least that is the hope and the goal of an eclectic band of legal scholars, writers, teachers, scientists, and activists, a few of whom you'll meet in these pages.

* * *

In the summer of 2013 I, along with my husband Chris, and Alice, a former sailing student, circumnavigated the lake aboard the schooner *Sara B,* a bit of a commons effort herself thanks to my spouse who believes in open source practice and uses it in his work as a software developer.

Sara B, a thirty eight foot gaff rigged schooner, now owned by The Schooner Sara B LLC, was about to slip over the edge and down to the bottom when we saw her for sale on eBay. After a five year battle with entropy to keep her afloat with the help of four bilge pumps, we attacked her ills and our savings account, gutting the latter, and attempted to stall entropy's advance. We purchased 1500 pounds of resin and fiberglass cloth, a truckload of meranti plywood and pressure treated pine, respirators, Tyvek suits, chemical solvents, chainfalls, trailer tires, steel, and thousands of dollars worth of other odds and ends. We then spent two years doing an unorthodox re-build of the hull with the ownership co-op's help. What emerged from the resin spattered work space was an old wooden boat with a tough re-enforcing shell of fiberglass up to an inch thick on the keel's bottom. Our boat was now strong enough to travel the lake again.

Sara B's unconventional rebuild was a redemption of sorts. Not permanent, but what in this weary old world is? The question, as we embark upon this literary voyage, is can we perform a similar redemption of the lake? We know we can't ever restore it and its sister lakes to the pristine condition that the first Europeans found here. Not any more than the *Sara B* co-op's limited budget could build a new traditional wooden schooner out of top grade tropical hardwoods, grown hackmatack knees, native white oak, and 18 foot long clear grain cedar planks. But nature's resilience is impressive if given half a chance. Just as we gave *Sara B* a new lease on life (admittedly in somewhat modified form from her original condition) we collectively can do the same for Lake Ontario and the other Great Lakes. But we do need to get started.

Back in 2010 Congress passed the first installment of funding for the Great Lakes Restoration Initiative. This was a multi year plan to clean up areas contaminated by toxic chemicals, combat invasive species, restore wetlands and protect near shore waters from polluted runoff. Since then problems have been defined and given priorities through a sort of triage system not unlike our effort for the boat which began with a four page list of 'tasks' (soon revised, then ignored, then ultimately discarded). Now, some of the contaminated harbors rivers and shoreline deposits of chemicals and radioactive materials are being cleaned up. Restoration efforts are bringing sturgeon back to some of our rivers and are hopefully buying time for the endangered American eel, the whitefish, and other icons of our lake. There is lots more to do, but we have made a start.

We got into this mess, one little abuse at a time. Not unlike deferred maintenance on a 60 year old wooden boat, you can only ignore the careless misuse of our watershed's resources for so long before it loses much of its ability to support life. We have cut corners and saved money to enhance the bottom line over the last 200 years on Lake Ontario hoping no one will notice. But Mother Nature noticed. Now we're left with nearshore 'dead zones' devoid of oxygen, outbreaks of murky green water, and in some areas, inedible chemical-laced cancerous fish. This is not where we need to be.

During the 2013 cruise I sought insight as to how Lake Ontario came to be colored so red on that map. Once back on shore, I further explored what was being done about it. First must come awareness of the problem, and the portion of this book based on that trip around the lake explores some of the current and emerging issues that are of greatest concern. But there are ways to start fixing the problems. We'll meet some people and learn of some of the projects now underway that are moving our lake towards a better day. They're doing good work, but they need our help. There is much we can do ourselves. Some of it is as easy as spending a few more dollars at the grocery store. Some of it requires grassroots work and some requires policy changes and governmental action. It's past time to begin the job. Let's get aboard and shove off for *Sara B*'s tour of the lake.

1. Adventures In Gasland

Sara B's longest Lake Ontario cruise began on a calm day in early June as we pointed her bowsprit for the channel from Little Sodus Bay to open water. Her route would take her around most of the lake's 634 mile perimeter over the next three weeks through much rain, some fog, calms and some very hot early summer days. Though Lake Ontario is the smallest of the five Great Lakes by surface area, we had plenty of territory to cover. The lake is 193 miles long and 53 miles across at its widest point. It and its sister lakes contain enough water to cover all the lower forty eight states to a depth of 9.5 feet feet. All that water is a legacy of the half mile thick sheets of ice that once covered the region 10,000 years ago.

Mariners know this is a great lake. Storm winds can kick up twenty foot waves here, and in the days of sail and steam powered commerce thousands of large and small vessels and hundreds of people died on its wave swept shores or slipped beneath the surface to rest in the icy depths far below. Lake Ontario so big that it makes its own weather, and it influences regional climate a hundred miles or more beyond its shores. *Sara B's* homeport lies at the eastern edge of a lake moderated area on the southern coast that is one of the country's most productive fruit belts. More than 20,000 acres of orchards produce about 12 million of bushels of apples here each year thanks to the lake's moderating influence on extreme winter cold and the protection from late spring frosts it provides to fruit trees during blossom time.

When we sail across the lake to Canada on a clear day from Fair

Haven, the distant blue rise of the Tug Hill Plateau marks the lake's end off to starboard. "The Hill" is one of the snowiest places in the U.S. east of the Rockies. Here, lake moisture picked up by west winds is deposited each winter as lake effect snow- up to twelve feet of it in a single storm. The heart of the snowbelt near the town of Redfield averages over 300 inches a year. I sailed with a man a few years ago who lived up there. He told me that one year he still had a little patch of snow under his deck on the north side of his house in June.

Water as far as the eye could see stretched before us on our day of departure, with nary a ripple from lake generated wind to fill our sails. Yet that seemingly limitless amount of liquid before us represents a tiny fraction of earth's water supply. Nearly all our planetary water is either salty, locked up as ice, or is concealed underground. Easily accessible surface fresh water in lakes and rivers is exceedingly rare and makes up far less than one percent of the world's total.

The Great Lakes contain a fifth of all that surface freshwater, making them of truly global importance. On this gentle June day as *Sara B* traveled along under diesel power, she carried her crew upon the largest freshwater ecosystem in the world. About thirty four million people live within the Great Lakes basin. It's an ecosystem that along with the St. Lawrence encompasses two nations, eight states, two provinces and more than forty tribes of First Nation peoples. Little wonder the politics of restoration here are so formidable.

Thinking back to a cross country drive through three of the continent's great deserts I made a few months before the cruise, I marveled to Alice, our shipmate, at the sight of so much drinking water.

However, the seemingly limitless supply around us was an illusion. The Great Lakes are a virtually closed hydrologic system. Only about one percent of the water within them enters or leaves each year. The other 99% recirculates within the watershed-evaporating, precipitating then vaporizing and moving aloft again in that amazing purifying dance of life we call the hydrologic cycle. Remove any more than that to irrigate orchards or fill swimming pools or frack gas wells, and the white bathtub ring so prominent on Lake Mead these days will soon appear. In just thirty years the Aral Sea in south central Asia, a body of water nearly the size of Lake Erie, was almost drained dry by irrigation.

Our first port of call was the hamlet of Pultneyville. *Sara B* chugged down the channel and into its tiny harbor late on a Sunday afternoon. A swarm of memories surfaced like the lake's annual spring midge hatch as I looked at the sandy beach just east of the creek mouth. I had entered this small backwater hundreds of times. Pultneyville where I learned to sail, had been my home port for over twenty years, and the harbor looked reassuringly little changed. A few members of the boat club where I had once kept my wooden sloop "*Ariel*" paused from packing up their picnics and camping gear to stare at the old gaffer as she glided past them. Ah yes, the WTF look, we said to Alice. You get a lot of those when you sail on *Sara B.*

Perhaps our antique boat looked like a ghost from the past to some of the boaters on shore, for this small harbor was rich in maritime lore and lake faring memories. Pultneyville has been a place of commerce, wealth building, good times, picnics, parties, and hard labor for 200 years. Once its harbor had been home port to a dozen wooden schooners considerably larger than *Sara B*. And before that, native Americans and French coureurs des bois traveling the lake with bark canoes and dugouts did business here during the fur trade times. Soon after settlement in 1806 a pioneer found a cache of ancient artifacts in the nearby forest that were said to be goods from a French trading pack.

Pultneyville's Salmon Creek was well known to the French. Perhaps the great explorer La Salle stopped here on his journey to Niagara along the south shore of the lake in 1669. The Marquis de Denonville may have camped here in 1687 as he led his army of 3000 French and colonial troops, Ottawas, Hurons, and assorted other native converts to Christianity into the Iroquois heartland to destroy the Senecas who had been meddling with the French traders.

Before the Erie Canal and railroad development siphoned lake trade away to places like Oswego and Rochester, this sleepy hamlet was one of the busiest south shore lake ports. In the 1850s, thirty schooners filled its small harbor at times, rafted three deep inside the creek's protection. They carried corn, wheat, lumber, barrels and boxes of fruit, and sometimes they carried runaway slaves to Canada. In those days splendid big passenger steamers like the *Lady of the Lake* and the *Ontario,* called here daily. The old wooden paddle wheelers were queens of the inland seas, with their crystal chandeliers, gilded and carved wood paneling, grand saloons trimmed in mahogany and brass, and hand painted stateroom doors bearing romantic scenes of castles on the Rhine and old wild west Pueblo ruins.

Today, the tidy white clapboard and cobblestone houses built by ship captains and owners still look out over the lake. But little trace of the working harbor remains. The "red barn", an old warehouse where schooners once loaded grain, is now an upscale restaurant and art gallery. The small weekender cottages boathouses and fishermen's shanties are gone. But thanks to legal arrangements by the deceased owner that stipulated the harbor remain in active use by recreational boaters, waterfront condos and general gentrification has not yet displaced the two sailing clubs.

We settled in at the yacht club guest dock, had dinner, and strolled around the very quiet harbor on a Sunday night. Everyone had gone home leaving us to contemplate past memories and the empty gray lake from the vantage point of Appleboom Point. That night, a bone chilling northeaster began to blow and rain and fog settled in along with temperatures in the lower fifties. The next morning we decided a day in port was in order. No sense in being miserable so early in the cruise with three whole weeks ahead of us we agreed. We whipped lines, read, listened to music and explored the topic of Pennsylvania's great natural gas rush and its implications for the Great Lakes with our shipmate.

* * *

Alice (her name and some of the facts concerning her have been modified for, I think, fairly obvious reasons) is a woman of courage, fortitude, lots of energy, and a strong sense of adventure. She had mastered many hobbies and several careers in her sixty some years of life before I met her as one of my sailing students. Early on, she was determined to work with animals, but upon learning how much veterinary school tuition cost, she shifted to nursing, an occupation she pursued for several decades. She now lives on a 150 acre farm, raises a few beef cows, and keeps a couple of retired harness racers and a pensioned off pony or two on her pastures.

Her farm sits squarely in the middle of Pennsylvania's portion of the gas bearing Marcellus Shale region, said by some to be one of the largest reservoirs of natural gas in the world. The Marcellus stretches from West Virginia northward into New York and Lake Ontario's watershed and may contain enough gas to supply the entire U.S for six years. When the landsman came knocking on her door and offered to buy her mineral rights, Alice considered her mortgage, her overdue payment charge on the property taxes, the leaking barn roof, the 12 year old farm truck, and other increasingly urgent needs and cheerfully signed up. A couple years later the gas rush was on. The trucks were rolling, a well pad had gone in on the farm next door, a pipeline and compressor had been installed under and on her farm, and the royalty money was rolling in. More money than Alice or her neighbors in this rust belt region of marginal farm land and high unemployment had ever dreamed of having in their lives.

Suddenly, in gas land when your well comes in everyone is your friend. And you're getting calls to serve on this board or that nonprofit in the hopes that you might build a new 4H barn at the fair grounds or pay to re-surface the riding club's ring. A certain wariness creeps into your relationship with former casual acquaintances. Everyone, it seems, wants something of you. And not everyone is happy with the transformation of their once sleepy small town or city into a boom town to rival that of the Klondike's glory days.

Rents skyrocket to double or triple the pre- boom era rates along with hospital ER admissions, heavy truck crashes, sales of alcohol, and venereal disease infections. Those people who don't get royalty payments or otherwise benefit from the boom frequently get pretty testy if not downright litigious about it. Along with industrialized agriculture, (which is totally dependent on natural gas as a feedstock for chemical fertilizers), fracking is one of the most polarizing industries in rural America as it sets neighbor against neighbor. But almost everyone including Alice, complained about the truck traffic. It takes steel, gravel, equipment, sand, chemicals, diesel fuel and lots of water all transported on trucks, to make a shale gas boom. Alice said ruefully the cleared level land across from her farm house looked like a "parking lot" for heavy trucks. Others said the whole town looked that way.

The shale gas rush started in Pennsylvania in 2003 shortly after the extraction of natural gas and crude oil from so-called tight shale formations by horizontal drilling and hydraulic fracturing were perfected in Texas. Since then hydraulic fracturing (often shorthanded as hydrofracking, slick water fracking or just plain fracking) has spread across the land and now is impacting the watersheds of Lakes Michigan Erie and Ontario. It seems almost certain to eventually further degrade other parts of the Great Lakes basin upstream from us.

Fracking has transformed the energy landscape of North America. A few years ago the concept of peak oil and our reliance on foreign supplies of it was a constant topic of bloggers and news media outlets and a cause for hope among advocates of renewable green energy sources. Suddenly, for better or for worse, we are now poised to become exporters of oil and liquefied natural gas. Oil production in the U.S jumped 39 % in just two years. Some energy analysts predict the U.S. could soon be the world's largest oil producer thanks to hydrofracking. Total U.S. natural gas production has increased about 25% since 2005, and the industry is working hard to get pipelines and storage areas in place to increase consumption of all that new supply.

It's impressive what a 545 billion dollars in capital investment (a figure cited for 2011 by the American Petroleum Institute) can do to change the energy picture. Unfortunately, this abundance of inexpensive fossil fuel is not making it any easier to shift our nation's energy mix onto a more sustainable footing by using renewables to generate power and heat our homes.[1]

The oil and natural gas locked up within dense low porosity shale rock was of little interest to the energy companies until fracking became feasible. In this process a well shaft is drilled downward 2 or

3000 feet or more. Then the bit is turned sideways to move laterally a mile or more through the layer of shale. Then millions of gallons of water and truckloads of a special sort of sand laced with an unappetizing "proprietary" stew of chemicals known to include dilute acids, benzene, antifreeze, acetone, and/ or other toxic and carcinogenic compounds are pumped under high pressure into the shaft to fracture the shale. The sand grains help prop open cracks in the shale allowing the gas to escape.

Some of that water, now polluted with brines from underground salt deposits, toxic metals like arsenic, a mixture of fracking chemicals, and, in the Marcellus formation, radioactivity, comes back up to the surface along with the gas and must be disposed of. This used flowback water is perhaps the biggest, (though hardly the only) environmental concern associated with shale gas wells in our region. It is sometimes stored in open plastic lined lagoons that can overflow during heavy rains. Or it may be filtered processed and re-used to 'stimulate' another well. That is, if any facilities exist near the well field that can recycle the water and deal with the left over residue sludge.

Alice did not know anyone personally with a contaminated drinking water well, but a number of groundwater supplies around her area have been polluted by hydrofracking. One that made headlines was the Dimock, Pennsylvania homeowner's water well that blew up after methane in the drinking water was ignited by a spark from the well pump. Gag orders, sealed court documents, and out of court settlements with nondisclosure clauses between gas drillers and paid off homeowners make it difficult to document the extent of the problem.

However, we do know from government documents that the cement around well casings is prone to leakage at failure rates of up to 50% within fifteen years. Pennsylvania well inspection records for 2012 surveyed by Cornell engineering professor Anthony Ingraffea, showed a failure rates of 6 to 7 % within a year after the well was drilled.[2]

Public health researchers and other scientists have criticized the wide use of non disclosure agreements as they make it impossible to collect data to assess the environmental risks of fracking. In 2012 two researchers at Cornell University's College of Veterinary Medicine published an article in a peer reviewed journal about illness reproductive failures and deaths of farm animals exposed to gas fracking operations. A college press release about their study stated *"making a direct link between death and illness is not possible due to incomplete testing, proprietary secrecy from gas drilling companies regarding the chemicals used in hydrofracking, and non-disclosure agreements that seal testimony and evidence when lawsuits are settled."* The researchers recommended that nondisclosure agreements be prohibited when public health is at risk.[3]

Other scientists have also criticized non disclosure agreements and the regulatory loophole that allows companies to declare their mixes of chemicals "proprietary". With a secret ingredient list of what they're pumping under the ground, it is not easy to prove the presence of a chemical in someone's water well came from a faulty gas well casing a spill or from waste lagoon overflow. The Union of Concerned Scientists has called for an 'evidence based debate' on the merits of fracking. Their report documenting the obstruction of access to data states that *"without strong chemical disclosure laws in place, it is more challenging for scientists to detect pollution when it occurs and study its potential impacts on the environment and human health."* In other words if you can't look for it, you'll never find a problem.

While we don't know exactly how bad it is, it's a good bet that drinking water wells have been compromised, and that people have gotten sick from either their water or from air exposures to toxins. An AP story surveyed Ohio, Pennsylvania, Texas, and West Virginia and documented nearly 3000 complaints relating to polluted methane laced water, while an EPA study in Wyoming found benzene at 50 times safe levels in ground water and concluded it came from fracking. A study published in a peer reviewed journal by Duke University researchers in Pennsylvania also linked fracking to drinking water contamination by methane. In this study wells drilled within a half mile of the drinking water supply caused contamination. (Methane can and does occur naturally in many water wells in Pennsylvania, as the gas drilling industry likes to point out. But gas from deep rock formations has a unique isotopic signature that allowed the researchers to determine the pollution's origin from fracking).[4]

More than 6000 wells have been drilled and fracked to date in Pennsylvania. Each operation involved several millions of gallons of water and many truck trips. Sometimes a hundred truckloads a day move on and off a well pad. More wells will be drilled throughout the Great Lakes watershed in the next few years. All of this polluted water and the residue of sludge left when the water is processed and "cleaned" for re-use in another gas well has to be disposed of.

Previously in West Virginia and Pennsylvania the industry considered that dumping it in rivers, or in standard sewage treatment plants (that do not remove chemicals and brines from water) was proper disposal. Specially built deep wells for storing toxic waste in Ohio are now used for some Pennsylvania waste, but it costs money to truck the wastes there. It's far cheaper to use it as a de-icer on highways which is being done in a number of counties in New York and elsewhere.

Some sludge comes to Lake Ontario's watershed in New York to be stored in landfills. And some of it is radioactive. So-called naturally occurring radioactive material (NORM) is a signature of the Marcellus Shale. Those materials come up to earth's surface with drill cuttings and flowback water and are concentrated in sludges and in mineral scale deposits on pipes.

The federal drinking water standard for radioactivity from radium is 5 pico curies per liter. Some flowback water can contain as much as 9000 pico curies per liter while pipe scale can be ten times more radioactive than that. Yet to date, New York's regulator, the Department of Environmental Conservation, has turned a blind eye towards the issue, allowing sludge of unknown radioactivity to be dumped in New York landfills. Leachate from some of those repositories has been 'treated' at water plants that discharge into the Genesee and other Lake Ontario tributaries. The water treatment plants do not remove all the radioactivity.

To make matters worse, several of the water treatment plants had relied on a testing lab in Syracuse, Upstate Laboratories, that had its certification yanked by the NYS Dept of Health in 2012 amidst some nasty allegations of sloppy record keeping, corruption and fraud.

Science writer Valerie Brown wrote in the peer reviewed journal *Environmental Health Perspectives* in 2014, *"the current patchy understanding of radioactive fracking waste's fate in the environment precludes making good decisions about its management."* 5

In 2013 the Pennsylvania Independent Oil and Gas Association, an industry trade group, put out a press release in support of a study by the Pennsylvania Department of Environmental Protection on the extent of NORM and its possible hazards to the gas field workers. This was after ten years of drilling and two years after reports surfaced of levels of radioactivity up to 200 times background levels in stream sediments below a 'treatment plant' that had discharged flowback water into Blacklick Creek in western Pennsylvania. Better late than never, I suppose.

Direct water pollution from fracking is not the only threat to Great Lakes water quality in general within the region and to downstream Lake Ontario in particular. Silt and polluted runoff from land cleared for access roads, pipelines, well pad construction and other infrastructure muddies tributary streams and smothers wetlands across the region. Fragmentation of forest habitat degrades the overall watershed, making it less resilient to damage by invasive species, disease, erosion and other forms of pollution. Nationwide an estimated 350,000 acres have been cleared, paved, graded, filled, or otherwise impacted by gas and oil extraction infrastructure.

Another issue is the widespread use of flowback brines as road de-icers in northern areas including some counties in Lake Ontario's watershed. This has been widely condemned by environmental and human health advocates even though it is on going in a number of areas especially in the southern tier. Brines and sludges from the Marcellus Shale under New York and Pennsylvania contain more than simply salt. Benzenes, styrenes, arsenic, lead, and that pesky hazardous NORM at least occasionally have exceeded levels of regulatory concern when brines have been tested. (Several scientific studies have suggested the saltier the water the more radioactive material it contains.)

Legally some of this stuff is too "hot" for landfilling and should be classified as low level rad waste and sent to special repositories along with the plastic suits booties and gloves from the lake's nuclear power plants. However, in New York and Pennsylvania (and elsewhere) authorities are allowing it to be spread on roads. In Pennsylvania where landfills have been required to monitor for radiation since 2001 alarms have been set off by fracking sludge. Yet radioactivity is not considered by New York State when it regulates the disposal of the brines for so called "beneficial uses" (such as road de-icers).

The vast withdrawals of water from creeks also threaten the well being of the Great Lakes. As water is pumped into tanker trucks for fracking, headwater streams may dry up or become intermittent destroying aquatic life. A report published in 2013 by Environment Michigan tallied water use across the entire country by frackers and came up with an almost certainly low ball estimate of 250 billion gallons of water used and polluted since 2005. (Most state regulatory agencies do not keep close tabs on water withdrawals by drillers). That amount of water approximates a month's worth of flow over Niagara

Falls.

* * *

Six months after Alice's description of the 24/7 industrial action surrounding her neighbor's well pad, I glimpsed a fracking boom myself during a drive through the Permian Basin oil country in West Texas. On a frosty morning just outside Midlands a dozen oversized truckloads of massive mysterious bright yellow or red machinery rumbled by the truck stop during the time it took to fill our car's tank with eight gallons of petroleum product. Tanker trucks of chemicals and water and loads of sand shuttled around town and down the highway, all enroute to the latest penetration into the arid desertified Texas plains. Here, millions of dollars worth of equipment aboard more trucks clustered around towers of steel to frack and crack rocks and extract more crude oil. All night long in our motel, doors slammed, voices sounded in the hall, and engines grumbled in the parking lot as the 24-7 race to frack went on.

We followed other tankers down Interstate 10 past the Midlands refinery humming away to crank out gasoline to fuel more cross country driving trips like ours. We flashed by "man camps", the small flocks of campers like roosting birds huddled together in the dusty flat lands among dried yucca and mesquite beside the Interstate, and we speculated on the composition of the liquid seen dribbling steadily onto the highway from a pair of red Halliburton tankers that we passed. That's one way to get rid of the fracking flowback waste we joked.

The sheer exuberance of all this hustle and bustle amidst the parched wide windblown ranch lands of West Texas was palpable. And seeing the glitz and raw power of all this pricey high tech gear in action was fascinating, (and wearing). Alice had toured the control room during the well drilling next to her farm. She said the numerous computer monitors and data readouts looked like Mission Control at Houston. But I was glad my green and growing wood lot's beech trees and sugar maples back home weren't being cut down and bulldozed aside to make room for a well pad and a plastic lined lagoon of toxic chemicals and a noisy compressor like Alice now has to live with. Fracking is bad enough out in the wide wild West Texas Plains, but it looked intolerable for the densely populated Great Lakes region. And even as I admired all the pricey engineering on display, I wished some of that ingenuity and intellectual creativity and the massive amounts of capital that were making all this happen could be directed at development of more sustainable energy sources.

Shortly after the rush in Pennsylvania began, David Patterson, then interim governor of New York, signed an Executive Order for a moratorium on horizontal hydrofracking. The move was intended to give the state's Department of Environmental Conservation time to re-write regulations that were badly in need of updating in order to protect water and other resources. That was back in 2008 and the moratorium remained in place until 2015 when the state issued a decision to put a ban in place. The decision was made because of "significant uncertainties about the adverse health outcomes that may be associated with (hydrofracking). A state Department of Health report in 2014 concluded that *it will be years until science and research provide sufficient information to determine the level of risk HVHF (High*

Volume Hydraulic Fracturing) poses to public health and whether those risks can be adequately mitigated. Until more information on those risks becomes available there will be no hydrofracking in New York, if the Department of Health has its way. (Already, though as of this writing so called dry fracking as described in the next chapter has been proposed..)

And hydrofracking continues upstream of Lake Ontario in Ohio and Michigan even as toxic and radioactive sludges from Pennsylvania are placed in landfills within the lake's watershed. Casting a long shadow over all the debate and discussion about hydrofracking is the elephant in the room of climate change. Climate change, as we shall see in Chapter Eleven, is already impacting the Great Lakes and the life within them. It will have far more dramatic and destructive impacts within the next half century if no effort is made to curb fossil fuel usage locally and globally.

Natural gas continues to be touted by the oil and gas industry as a greener cleaner alternative to coal. But a growing number of studies have cast doubt on this assertion. After reading dozens of articles on the question I conclude we really have no idea how much "cleaner" gas is compared to dirty smoky carbon intensive coal. Some models suggest that airborne soot from coal has a cooling effect in the atmosphere that at least partially offsets its green house gas impact. And it appears the green house gas footprint of natural gas has been badly underestimated in the past. It may be as big as that of coal in the short term at least.

Natural gas is methane, and methane is a potent though relatively short lived greenhouse gas. It traps heat at up to 30 times the rate of

CO2 over a 100 year period and 72 times faster over a 20 year period. We don't know how much methane escapes from well casing failures, leaky valves, pipe connections and storage tanks, and how much is deliberately allowed to escape during the transport and use of LNG (Liquefied Natural Gas). LNG storage tanks have to vent liquefied stored gas into the atmosphere (so-called boil off). We don't know how much methane escapes from abandoned wells. And we have no idea how much methane escapes from the underground lines that feed gas into people's homes. But recent studies that measured "fugitive" emissions have documented a range of numbers that are disturbing at best. They cast serious doubt on claims that natural gas is 'cleaner' than coal from a green house gas emissions standpoint.

One study by researchers from the University of Texas at Austin published in 2011 found that emissions of methane from all phases of natural gas production totaled about 2.3 million tons a year. The same study monitored emissions from 150 wells and found methane escaping at rates up to 67% higher than the EPA's best guesses had been. Another study by EPA and University at Boulder Colorado scientists who sampled the air over an area of working gas wells in Wyoming found a cluster of wells there were releasing about 4% of their production into the air. In Pennsylvania researchers measured methane losses from 19 abandoned wells. They assumed their samples were representative of the thousands of abandoned wells statewide and estimated 4 to 7% of total Pennsylvania methane emissions were from abandoned wells.

Methane leaks from old wells have not been studied enough to estimate the true green house gas effects of natural gas compared to coal or oil. But there are huge numbers of unused wells around the country, and more are being abandoned every year.

Then there are those tens of thousands of miles of gas lines, some of them cast iron pipes over a century old in northeastern cities like Boston and New York, that are leaking natural gas into sewers, next to waterlines, into the air, and once in awhile into buildings that sometimes then blow up. According to a report commissioned by Senator Edward Markey of Massachusetts gas leaks killed 116 people between 2002 and 2012, and caused more than 800 million dollars in property damage. To this day, I retain a vivid memory of the rubble remaining after Steven's Hardware Store in Ontario Center near my childhood home blew up from a gas leak forty odd years ago.

A few years ago Bob Ackley a private contractor teamed up with a Boston University plant physiologist named Nathan Phillips to try to quantify just how much gas the gas companies were losing. (Phillips initially became interested in the problem partly because of the harmful effects of gas leaks on city street trees.) Their results were eye opening.

No one, not even the gas companies, knows how much greenhouse gas is being added to the atmosphere by this particular source of methane, but the Boston study found 3,356 leaks suggesting it's considerable.

Ackley and Phillips along with other Duke University researchers also drove around Washington DC with a mobile monitor and found 5,893 leaks in that city. Their paper states these countless little wisps and spurts and burps amount to the single largest source of green house gas methane from human activity. They found one leak releasing enough gas to heat seven homes.6

After New York's moratorium on hydrofracking began, several other counties and municipalities around the country declared similar holds or bans while they considered tougher regulations. The biggest obstacle to protection of public health and the environment is without doubt, the Halliburton loophole which exempts fracking from federal regulation under the Clean Water Act. In addition to budget limitations and constant "catch up", individual state rule makers and inspectors are all too prone to something the activists call "regulatory capture". This occurs because state regulators often have limited resources to draw up new regulations and so depend on the gas and oil services industry for technical assistance as they re-write them. And the individual states also lack the manpower to monitor potential health issues. Consider, for example Pennsylvania's belated decision to begin studying the radioactivity of drill cuttings and flowback water a decade after drilling began.

Many critics of New York's regulator, the Department of Environmental Conservation, pointed out that permitting for new wells and using money from the permits for funding is inherently in conflict for the agency's mandate of protecting the environment. Some states divide the two functions between a minerals management agency and a separate autonomous environmental protection agency. And then there is the problem of that 'revolving door' between industry and regulatory body that exists in so many situations in our complex world. The SEC that is supposed to regulate Wall Street deal makers, the NRC regulators who frequently leave the government go to work for the nuclear industry and countless other examples of too cozy relationships between industry and regulator at the state and federal level come to mind.

New York, like many states, is facing budget cuts and rising costs. It has cut staff and in constant dollar amounts reduced the budget of the Department of Environmental Conservation, the state agency that will oversee and enforce shale gas extraction when and if it ever begins. The agency had just 17 inspectors to oversee and monitor compliance at the 14,000 currently operating gas wells state wide in 2011. According to a report published by the non profit advocacy group Earth Works for its Oil and Gas Accountability Project, three quarters of those wells were not inspected in 2010.7 In late 2014 the State Comptroller issued a report on environmental funding in New York State and wrote *"The combination of increased responsibilities, reduced staffing, and ongoing fiscal pressure raises questions regarding the DEC's capacity to carry out its critical functions"*

These factors along with the surplus of natural gas from fracking in other areas, may have contributed to the decision in late 2014 to put a hold on fracking. For some ideas on how to reduce our dependency on natural gas read on.

2. Some Sustainable Solutions

A few months before *Sara B's* cruise around the lake, I drove to Dansville, New York to a public hearing. The assembly was held in a packed high school auditorium and was on proposed new regulations to allow hydrofracking in New York State. Emotions were high in the crowded room. State troopers stood by every door and were stationed around the auditorium. I listened to dozens of three minute statements from farmers, retirees, small business owners, town elected officials, teachers, industrial chemists and oil field service workers. Hundreds of people signed up to speak. Some had waited in line overnight to be sure of getting a spot on the schedule. The three minute limit on speaking was strictly enforced. Some of the speakers choked with emotion as they delivered pleas to make the moratorium permanent. Others, mostly landowners with fat royalty offers begged for desperately needed income or stridently demanded their share of the possible pot of gold lying under their farms.

One of the speakers that day was Jodi Andrysick who, along with her husband Jeff, grows organic vegetables and fruits near Keuka Lake. Visibly nervous but determined, she spent her three minutes asking for sanity in this mad rush to extract gas at any ecological price. Afterwards I talked to her and her spouse about the documentary "All Fracked Up" that she and Jeff had made to spread the word to New Yorkers about the many issues associated with fracking. Jeff and Jody believed that the best way to avoid a Pennsylvania style mess was to educate people about the consequences of yet another gold rush to extract wealth from the land at a breakneck pace.

Jeff and Jodi live in a house they built with their own hands on fifty acres where they planted nut and fruit trees and berry bushes. In the winter of 2009 they were happily planning the lay out and construction of a multi vendor farm and craft store on their land (their Harvest and Artist's Market has since been built) when a headline in the local paper changed everything, sending them off on a year long quest to prevent hydro fracking in New York.

The news story described a proposed deep injection well for storage of toxic waste water sludge generated by Pennsylvania gas well drillers. Jeff recalled, "That twisted me around. They wanted to start with a billion gallons. I've heard of this sort of 'pump and dump' in Ecuador or Africa, but this is America!" After their initial outrage, Jeff and Jodi, his wife and soul mate of 27 years, mobilized hundreds of neighbors for an informational meeting just three days before a critical town board vote on the proposal.

Incredibly on Super Bowl Sunday, a bitter February day, they packed the meeting room to over capacity and then turned people away. Six hundred residents learned from nationally known experts about the potential for pollution of ground water, wells and streams, and Keuka Lake. They learned of traffic, of air pollution from methane leakage and constant diesel emissions, and other issues associated with the proposal. Despite the town supervisor's entanglements with the gas company (as revealed by Freedom Of Information requests), the outpouring of opposition convinced the gas company to rescind their application. Jeff and Jodi then launched a campaign to educate people across the state about shale gas drilling.

Knowing the visual impacts of video and on camera testimonials, they decided a documentary was their best hope. They determined to make a movie "that a PhD or a sixth grader could learn from". But neither Jeff nor Jodi knew anything about making a documentary. They started climbing a steep learning curve. "We bought a used high def video camera. I figured out how to put it on the tripod and stepped back. I didn't even know how to turn it on," said Jeff. But those who live on small farms are nothing if not resourceful. It wasn't easy though. Jeff quotes an old saying "Success has many mothers, but failure is an orphan."

Many doubted they could do it and felt free to tell them so. Comments like how's a farmer going to make a movie? You can't do it- they'll be fracking long before you'll ever get it done and other such helpful remarks were legion. Jeff remembering the discovery method of learning, told me, "Their negativity was understandable."

They went at it full time, using the money they had set aside for their farm market. They traveled thousands of miles and interviewed dozens of experts and people in northern Pennsylvania who had been impacted by the gas rush. But people wouldn't talk on camera. Many were involved in litigation with the gas drillers, and their attorneys had told them don't say anything. You'll compromise your case. They said plenty to Jeff and Jodi about polluted drinking water wells, asthma, noise, air pollution, dead animals, and insane amounts of heavy truck traffic over running their towns. But all off the record.

The would-be documentary makers had hit a brick wall. Jeff and

Jodi fell into despair. With Jodi in tears, Jeff recalls pulling off to the side of a back road in Pennsylvania and hitting the steering wheel in frustration. "Here we are trying to help and no one is going to open up." They were about to call it quits. Then they decided to go back and ask one person one more time. This time the woman agreed to talk on camera. As soon as her neighbors heard that she had agreed to an interview, they, too, began to tell their stories.

One home owner showed off his basement. It was filled with tanks, filters, plumbing, de-gassing equipment and enough gear to do justice to the neighborhood nuke, all installed in an attempt to purify his water. This same cheerful Pennsylvanian on camera lifts up and shows off a jug of lemonade colored liquid from his well to show why the gear was installed. A young girl told of dirt roads being sprayed with waste water for "dust control". She said "It made the road really slippery. My little sister on her bike would slip and wreck because the road would be really slimy – there would be a lot of foam..."

Jeff is fond of quoting folksy bits of wisdom. In trying to explain why he and Jodi burned through their life savings and devoted two years of their lives to fighting Frack, he said "My grandmother used to say 'tell the truth, shame the devil, and do right in this world.' "

As of 2014, Jeff and Jody had their farm store going and New York had put a ban on hydo fracking. Without doubt the state's moratorium happened because Jeff and Jody and hundreds of other equally determined people devoted thousands of hours of unpaid effort to defending their land and water. They included academics and researchers with expertise in engineering, toxicology, radiation, and geology. They included lawyers, energy investors with knowledge of the gas and oil industry, and self employed musicians and artists. New York City based celebrities, upstate teachers, and people from all walks of life organized rallies circulated petitions and held informational meetings. Thanks to their efforts tens of thousands of New Yorkers wrote their governor to say 'don't frack New York'. As the moratorium dragged on, the peer reviewed studies piled up, making an increasingly strong case against the practice.

An obvious solution to the problem of weak state level regulation is to close the so called Halliburton loophole tacked onto federal energy related legislation in 2005 that exempts the industry from the 1972 Clean Water Act. The need for federal authority over water quality became glaringly apparent back in the days when Cleveland's stretch of the Cayahoga River caught fire, and Lake Erie was declared dead. Regulation by the states had resulted in weak and inconsistent oversight of politically powerful industries and to smoggy skies, poisoned farm fields, burning rivers, dead lakes, and leaking toxic dumps. But to date attempts to get legislation through Congress to regulate hydrofracking have failed, not surprisingly, considering the vast amount of money spent by the energy industry on lobbyists and political campaigns at all levels of government.

Grassroots opposition to fracking continues to grow within the Great Lakes region, though local bans under the legal doctrine of "home rule" have been successfully challenged by the gas drillers in several states. Downstream from Lake Ontario Quebec currently has a moratorium in place that is being challenged by the industry, while Nova Scotia extended its moratorium in 2014. Michigan activists are working on a referendum to ban fracking and Vermont has banned fracking. Even frack friendly Ohio saw one city place restrictions on the industry in late 2014.

One way to make fracking less damaging to water resources is to use something else like propane or compressed CO_2 gas to recover shale gas or oil. Several big companies including GE, Praxaire and Statoil, a company with large interests in Pennsylvania's gas fields, are researching and experimenting with liquid CO_2 as a substitute for water. In "dry fracking" a well owner could re-use the CO_2 at the next well fracked, since nearly all CO_2 injected would return to the surface. In theory, at least, CO_2 can also be used to displace natural gas left behind in a fracked well. Once the methane is pushed out, the well could be capped and the CO_2 left underground. If the CO_2 was captured from coal or natural gas burning power plants or from other fossil fuel using industrial sources, then a portion of it would be returned to the earth to be 'sequestered' for centuries. In theory. China, with its large arid regions of shale gas reserves and abundance of coal fired power plants is said to be interested in the technique. But industry experts caution that dry fracking with CO_2 produced by fossil fuel burning is years away.

Efforts to use less water to extract shale gas and oil are getting a boost from droughts of historic severity on the Texas plains and in other areas of fracking activity. (Those droughts, ironically, are believed to be enhanced by climate change caused by burning gas and oil and coal.)

Even if we could extract gas and oil without water, there are still the many other adverse impacts on land, air, wildlife, climate, and society associated with fracking. In the long run, the problems that hydrofracking in particular and gas and oil use in general pose to Lake Ontario's health and well being will only be solved when we reduce our dependence on fossil fuels. Thousands of people in and near the Lake Ontario watershed are working to do just that. They include two neighbors of mine who have installed their own wind turbine and roof top solar generation array respectively, and a third former neighbor who moved to Ithaca and built a energy efficient "net zero" house.

There's wide spread agreement among policy makers about the value of efficiency. Nothing else comes close to the payback time of simply not using as much energy. Nationwide, residential and commercial buildings use 40% of all energy produced in the U.S. and about 40% of that energy goes for space heating. In the Lake Ontario area a growing number of homes use natural gas for heating.[1]

I had occasionally crossed tacks with Ray Stiefel, a genial wandering free spirit with a successful eco- touring business. He returned now and then to look after his affairs near my home. When I encountered him in the local grocery or the post office and asked how his new house was coming along, he always answered, "Slowly." When I heard it was finally finished, I asked if I could visit him to check it out. "Sure, come on down," he said, so on a brisk gray December morning I headed to the south end of Cayuga Lake, near the limits of Lake Ontario's watershed to the Ecovillage development perched atop a lofty ridge overlooking Ithaca and Cayuga Lake.

I learned of Ecovillage nearly twenty years ago from another Lake

Ontario advocate who visited this experiment in co-housing and intentional community shortly after it broke ground for its first energy efficient homes. Ecovillage's philosophy, design, and management is based on the practice of sustainable living, and it now has more than two hundred residents in three "neighborhoods" each consisting of about thirty state of the art energy efficient homes. The most recent development includes my neighbor's net zero home.

A net zero house, also known as a passive house after its German 'Passivhaus' derivatives, goes beyond being super efficient. It actually produces more energy than it uses. Houses have been built without furnaces for years in northern Europe, but at the time of my visit there probably were less than a hundred such occupied residences in the whole U.S. However, interest in them and other energy efficient residential and commercial construction is growing. In 2007 New York

City launched an effort to reduce green house gas emissions 30% by 2030. After Hurricane Sandy hit the Big Apple hard few years ago, the program picked up considerable momentum, and currently the city's goal for building energy use is a 30% cut by 2025. Much of of the reduction is being done through efficiency upgrades. Older buildings are now being re-fitted to reduce heating and power consumption by up to 75% under the city's Carbon Challenge initiative.

My neighbor came by his interest in energy efficient housing from a long passion for sustainability. His parents built a passive solar home around the corner from my own residence in the 1980s. Before that in the early 1970s as a newly minted marine biologist he was involved with baseline studies for the Prudhoe Bay oil terminal and trans Alaska pipeline project. "I flew that entire line in helicopters. I saw jeep tracks from the 1940s down there in the tundra," he told me. The potential damage to that pristine and fragile wilderness environment should a spill occur reinforced his already keen interest in preservation and sustainability.

Stiefel, along with two other residents, began planning an expansion of an additional thirty homes to Ecovillage several years ago. These had to be designed, financed, and sold, so it took them awhile. "At first we talked about all kinds of ideas-underground houses, straw bale houses, shipping containers-then we got real and started looking at state of the art high efficiency housing. The more we looked into Passivhaus the more interesting it sounded."

Stiefel explained that he and the contractors, local code enforcement people, bankers, and architect all learned together. This took more time, and the homes weren't particularly low cost when finished. (Ray's 1450 square foot house, the first one built, came in at around $250,000). All the residences were finished, and many were already occupied at the time of my visit. Eight of them were designed to be net zero homes.

On a gray 20 degrees Fahrenheit day with a brisk wind and minimal solar inputs through the big south windows, Ray and I both had sweaters on and a supplemental electric heater was gobbling up watts to boost the house temperature to around 70. Yet he assured me that over a one year period, he and his roommate had consumed just slightly less electricity than their house had fed into the grid. The all electric home with solar panels and a roof top solar water heater is modeled after the northern European structures. Along with passive solar design, super insulation, extremely tight construction, advanced triple pane windows and special ventilation for air exchanges that recovers exhaust air heat, the houses are equipped with the most efficient appliances and LED lighting available. The house stood on an insulated concrete slab and had no geothermal heat or furnace. "We didn't think we'd need it," Stiefel said. Since his first year in the house had included the winter of 2013-14, one of the coldest in years when over 90% of the Great Lakes surfaces froze over, the design had been well tested. In addition to energy efficiency, the home designer specified 'eco friendly' materials where ever possible such as recyclable steel roofing and durable light weight composite cement fiber siding.

There are complications to net zero life. During periods of prolonged cloud cover in the winter, for example, your shower might not be as hot as you'd like unless you flip the electric heater switch on for the hot water tank. But summer sun makes up for it as does the year around lack of utility bills. Stiefel said this sort of housing is best suited for occupants who are willing to "work with" their house. "We have moved away from thinking as a society," he told me. In this type of house he explained you have to do some management (at least you do if you want to be net zero).

I grew up in a huge drafty cobblestone house. We closed off rooms and used a small wood stove to keep the kitchen toasty on winter nights, so I get the concept of 'interacting' with one's house. And I appreciated the comfortable airy feel provided by the natural lighting of the house's large south facing windows in its main living room.

Net zero homes must be designed for their location. Architectural features appropriate to upstate New York won't work in California, so this lack of standardization may add to the cost. But in my view it also adds to the appeal of a house in an age of homogenized mass produced everything when mini mansions all look alike whether in Texas or Toronto.

Perhaps someday people will look at house efficiency in much the way they now consider gas mileage when buying a car. Especially when gas and heating oil prices go up again. As of this writing at least a half dozen highly efficient apartment buildings and housing subdivisions that will use up to 90% less energy than conventional homes were either complete or under construction within a hundred miles of my home. As they become more common, the costs will come down and the 'pay back' time on utility bills for any upfront cost difference will decline.

* * *

The best solutions are those that take care of more than one problem. Biomass fuel used in conjunction with energy efficient houses, sustainable agricultural practices, and improved gasification technology has potential to do that. It could improve water quality in tributaries feeding the Great Lakes while reducing fossil fuel use in the area. But only if it's done right.

More than half of the natural gas consumption in the U.S. is used for space heating. And space heating is by far the largest portion of household energy use in the Great Lakes region where a growing number of homes use either propane or natural gas. Given that a modest sized poorly insulated old house like the one I owned in the 1990s can go through four or five hundred gallons of fuel oil in a winter while the owner wears lots of sweaters and sleeps in a very cool bedroom, it's not surprising that interest is growing in both high efficiency houses and in biomass fuel made from perennial grasses or fast growing trees. Biomass is a clean renewable alternative to natural gas for home heating. Along with "eat local" there is now a "heat local" movement underway in the Northeast.

Deep rooted perennial plants hold soil on steep slopes, soak up excess nutrients from farm fields that would otherwise run off into streams and lakes, and provide at least some habitat for wildlife while also taking up and "sequestering" CO_2 into leaves stems and wood. Think of a firewood log or a bale of hay as a battery of sorts. It holds a surprising store of solar energy stashed away in the form of cellulose and lignin. Combustion releases that energy months or years later. One form of energy release called gasification can extract 75 % of that stored up solar energy.

Gasification converts solid wood into char and a mix of combustible gases through pyrolysis. The resulting gas is often called synthetic gas (syngas) or 'producer gas'. In gasification the wood is 'cooked' at high temperatures with steam and a small amount of oxygen, unlike normal combustion where oxygen fuels the reaction and large amounts of CO_2 are released.

According to Wikipedia, 1.1 kilogram of wood (about 2.4 pounds) can produce a kilowatt of electricity using gasification. During World War II tens of thousands of cars and trucks were converted to run on "wood gas". More recently foundations like World Stove and the Global Alliance for Clean Cook Stoves are working to introduce high efficiency gasification stoves to third world homes. The stoves burn clean and hot with far less indoor smoke and adverse health effects. They also consume less fuel than conventional cook stoves.

Gasification is receiving much more development support in northern Europe than in North America. Sweden with its abundant forests and lack of offshore oil has been a center of commercialized gasification technology. In the Lake Ontario region, the technical challenges of gasification along with abundant supplies of cheap natural gas and oil from hydrofracking have prompted interest in a simpler though less efficient way to extract energy from biomass. Two universities within the lake's watershed, Cornell and Syracuse University's School of Forestry and Environmental Science, are researching pellet fuels for residential and commercial heating.

Biomass pellets can be made from wood, sawdust, agricultural waste like corn stalks and cobs, straw and other dried plant fiber. Such fuel has a small green house gas 'footprint' because the CO_2 that is released from burning plants is taken up by other growing plants.

The Lake Ontario region is blessed with abundant rain and open rural land where biomass flourishes. It's not unusual to take three hay crops a year off a field here, something a rancher could only dream of doing in West Texas or on the Colorado plains. And if a field isn't mowed it's likely to be growing fifteen foot tall trees within a few years. Biomass fuel is still largely experimental in New York, but funding by the state for its development is on going. There are at least two large commercial boilers running on wood chips or pellets on the New York shore of the lake. A 60 MW coal fired power plant near Watertown was recently converted to use wood chips, while the Syracuse University School of Environmental Science and Forestry has installed a boiler that supplies heat and electricity using biomass pellets and gasification as part of a goal of campus wide carbon neutrality by 2015.

By far the most common biomass fuel in upstate New York is a cord of hardwood cut split and delivered to an inexpensive and inefficient wood stove like the one in the author's house. But in Europe, where land resources are less plentiful, renewable biomass is a viable alternative to uncertain foreign supplies of natural gas piped in from politically unpredictable entities like Russia. Often it takes the form of wood or sawdust pellets used in a clean burning airtight stove designed for pellet use.

Perennial switch grass and other mixes of grasses like those planted for animal forage and erosion control are good candidates for biomass heating. Several research programs are underway within the lake's watershed to determine the commercial viability of pelletized grass for space heating. Perennial grasses grown for fuel hold soils in place year around reducing nutrient losses and silt that clogs lake tributaries and wetlands, even as they store solar energy through summer's long days. They are essentially 'carbon neutral' because the CO_2 they release will be taken up by next summer's growth. Dr. Jerry Cherney of Cornell points out that it takes 70 days to grow a crop of grass that can go into a bag of pellets for home heating, while it takes 70 years to grow a decent sized tree for firewood and 70 million years to make a 100 pounds of fossilized grass in the form of coal.

Grass fertilized with excess manure that is harvested for space heating provides at least eight times as much green house gas reduction as ethanol from corn pumped into a automobile gas tank. And a Canadian group called REAP (Resource Efficient Agricultural Production), a non profit founded to promote sustainable farming, claims switchgrass produces three times more net energy gain per acre than corn in cellulosic ethanol production.

Most small pellet stoves currently sold in the U.S. are not designed to deal with the higher amounts of sometimes more corrosive ash produced by grass pellets. Some pellet stoves can run on a mix of wood and grass pellets, however, and in tests by Cornell researchers some corn stoves seemed to operate tolerably well with straight grass pellets depending on how the grasses were grown and cured.

In Europe small furnaces that heat water for home heating have been adapted to use grass pellets according to Dr. Cherney. He writes in a report posted on line that there is a long litany of social benefits associated with using grasses for pellet fuel including big reductions in the uses of chemical fertilizers and pesticides. And the machinery "infrastructure" needed to grow and bale grass is already available on farms. If grass (or mixtures of other perennial plants or fast growing woody trees or shrubs) became a viable energy crop, it would help keep small farms and rural communities afloat with cash infusions and new jobs. The benefits to our local waters and the creatures that depend on them will become obvious to anyone who wades into the next chapter.

One big challenge to biomass energy crops like the perennial grasses is our current system of market distorting subsidies that promote soy and corn production. Perennials can't compete against corn in the present marketplace of price per acre returns to the farmer. "Ecological services" like reduced green house gas emissions, top soil retention, and clean water are not currently recognized by our outmoded economic system's accounting. Sales of Round Up and chemical fertilizers contribute directly to the GNP and are easy to measure. But so called 'external costs' of blue green algae blooms or increased cancer rates are not so easy to quantify. And the economic benefits of greater biodiversity and environmental resiliency in the form of clear running creeks and habitat for wildlife and songbirds are considerably harder to quantify. However, they are real.

The irony of encouraging corn production for ethanol with tax payer supplied subsidies to reduce fossil fuel dependency is that we are far more dependent on fossil fuels than if we used our fields to grow grasses for pellet fuel. Corn production on conventional farms depends on fertilizers and pesticides derived largely from fossil fuels. It takes huge amounts of ammonia fertilizers produced from natural gas and atmospheric nitrogen to grow that corn, and it takes plenty of diesel fuel to plant, spray, and harvest it. Our current agricultural system is utterly dependent on synthetic fertilizers derived from fossil fuel. We'll see in the next chapter how such agriculture pollutes our water directly as well as indirectly by using hydrofracked gas and oil to grow the food.

Biomass for space heating and or electrical generation could supplement geothermal energy and renewables like wind solar and hydropower to completely replace fossil fuels. Sweden is doing just that. Sweden lacks the offshore oil resources of Norway and Denmark. After the first "energy crisis" of the 1970's when OPEC pushed oil prices sky high, Sweden put in place a national policy goal to completely eliminate fossil fuels from its energy mix supply. The country now supplies about a third of its entire energy needs from biomass including methane gas produced from agricultural and food wastes. Sweden uses a mix of wind hydro and nuclear energy to power its electrical grid and fossil fuels are now mostly used in their transport sector.

Perennial plants grown for biomass fuel protect water quality instead of degrading it. But unless we reduce our overall energy use through high efficiency homes and transportation, we run the risk of deforestation, more lost biodiversity, unsustainable top soil loss and rising food prices. Taking trees and converting them into pellets is not a sustainable way to produce pellet fuel. Unfortunately, however, it is now happening in the southern U.S.[2] And biomass fuel production from crops makes no sense at all in areas lacking abundant rainfall. Corn for ethanol grown with irrigation from non renewable aquifers or the Platte River is an extremely poor use of scarce resources.[3]

In Chapter Nine we'll see how New York State might take a lesson from Sweden to completely replace fossil fuels for electricity heating and transportation with 100% green energy from renewables within 30 years using existing technology and increased efficiency.

3. Dead Birds and Cheap Food

The heavy rains of the last two days that had kept us in port and brought area creeks up over a foot impacted Wilson Harbor, too. A thick brown stain of silt spread a quarter of a mile out from the harbor entrance as *Sara B* chugged along heading for the twin jetties of the channel on our fourth day of travel. It contrasted sharply to the clear green waters of the near shore lake. We entered Wilson's harbor and narrow backwater bay formed by Sunset Island and pointed *Sara B's* bowsprit at the Wilson Yacht Club. Earlier in the day I had phoned an old sailing friend about stopping by for a visit. He lived up to his club's self proclaimed title as "the friendliest yacht club on the lake" and invited our unaffiliated 'yacht' to stay at the guest dock. It's the only one we have long enough for you, he told us.

With the help of our friend and another bystander we crammed *Sara B* into a tight little berth and settled her for the night. "Come on up to the club house, I'll buy you a beer," our friend said. It had been a long day of motoring with a hot diesel on a real scorcher of intense early summer sun reflecting off glassy water, so we were quick to follow him. We climbed the little hill to the yacht club cottage on its summit and settled in on a cool screened in porch shaded from the late afternoon glare by a grove of big oaks and hemlocks. Wilson is a working man's yacht club. No mega yachts or paid stewards or fancy facilities here. Just a little member built club house on the summit of Treasure Island with a self serve refrigerator full of cold beer and a cash box to drop the money in.

Below us the island's edge sat *Sara B* looking decidedly out of place in a line up of a dozen nearly identical white fiberglass sloops. With her black hull, two wooden masts, square deck house and long wooden bowsprit she looked a bit like a dignified old lady in full Victorian dress hanging out at a party of bikini clad twenty-something beach babes.

But we drank a toast to her old diesel and said kind things about her to our friend. She had gotten us down the lake on a long hot windless day with just twelve miles to go to the Niagara River and the Canadian border.

Walking back to the boat I noticed a dead goose floating in the backwater behind the yacht club's island. A small knot of dread settled in my stomach at the sight of its body. Could it be the start of a blue green algae bloom? The conditions had certainly been favorable for one. The last few days had been a mix of hot calm conditions and vast amounts of nutrient laden run off from heavy rains. (And two days later in Burlington Bay I did see an unmistakable small bloom underway in our backwater anchorage.)

Blue greens, also known as cyanobacteria, are indicators of polluted water. Too much fertilizer from animal waste or human sewage is a common cause of a blue green bloom. When conditions are right, the one celled blue greens can explode in abundance turning the water bright green or turquoise. Some species also produce toxins which can be deadly. In the late summer of 2010, Sodus Bay near *Sara B*'s homeport, suddenly produced a thick green scum speckled with rotting fish and a few dead birds. No one had ever seen anything like it before on the bay. This was new to our region. And frightening.

Within days, the New York State Health Department had posted warnings to avoid swimming or other contact with the water. Anger, angst, indignation, and protests from cottage owners, anglers, boaters, business owners and other bay users followed. As public swim beaches were closed and dead fish and rotting plant material washed up in front of $400,000 homes, another community was rudely awakened to the true costs of 38 cent a pound chicken, cheap milk and industrialized farming across North America.

One common species of cyanobacteria produces a toxin called microcystin. Microcystin shut down the water supply of Toledo, Ohio in August 2014 after a massive blue green bloom hit the west end of Lake Erie. Half a million people scrambled to find bottled water after they were told not to even cook with their tap water. (Neither boiling nor many standard water treatment plants remove the toxin of a severe bloom). If ingested in sufficient amounts, microcystin causes liver failure. Mostly cattle and other livestock are at risk, but there have been several dog deaths over the years on various bays and small lakes in my immediate neighborhood. The pets had gone for a swim and then probably licked the algae off their fur. There is a suspicion, as yet unproven, that liver damage in humans who have ingested smaller amounts of the toxin can lead to cancer. And as residents of Sodus Bay saw, it also can kill fish and birds. Some researchers suspect that a toxin known as BMAA (beta-methyl amino-L-alanine) produced by many species of blue greens may be linked to various scary neurological diseases such as Parkinson's dementia and ALS, a gruesome disorder that kills slowly by paralysis.

Some intriguing clusters of ALS (Lou Gehrig's disease) have been mapped around several lakes in Maine and New Hampshire that are subject to blue green blooms. One study showed a tenfold elevation over the normal rate of ALS for people living by Lake Mascoma in New Hampshire. Toxins are suspected of possibly bio accumulating in fish that might then be eaten by humans. There is as yet no smoking gun to definitively prove a connection between blue greens from lakes and bays and neurological degeneration in humans, but everyone agrees there are plenty of reasons to try to minimize deadly blooms.[1]

Toxic cyanobacteria were not part of my past association with Lake Ontario. I'd seen them on small farm ponds, reservoirs surrounded by Iowa corn fields, and on Oneida Lake. But except for the unfortunate Bay of Quinte where I noticed a few blue green blooms in the 1980s, I had never seen them on my home waters until few years ago. However, they now seem to be here to stay on the Great Lakes. Lake Erie has been slammed with several huge blooms in recent years, some of which covered the lake's entire western basin. In 2011 an intense bloom covered over 1700 square miles of western Lake Erie. It shut down swim beaches and fisheries over long stretches of the lake's U.S shore. And each year the blooms pop up in areas that had previously been clear of them. A scientist, Raj Bejankiwar, was quoted in a September 2013 Buffalo News story "It is really concerning. We are seeing it in places we didn't see it before. Obviously...something going on in the lake."

While there appear to be several things contributing to the increase in "HAB's" (hazardous algae blooms), a good portion of that "something" is cheap food, specifically meat dairy and eggs. Large industrial factory farms, also known as concentrated animal feeding operations, or CAFOs, feed thousands of animals or tens of thousands of birds in huge warehouse-like buildings. The animals never see the sun or a grass pasture and are fed largely or exclusively on grain-based prepared feed, often grown on another farm and then imported to the animal holding area. The animals produce massive amounts of manure, which must be disposed of on surrounding crop lands. The 3000 cow dairy a few miles southwest of *Sara B's* home port produces four times as much waste as the city of Syracuse.

The CAFO is a recent development. Back in 1972 when the Clean Water Act was passed in response to 'point source' pollution from individual factory drain pipes and city sewage plants, manure was a useful and valued fertilizer and agricultural runoff was a much smaller contributor to the lake's water quality problems. Farms got big mainly in response to consolidation in the food processing business and to government policies and subsidies like cheap credit to encourage expansion that were rooted in events of the early 20th century.

By financing new equipment, the reasoning went, farms could become more efficient and food would become cheaper. It seemed like a good policy at a time when memories of the Great Depression's social unrest and mass marches on DC were still vivid. In 1932 the average household spent 22% of its income on food. Today the average household budget for food is a little over 9%, an all time low. (And of course a lot of that spending is for highly processed 'value added' food products like ready to eat frozen dinners, and colorful breakfast cereal loaded with sugar).

In the 1930's mechanization of the pork slaughter houses allowed them to ramp up production and the markets for individual farmers began to consolidate. Before long the neighborhood butcher shop was mostly a memory and the marketplace was almost completely controlled by a handful of huge corporate processors. Today Cargill and Tyson Foods control 83% of the U.S. beef markets and more than two thirds of pork processing. (According to economic theory a market typically becomes uncompetitive when 40% of it is controlled by oligopoly or monopoly). It is a rare farmer who has more than one possible buyer for his pork or beef today. (This same concentration of food processing has also occurred in the fruit and vegetable business. In the 1950s in my immediate neighborhood there were a half dozen canneries and farmers had at least had a couple of places to sell their corn or tomatoes or fruit for processing. Today just one very large one apple sauce factory remains in operation near my home).

In the 1950s corporate contracting, where farmers grow birds supplied by a big processor who directs the process, accelerated the trend towards CAFOs and lower meat prices. The cost of chicken has actually declined in inflation adjusted dollars over the last thirty years. A story posted at Farm Aid's website cites a typical example from Arkansas where the farmer contractors were given five cents a pound for their labor and animal housing facilities with no inflation adjustment for twenty years. When the contractor, in this case Tyson Foods, required the grower to install 300,000 dollars of computerized updated housing for the birds, the already indebted land owners were forced into bankruptcy. [2]

Chickens ducks and turkeys were the first animals to be raised in closely confined "animal feeding operations" and the waters of Long Island Sound, the Chesapeake Bay and other areas soon began to suffer from excesses of bird manure. Twenty years later hogs were being crowded into industrial settings that were 'scientific' and 'healthy' with no mud for wallows and no space for hogs to root. But there were still plenty of smells. In Lake Ontario's watershed, dairy was the last agricultural industry to consolidate. In the 1980s a family could still make somewhat of a living from a 80 cow dairy, though often their income was supplemented by a school bus driver's or substitute teacher's pay check. But in the 1990s a wave of consolidation swept through upstate New York's dairy business, much as it had earlier for pork and egg producers. Today many of those small dairies are gone, replaced by huge CAFOs with thousands of cows. The manure production had concentrated accordingly.

Regulation has not kept up with the consolidation of animals and manure and the impacts on water quality. Dairy farmers in Lake Ontario's watershed are a little better off than the poultry growers in the south, but the big farms generally operate with low wage high turnover labor, much of it Hispanic. With computerized feeding, automated milking carousels and milk production amped up by bovine somatotropin growth hormone, it's a very different day from that of the family farm of thirty years ago with fifty milkers that rambled around in a green grassy pasture and lay in the shade to chew their cuds on long lazy summer days. And all those cows produce staggering amounts of waste- about 80 pounds a day per milking animal.

Because the typical CAFO doesn't have enough acreage to absorb the waste, many of these large farms routinely over-apply manure on their fields. Some of the dairy and hog farms near the lake also apply liquid manure during the fall and winter when there is no plant growth to take up the excess nutrients and when soggy muddy fields or frozen fields and frequent rains allow plenty of run off to enter tributaries of the nearby lake. Farm waste also contains pathogens, antibiotics and endocrine system disrupting chemicals. In the summer liquid may soak into the soil to contaminate underground aquifers. But when there's a heavy rain it often runs off into into the nearest waterway, potentially spreading disease and fueling excess algae growth.

It's a nationwide problem. Across the Great Lakes basin and the rest of the U. S. surface and ground-water sources alike are at risk from excess manure spreads. Nitrate contamination in excess of federal drinking water standards from agricultural runoff, is estimated to have impacted 24 percent of America's groundwater supplies. Nitrates in water are dangerous to infants and are suspected of having other adverse human health impacts including cancer if enough of the compounds are converted to nitrites in the digestive tract.[3]

Phosphates, another component of human and animal sewage, fuel those toxic blue green cyanobacteria blooms, while nitrates from manure and farm field fertilizers also encourage excess plant growth that causes additional problems such as 'dead zones' that develop after algae rots and uses up oxygen at summer's end.

On that sweltering summer day in Wilson more than just blue green blooms was on my mind as I pondered the dead goose. I also was remembering another sultry summer in 2006 when massive amounts of rotting seaweed produced our first big botulism outbreak. That year while chugging in and out of the bay with sailing charters, I saw several dead ringbill gulls or common terns floating in the channel with their heads flopped to one side. The wildlife techs call the affliction limber neck, and it's caused by paralysis of the neck muscles. The birds couldn't keep their heads out of the water so they drowned. They were paralyzed by a neurotoxin produced by *Clostridium botulinum*- a ubiquitous bacteria that can only grow in an oxygen free environment such as a jar of home canned beans or a mass of putrid algae in the shallows of Lake Ontario. The poison is one of the deadliest known- the amount in the gut of a single maggot can kill a mallard duck. It's right up there with plutonium on the toxicity scale

Later that summer I rowed out to check on *Sara B* on her mooring and discovered a dead gull sprawled on her deck. And reports began to come in of widespread deaths among the colonial nesting terns and gulls on the rookeries of Little Galloo island where tens of thousands of birds of various species breed each summer. About 800 dead Caspian terns were collected by state workers, perhaps a third of the estimated population of the entire tern rookery. And in the fall, the first (but not last) big outbreak of botulism poisoning occurred on Lake Ontario among migrant fish eaters, killing thousands of birds. Loons, mergansers, grebes, and gulls washed up all along the lake's south shore. During a dreary walk on the short stretch of sandy swim beach at Sodus Point in October, a friend and I counted a dozen victims. More than 340 loons were picked up near Rochester in a two mile stretch of shoreline.

One writer has called these widespread outbreaks of poisoning on all the lakes a "reoccurring nightmare." That sums it up pretty well for me. I peered anxiously at every dead bird I saw floating in the water during the rest of our cruise (and I saw a half dozen). I failed to see the loon pair at Main Duck Island that summer. Then came the news late that fall that once again bodies of fish eating birds were washing ashore this time on the beaches at the lake's east end.

Botulism is produced from a strain of *botulina* that thrives in the 'dead zones' of the lake that develop after an excess of plant matter collects and rots. The plants involved are mostly a type of "seaweed" known as *Chladophora,* a filamentous algae that grows on rocks and other underwater hard surfaces like boat bottoms that didn't get a coat of antifouling last spring. The algae grow and flourish because of nutrients reaching the open lake from sewage and farm field run off. And the vast numbers of recently introduced zebra and quagga mussels contribute to the problem by filtering one celled algae from the water for their food. This increases the water transparency which in turn has greatly increased the area of lake bottom that gets enough sunlight to support the attached *Chladophora*. These days algae can grow at depths of 40 feet (or more) much deeper and farther offshore than it could grow back when I was walking around on those dried six inch thick mats of it in the 1960s.

When the vegetation on the lake bottom dies and decays it uses up oxygen and provides a perfect anaerobic environment for Botulina bacteria growth. The bacteria or their spores and accompanying toxins are then taken up by bottom dwelling zebra mussels. Various birds are exposed to the toxin either by eating the mussels or by eating the round goby, another invasive species from the Caspian Seas, the same area of the world that the zebra mussel immigrated from. These small bottom dwelling fish frequently dine on mussels and may acquire enough poison in their gut to kill the birds that eat them.

Most cities now treat their sewage, so it is known that the majority of the nutrients fueling these algae blooms are coming from farm fields. Excess manure from CAFOs heavily dependent on corn and soy production is part of the problem, but one has to also draw a connection between blue green algae blooms and dead zones and the federal subsidies and mandates of corn produced ethanol now being used to spike the nation's gasoline supply. Not only is use of gasoline with 10

% ethanol questionable and 15% downright incompatible with many elderly inboard boat motors and two cycle outboards, it is also elevating corn prices prompting a huge increase in acreage planted in corn. That acreage is shedding silt, herbicides and pesticides and chemical fertilizer into the lake.

Robert Howarth of Cornell University, an oceanographer who has studied nitrate pollution for decades has a video up on line that I showed to a group of unhappy cottage owners on Sodus Bay at a public information presentation shortly after the first big blue green bloom. In it he says "Corn is particularly 'leaky' as a crop for losing nitrogen." He explains on camera that the fertilizer used on Midwestern cornfields is the principle culprit responsible for the Gulf of Mexico's dead zone, a huge swath of ocean devoid of fish and shellfish. Although no crop can absorb all the fertilizer applied to it, corn is especially wasteful. Its shallow roots use only the nitrogen in the top few inches of soil, and unlike most plants, corn takes up nitrogen for only two months of the year. Howarth said, (typically), "a quarter or more of the nitrogen fertilizer (applied to corn) is wasted, running off the fields and into rivers and streams..."

A few months after Sodus Bay's massive blue green algae bloom, a group of concerned residents, your author among them, launched a public education and outreach campaign against factory farming in general and winter spreading of manure in particular in the small town of Rose a few miles south of the bay. Ironically, the initial spark for organizing came from a big dairy farm's expansion of its manure storage capacity, presumably done in part to minimize winter spreading. The dairy built their new lagoon a short distance from the town's drinking water well field in an area of town that had been supplied with public water a few years before and designated as "residential" with the idea of encouraging future home building in that part of town. The unhappy neighbors invited Barbara Sha Cox a nationally known expert on CAFOs and health and environmental issues associated with them, to speak to farmers and concerned residents at a public meeting.

Cox, a former dairy farmer and retired nurse, is the founder of Indiana CAFO Watch. Her focused tireless approach to educating and lobbying in the state legislature and in rural communities throughout Indiana Ohio and elsewhere caught the attention of Dan Kirby, a former New York Times reporter and the author of *Animal Factory:The Looming Threat Of Industrial Pig Poultry And Dairy Farms To Humans And The Environment.* He calls this matronly woman "indefatigable" and included an account of her work in his book .

The Rose meeting took place in a former elementary school building on a clear frosty November night. Fields of corn stubble and crusty mud lay under a serene silver moon as a large group of unhappy people gathered in the auditorium of the Rose Community Center. The program organizers were a little nervous. Cox, an experienced campaigner of many years who has spoken hundreds of times, told them to expect a strong contingent of Farm Bureau members who would attend in solidarity with their beleaguered dairyman confederate. "I know I'll be talking to a hostile audience."

However, her cheerful pragmatism and her genuine empathy for both neighbor and farmer set a tone of civility and to everyone's relief the meeting went well. This former nurse who knew plenty of family farmers in her home state, understood exactly what they were up against. Low milk prices. Get big or get out. My neighborhood grocery each week sells a few gallons of organic milk for around five dollars a half gallon and hundreds of jugs of $3.50 a gallon regular milk. The relentless consolidation of the dairy business that now depends on thousands of cows and on low wage workers and big cap management of cows and humans alike as "units of production" to produce cheap milk has profoundly changed the upstate New York landscape. And not for the better in many respects.

Along with shale gas extraction by hydrofracking, factory farming is one of the most polarizing and divisive issues in rural America today. Both set neighbor against neighbor in a particularly nasty way. Right To Farm Laws which trump local zoning restrictions leave small farmers and other rural neighbors of CAFOs feeling helpless and angry. The big scale farmers fighting low prices, feel isolated and besieged. "Respect," said Cox. "Both sides need it."

The large room was filled that night with dairymen, unhappy manure lagoon neighbors and waterfront home owners still angry about the summer's toxic bloom on Sodus Bay. The bay residents muttered about declining property values and a suggestion was floated about putting their property taxes in escrow as a protest to get the county government's attention. The manure lagoon neighbors groused mostly about the stink, the flies, cow crap on their roads and mailboxes and the truck traffic consisting of large manure tankers traveling at brisk speeds on narrow curving roads as they shuttled back and forth between field and lagoon. The town supervisor fretted about his water supply.

"The right to farm is not the right to do harm. Farming can't be up there on a pedestal. It has to be subject to regulation like other businesses," Cox told the group.

She was referring to Right To Farm laws enacted in a number of states including New York in the 1980s after suburban sprawl led to conflict between established farmers and new home owners in the exurbs who disliked noise, smells and pesticide applications. Those right to farm laws were not intended to protect gigantic operations with 5,000 cows or 10,000 hogs from air and water pollution standards that other industries must comply with. Toxic ammonia emissions and dangerous levels of hydrogen sulfide in excess of clean air act mandates must be curbed to protect land and home values and human health as well as the environment. Currently CAFOs are not subject to regulation under the Clean Air Act.

Big CAFOs, like the hydro frackers, are also exempt from key federal water quality regulations that have been imposed upon smaller point sources of pollution like municipal sewage treatment plants under the Clean Water Act. Recently the EPA has made a few attempts to increase oversight of industrial scale farms against stiff well organized resistance in Congress but progress has been slow. Various court cases have sought to change that, but to date courts have ruled in favor of the farmers 'right to pollute'.4

For now, as with shale gas fracking, the states are largely responsible for regulating pollution from industrial agriculture. And as the waters of

Sodus Bay and Lake Ontario's botulism outbreak suggest, New York isn't doing a great job. All too often when state regulation is up against large well financed industries like the food processors or the oil and gas industry, the result is "a race to the bottom" through reduced regulation. Or sometimes states seeking economic growth will slack off on enforcement of existing regulation. Recently, New York's Governor sought to ease regulation of CAFOs with the goal of increasing yogurt production in the state.

In a 2006 report by Environmental Integrity Project, a non-profit established by several former EPA attorneys, the failure of both regulation and the enforcement of what weak laws are on the books is laid out in depressing detail. Budget limits are a big part of the problem. In Lake Erie's watershed the few permitted CAFOs were visited every five years by a state inspector. The report stated *"In general, state agencies are receiving less than half of the resources they need to fully implement the Clean Water Act permitting program for all sources."*

Cox showed photos of a lagoon liner inflated by giant bubbles of methane, massive applications of liquid manure laying thick and brown on barren fields, and a sadly degraded man made lake in southern Ohio called Grand Lake Saint Mary's that the state had spent millions of dollars on to clean up after intense toxic blooms of blue greens threatened human health and made recreation impossible. She spoke of deadly ammonia fumes and of massive antibiotic use by CAFO owners, promoting antibiotic resistance among important and deadly human pathogens. The farmers listened. So did the rest of the audience.

Sadly however, the winter spreading continues on the New York shore of Lake Ontario. Ontario Province outlawed the practice some years ago and Vermont on the shore of the almost great lake Champlain bans winter spreads but New York like most of the Great Lakes states simply says 'it should be avoided'. Recently, perhaps with the memory of a five day ban on drinking water in Toledo after a hazardous algae bloom in Lake Erie, Ohio did ban winter spreads.

A few days after *Sara B's* cruise concluded at the end of June 2013, the Sierra Club and River Keeper sued New York State over the decision to deregulate manure spreading practices even further for smaller CAFOs in a bid to promote milk production for a booming Greek yogurt markets. Maybe as one cynic remarked all the fracking water from Pennsylvania will take care of the problem by killing the algae.

4. Cow Power And Other Clean Water Solutions

Loon killed by botulism Lake Ontario in 2006

Big farm operators are currently polluting water and killing birds and fish because of loop holes in federal regulation that prevent the Clean Water Act from regulating runoff from their fields. Currently only "point sources" of water pollution are fully regulated. General runoff from a farm field is not considered a point source unless it collects in a ditch and then moves into the lake. So most of it escapes the permit process. And even the point sources of pollution are not well regulated. In 2008 the Government Accountability Office (GAO) in reported "no federal agency collects accurate and consistent data on the number, size, and location of CAFOs." As we have seen before and will see again (most notably in the chapter on Lake Ontario's nuclear industry,) this is an effective way to not solve a problem. If you have no data, then there's no problem. And no regulation.

The EPA estimates (remember, they have no way of knowing) that less than half the CAFOs have permits to discharge pollutants from point sources. And the likelihood that anyone is enforcing the conditions of those permits is nil. So it's mostly suggestions and voluntary compliance on the part of the agriculture industry that protect water from excess manure applications. Recommended "best management practices" do little to keep the nutrients in the fields if they aren't followed. The author has observed a number of occasions in her small sector of the lake's watershed when manure disposal has sharply differed from the recommendations promoted by all those paid professional manure managers. (Two weeks before this was written in February 2015, I drove by a field of brown snow and a manure spreader on a field beside Wolcott Creek, that feeds into Port Bay).

One reason often cited for withholding information on farm manure management from the public is that, like the composition of fracking fluid, it's "proprietary". It's nobody's business but my own how I run my farm. Some CAFO operators say they fear reprisals from fanatical destructive terrorist animal activists if their information is made public. It seems like a bit of a stretch to keep information on farm manure management plans private because of some imagined advantage to competitor CAFOs or because of eco-terrorists. But it does seem logical to withhold information about the farm's potential to pollute local water from inquisitive downstream neighbors and owners of waterfront property. Then it's possible to blame the blue green bloom in the bay on leaking septic systems or Canada goose poop. Nobody can prove otherwise.

Leaving regulation up to the states is not a great option either. Water, botulism toxin, blue green algae, and manure readily cross state lines. Already there are tensions between two states within Lake Erie's watershed about different regulations on manure that prompt the CAFOs near the state line to 'export' their waste across the line to the other state. Some of this has been done with federal subsidies to the tune of over 200,000 dollars in transport costs in the name of protecting the previously mentioned Grand Lake St. Marys.[1]

Some farmers in the Lake Ontario watershed are working to fix the problem of too much manure on too little land. Despite low milk prices and tight profit margins they are finding ways to deal with anaerobic methane belching manure lagoons by using digesters to process their animal waste. The methane digester for treating manure has been in wide use in Europe since mid 1980's. Today Germany has almost 7000 large digesters producing and collecting "biogas" (methane) from manure and food wastes. The country generates around 2300 MW of electricity by doing so. Recently a handful of farm operators have begun installing digesters in Lake Ontario's watershed using grants and low interest loans from the USDA and other government sources to finance them.

When I heard there was a big dairy farm in Lake Ontario's watershed that had a digester feeding power into the grid and also had an owner willing to show members of the public around the place, I went for a visit. Patterson Farms, a family dairy for six generations that had about 1700 cows when we visited is located an hour's drive south of *Sara B's* home port. I and two other environmentally minded factory farm neighbors took a land cruise to the farm on a chilly early March morning to check out 'cow power' in upstate New York.

New York ranks near the top in the nation in dairy production, and southern Cayuga County has one of the largest concentrations of cows in the state. One of the bigger operations, Willet Dairies, had a 5000 cow herd in 2010. With abundant precipitation for forage crops and a large market for fluid milk downstate, this area of rolling hills and deep narrow lakes has long been a stronghold for dairy farming. And since each milking cow also produces about 18 gallons of manure daily, we're also one of the top manure producers in the country with plenty of water quality impacts from farm waste. Oneida Lake was a poster child for blue green algae blooms for half a century and nitrate/nitrogen levels remain stubbornly high here despite millions of dollars spent for remediation over the last thirty years.

"It all started with the smell," Connie Patterson told us. About fifteen years ago the farm's dairy barn burned, and her family had to decide- keep farming or quit. They decided to keep farming, but to do so, they had to grow. Low milk prices forced them to follow the advice of Ezra Taft Benson who back in the 1950s told farmers "get big or get out." Farmers have been doing so ever since with subsidies encouragement and advice from the U.S. Government. In fact consolidation has been so relentless that the U.S. Census no longer recognizes "farmer" as a job category. Farming is now lumped in with fishing and forestry. Less than 0.7% of the U.S. population works at those collective occupations. Most of those farms are huge. There are dairies out west that milk 30,000 cows. In New York the pattern for at least twenty years has been for a dairy farmer to quit and sell out to his neighbor who gets bigger. But as Connie put it, she didn't want to be the one to decide to give up the farm. Instead, she opted to keep it going so her children could decide if they wanted to stay on the land.

The Patterson's increased their herd size and installed a "modern" manure handling set up with manure and liquids stored in a large pit near the barn. The stench was staggering. And there was too much manure for the fields to absorb. The excess fertilizer ran off and polluting nearby streams and drainage ditches clogging them with weeds and green slime.

"Manure management" I had learned previously from Barbara Sha Cox is today a well organized discipline of ag engineering with consultants, university researchers, college courses and lots of tax payer supported grants and federal financial incentives for farmers to reduce smells and water pollution. Big farms have full time "manure managers" (yes, as Dave Berry would say I'm not making this up. It really is a job title). These paid professionals take care of all the bulls...t and the paper work, too. Clearly the Patterson Dairy was in need of improved management of their manure. They decided voluntarily to do something about the problem. And the smell. They invested in a manure digester.

Digesters used on dairy farms are waterproof pits with air tight covers. The pit is filled with liquid manure and/or other organic material. Bacteria rot the manure in a warm oxygen free environment to produce compost, liquid, and a mix of gases that is mostly methane. If food wastes are added enough methane is produced to make it worthwhile to collect and burn it to produce electricity. More importantly for Lake Ontario's ecosystem, digesters greatly reduce the quantity of liquid that has to be disposed of so that the farm fields can absorb it. These nutrient rich liquids are almost odorless and can be stored until needed at planting season. Solids from the process are typically composted and used for animal bedding on the farm or sold to landscapers and gardeners. Digesters capture smells and gas that would otherwise be released into the atmosphere from an open manure pit.

The reduced volume of liquid costs less to truck or pump onto the land than conventional liquid manure. It is injected into the soil beside the growing plants for immediate take up. With less volume there's no need for winter spreading. And far less fertilizer leaks from or otherwise leaves the field.

As has been documented in Pennsylvania's shale gas rush and elsewhere, methane released into the atmosphere is a potent greenhouse gas. Currently methane produced by ruminant farm animals and manure lagoons that hold their wastes is believed to add up to more methane emissions globally than from all gas and oil production and transport. The huge uncovered lagoons on factory farms like the one that riled up the neighbors in Rose release vast amounts of green house gases, equivalent in climate change impact to tens of thousands of automotive road trips. Why not capture and produce power with it?

While digesters have been in wide use in Europe for decades where limited land and water resources are more valued than in North America, the Patterson family found themselves on the cutting edge of biogas production technology here after their digester went on line, and it wasn't a comfortable place to be. For one thing there was the paperwork.

Connie, a former business teacher, estimates she spent over 1700 hours on grant and loan applications, permits, engineering, and other paperwork. Imagine doing your federal income tax long form 1040, add in forms a,b,c,d,e, and multiply by twenty. Then while you're at it, try to run a farm and raise a family. Remember the herd has to be fed, watered, and milked two or three times a day seven days a week, 365 days a year. Either you do it, or you supervise somebody else to do it.

Not many farmers can afford the time and regulatory hassles of installing a digester. There are currently only a few dozen in New York State. You have to be passionate in your belief that it's the right thing to do. But Connie managed. Today her farm puts over 4000 kW a day into the grid, enough to power a hundred homes. She boosts her methane output by accepting food wastes from a dairy products plant. It's like adding gasoline to a fire, she explained. Without that additional input, the digester would do little more than maintain itself. But with added food waste the farm was able to add a second engine and generator and actually make a bit of money by selling power back into the electrical grid.

Operating and maintaining the digester and its associated electrical generating machinery takes considerable time. That's why some farmers share labor,set up costs, operation, and maintenance with co-operative digesters.

In Vermont a public utility and a half dozen dairy farms established an agreement to generate electricity from digester biogas. Customers sign up for "Cow Power" and pay a premium of four cents a kilowatt hour, most of which goes back to the farms to help with set up and maintenance costs. (Big twenty foot deep methane digester pits lined with steel reinforced cement, generators, engines, wiring, electrical controls and other gear don't come cheap. The Patterson's set up ran over 1.7 million dollars). The Vermont utility believes that in a few years ten percent of its power could be produced from manure and food waste.

But in New York, Connie told us, public policy must catch up with the technology before biogas can be a serious power producer. Under current law in New York a small power producer can't get a good price for electricity fed into the grid. In 2009 she was being paid only 3 to 4 cents per kilowatt hour for her production. That's because if you make more electricity than you consume, the excess is sold into the grid at widely varying "avoided cost" rates and is reconciled annually. This makes revenue projections (and financing of equipment) difficult. Long term purchase agreements that guarantee the cow power producer will get a set amount of revenue over a set time are needed. One consultant suggests that for farmers to get serious about power sales they would need to receive around 12 cents a kilowatt hour.[2]

The outdated electrical grid is another problem as it was designed many years ago to deliver power to rural areas over long distance. It was not designed to deal with numerous small producers feeding into it.

And the grid operators are not particularly friendly to dealing with "distributed" generation spread around the countryside, since it involves engineering and expense to re-design the grid. In Vermont a safe reliable interconnection between farm and the grid had to be designed by the electric utility to satisfy the grid operator. In New York the small producers are hit with a stiff fee to connect up.

Vermont has managed to do it. Some 10,000 dairy cows are now contributing "Cow Power" from biogas generators. Farmers are paid an extra 'incentive' each month to help cover the labor involved in operating their plants in addition to regular market rates for power. The Killington Ski Resort website states that they're purchasing enough power from the program to run one of their lift lines.

In other countries biogas from various sources is replacing fossil fuels. Sweden runs a fleet of buses on biogas and one study done in California suggests half the cows in that state could power the entire California vehicle fleet that now uses natural gas. And if food processor waste and other organic materials supplemented dairy manure, California's cows could generate over 200 MW of power. We might not be able to retire Lake Ontario's fleet of nuclear plants yet, but biogas is well worth consideration as a way to reduce green house gas emissions and keep excess nutrients out of the great lakes.

Last summer I visited a small scale effort to clean up nutrient laden water that took a very different approach than the 1.7 million dollar digester on the Patterson dairy farm. It involved something called 'mycoremediation' and was initiated by a 73 year old adjunct biology professor and life long environmental advocate named Eugenia

Siracusa. She had teamed up with the local Soil and Water office to build a living water filter of sorts on a small polluted drainage creek running into Owasco Lake, part of Lake Ontario's watershed near Auburn.

Mycoremediation is an experimental but promising field of research that uses the mycelial growth of various fungi to treat pollution. Fungi, like the bacteria with which they compete in many environments, use an astonishing array of biochemical processes to break down material for their food. They typically grow as a network of fine threadlike filaments called mycelium on a substrate that they digest using enzymes produced by the mycelial strands. (The actual mushroom familiar as an item on the dinner plate is the spore producing part of the much larger mostly unseen organism).

Some species of fungi are capable of reducing toxic pesticides and chemicals into harmless sugars and ultimately into CO_2 and water. Fungi in the lab have degraded nerve gas and have been used in the field to break down crude oil and diesel fuel in soil. Some fungi are able to actively concentrate heavy metals like lead and cadmium making them easier to remove from contaminated soil. One species even managed in a trial to concentrate radioactive cesium 137 10,000 fold over the amount present in the environment. Another can exist solely on polyurethane plastic. So called bio beds, shallow basins filled with organic material like waste straw or wood debris that supported bacteria and fungi have successfully treated pesticide laced water in Europe.

Fungi often compete with bacteria in soil and it's not surprising that some can destroy certain bacteria (the first antibiotic, penicillin, was isolated from a mold). The ditch water Siracusa wanted to clean up was heavily polluted with fecal coliforms, so she chose to try the mycelium of a common edible mushroom. This species has reduced coliform concentrations in a number of small scale lab experiments. In a field study in coastal Washington State funded by the EPA, polluted run off from a dairy lagoon was successfully treated by running it through a retention basin lined with wood chips that had been inoculated with mushroom spawn. The *Stropharia* mushroom, commonly called the garden giant, actually feeds on coliform bacteria and removed 90% of the coliforms in the Washington study when water was passed through a 'filter' of living mycelium filaments. However, other experiments with it in the field have been less conclusive. Retention times, varying rates of flow, and changing temperatures make working with living filters in the field a challenge.

Siracusa and her collaborators attempted to create a quick and dirty "retention cell" (a small artificial wetland of sorts) that would allow the polluted ditch water to trickle through a bed of wood chips that had been inoculated with mushroom spawn. Unfortunately, for the cause of science and clean water, two days after the ditch had been scooped out and the wood chips had been dumped in and sprinkled with mushroom spawn, a gully washer thunderstorm hit the area with five inches of rain. It washed out a good share of the freshly created wood chip bed. Undaunted, the crew re-built it and sat back to wait. As of this writing, the results were inconclusive though it did appear some reduction of bacteria concentrations had occurred.

Despite the challenges, there is plenty of interest in living filters as a possible inexpensive way to clean up farm field runoff. A number of variations on mycoremediation are under study. In the Midwest so called "bioreactors", trenches filled with wood chips that take runoff from tiled farm field drains, have reduced nitrogen nutrient run off up to 50% through microbial action. Cornell researchers have installed several experimental bioreactors in the Susquehanna drainage area of the state and initial results have been promising, being similar to those in other areas. As with any new technology there will be failures and sidetracks enroute to success. But the pay off with living filters ultimately is an efficient and cost effective clean up.[3]

All farming and manure production take place in a watershed. A lake cannot be healthy without a healthy watershed. Until a little over two hundred years ago Lake Ontario's watershed consisted mostly of woodlands and thousands of acres of marshland and swamp. Forests act as living purifying water filters. The intricate structure of trees, roots, fungal mycelium, forest litter and living soil slow water's movement giving it time to be cleansed and allow the recharge of underground aquifers. Wetlands also allow materials to settle and be absorbed and filtered. Today, most of the watershed's historic wetlands have been drained, and our American food system is built largely on a vast acreage of row crops like corn and soybeans and on other annual grains. Much of this acreage is subsidized by taxpayers through various U.S. Department of Agriculture programs ranging from low interest loans and crop insurance to direct payments and crop price supports. The result is lots of bare compacted soil in the Great Lakes watershed.

Fields are doused with chemicals and fertilizers each growing season and then filled with a single crop of vegetation. After harvest much of the soil is left exposed to erode for long periods. Winter spreading of liquid manure when no plant growth exists to take up the nutrients is permitted in New York's portion of Lake Ontario's watershed. (Though Ontario Province prohibits the practice and Ohio recently passed a law to ban it in Lake Erie's watershed). It would seem obvious what the problems here are. But regulation and common sense elude us.

Humans have a need for security and predictability. Since the invention of agriculture, that relentless drive has accelerated through the industrial age to our present consumption based economy. But agriculture (as with other man made landscapes) invariably simplifies the natural environment. Unwanted life must be eliminated in the name of maximum production of the desired plant or animal. Weeds, predators, pesky plant eating insects, or pathogenic bacteria and other organisms must go.

But the vast sameness of a cornfield or a close clipped lawn of grass has high ecological costs, and the lake is bearing them. These unnatural monocultures can only be maintained by vast inputs of energy in the form of fossil fuel powered machinery and by petrochemical based herbicides and fertilizers, a lot of which end up one way or another degrading our water quality and the aquatic life of the lake.

We like our mowed lawns. There's no chance of encountering a large dangerous predator or a small harmless snake in the clipped grass. But simplification in the name of a predictable secure environment and crop revenues comes at an unacceptable price in the long run. It's been said that creativity is the natural order of life. Only by the constant addition of fossil fuel based energy can we keep the cornfield or grassy lawn uniform, predictable and safe. Nature, the great and tireless creator, seeks to place dandelions and thistles in our predictable world. Diversity is the natural end result of creativity. In the long run, farm fields and lawns are fighting nature's relentless trend towards complexity and intricacy. It is a trend that has prevailed on this planet for over 3.8 billion years as one-celled life evolved into worms, whales, herons, and humans. There isn't much doubt about who the ultimate winner in this particular contest will be.

There are solutions. Reducing food production from CAFOs is an obvious one. Eating less meat is another. However, meat produced on smaller farms would shift some costs away from Lake Ontario and its watershed onto the consumer. Are we ready for that? Until society and government regulation recognizes pollution's "external costs", if you eat meat, consider eating less grain fed meat. If you can afford to buy grass fed beef, organic free range eggs, and milk and cheese from cows kept on pasture, do so.

5. Water And Power

When *Sara B* chugged into the Niagara River and slowly pushed her way upstream against the current to Youngstown, the power of the unseen falls a few miles upstream was apparent. Travelers' accounts from a quieter pre-industrial age say the water's roar could be heard at a distance of fifteen leagues on a calm day, while mist from the falls was visible twenty miles or more. We saw and heard no sign of the falls, but the river's outflow was undeniable. We had reached the end of the lake.

Except for several brief cruises in the Caribbean, three years in coastal saltwater, and one venture offshore to Bermuda, all my sailing has been in a single watershed. I have explored a tide-less salt-free sea for nearly four decades.Like all lakes it is essentially static. Summer squalls and strong winds whip up the surface now and then, but the main body of stillness remains with no daily ebb and flow of tides. So when I have ventured into the rivers at the head or the foot of the lake, their ceaseless movement fascinates me.

As you enter the St. Lawrence or Niagara River, you realize Lake Ontario is part of something very much bigger. The water has only paused here in short term parking in the last basin of a vast system. Then it's off again on its ceaseless travels. Looking up the Niagara River, I wondered what would it be like to turn around, head east along the length of the lake, and steer down the St. Lawrence River to the gulf and on to salt water. For four centuries people have traveled that long liquid highway through rock bound islands, past busy Montreal and Quebec City's old stone walls, and on to the sea.

This water road once transported trappers, priests, traders, treasure seekers and armies. Since Jacques Cartier's day it has been a wealth builder and a pathway of dreams. And a few nightmares. As we entered the river we passed the grim gray walls of Fort Niagara and its landmark French Castle, one of the oldest stone buildings in all the Great Lakes region. Niagara was second only to Quebec as a strategic point in the struggle between France and Britain for control of North America. The first fort built here dates back to the late 1600s. Although the French Castle was originally built as a trading post in 1726, it did not look particularly welcoming that afternoon as it stood vigil at the very edge of the land. Its gray stone walls reminded me of Hamlet's castle enduring grim and alone on the strait between Denmark and Sweden.

The French Castle has seen its share of dark history. Disease, starvation, and battle have visited its four foot thick walls. The castle was built around a well to help it withstand sieges, a well said to be haunted by an unhappy ghost whose body fell in after he was beheaded during a dual. I'm not a big believer in ghosts, but a restless spirit prowling that dark stone chamber by the well felt plausible to me. The massive castle has an almost medieval feel.

After we settled *Sara B* on a mooring in front of the Youngstown Yacht Club, we called up the water taxi on the VHF and took a ride ashore. The fort was a short walk away on this overcast day of light drizzle. About when we passed by an old military cemetery just outside the restored fort, the rain let up. By the time we were finished exploring the fort, a brisk offshore wind was tossing the gulls around blue skies.

Fort Niagara had played a key role in three conflicts before the Treaty of Ghent ended the last one, the War Of 1812. Today, the Rush-Bagot Memorial beside the French Castle overlooks the lake. It's a monument to the 1817 agreement that established an unarmed 5500 mile long border between the U.S. and Canada, (at least it was unarmed before the era of Homeland Security). The memorial is built on a common grave for dead soldiers. Men from the First Nations, Canada, Great Britain, America and France all shed blood here. I turned away from the monument and watched the swallows skimming now silent grassy grounds. Perhaps their ancestors had hawked for insects over a parade ground of drilling musketeers defending this far flung outpost of the Sun King's empire.

During our visit to the very quiet fortress and parade ground, we met a large orange cat who escorted us through the upper floors of the French Castle and saw about a half dozen tourists during our weekday stroll. When we departed the fort and headed back to *Sara B* we noticed a little red fox curled up for a nap in the sun on the grassy ramparts. It wasn't always so quiet here. Once this place teemed with activity.

The first fortification built here was Fort Conti created of logs and earth in 1678. A few years later, the outpost was strengthened as Fort Denonville, built to protect the trade route portage around the falls and to establish a French presence in the lands of the hostile Seneca. A garrison was left here during the winter of 1687-88 under the command of Captain Pierre de Troye, a bold and capable military officer. Historical accounts of the time said of him that he was 'wise sensible and of good will'. But skilled leadership was no match against a northern winter and the surrounding Senecas. Only twelve men were left alive when spring came. Disease, starvation, and scurvy had finished most of the company off. A number of old graves were found inside the fort in 1929. Perhaps they contained the bones of these desperate men.

In the days of the French fur trade, the Niagara portage on what is now the New York shore of the river was especially hectic when the flotilla of canoes and bateaux arrived laden with trade goods from Montreal. Their appearance each August was the great event of the year for the lonely outpost. Then hundreds of Frenchmen, Indians, and Metis voyageurs toiled up the steep portage carrying packs weighing as much as 90 pounds. The Seneca name for the portage on the western shore was said to translate as 'walking on all fours'. Wikipedia notes that hernias were common among the voyageurs. English rum and French brandy no doubt flowed freely at the end of the day among French and

Indian porters alike.

Fort Niagara remained one of the continent's most important military posts for nearly 150 years. Command of Lake Ontario and the all important portage around the falls that gave passage to the four upper great lakes was key to control of North America's interior until after the War of 1812. Starting around 1750 two clusters of settlements grew up on either side of the river both eventually acquiring the name Niagara Falls. After the Revolutionary War, New York State auctioned off a strip of land with water rights along the river and several water powered mills and factories soon sprang up. After the U.S.-Canada boundary was settled once and for all and the British left town in August 1796, the American village population increased rapidly and the destinies of these two sides of the river began to diverge.

By 1842 various canals and wing dams were diverting large volumes of water through dozens of factory penstocks to turbines on the American side, while the Canadian settlement remained considerably less industrialized. A Canadian history of the area refers to the New York side development as "unsightly and unwelcome". On the Canadian shore the old Portage Road and later the Welland Canal and the suspension bridge contributed to the region's rise as a transportation hub and key link to the interior of upper Canada. The area also became an increasingly popular tourism destination with a half dozen hotels standing along the river by the Horseshoe Falls. Within twenty years of war's end, a sixty room three story hotel had been built along with numerous smaller hotels and taverns.

The now famous *Maid of the Mist* boat ride originated as a ferry service from Canada across the river just below the falls. After the first suspension bridge was built in 1848, the boat began making sight seeing trips upriver to within a few yards of the Horseshoe Falls. By now, about 60,000 tourists were visiting the Canadian falls each year. Around 1850 one visitor, William Chambers, wrote, *"the Canadian side had a series of paltry curiosity shops and at the Table Rock a labourer wheeling rubbish into the cataract. The road we took was lined with museums, curiosity shops, refreshment booths and raree-shows, a number of chinese pagoda looking edifices and other incongruous buildings had been erected on the Canadian bank. The banks on the American Falls had saw mills built up..."*

About this time, the Niagara Falls Hydraulic Power and Manufacturing Company of New York changed its name from the less euphonious Hydraulic Tunnel and Sewer Company and began drawing water from the rapids above the falls to run through a canal as a power supply for a cluster of mills and factories. The canal filled a reservoir, and the mills then drew water out for power. They discharged water through tunnels bored through the rock of the gorge. Old photos show a series of tailrace cataracts gushing down the side of the gorge to the river below. By the Civil War the American side of the gorge below the falls was a solid wall of large mills, and the upstream rapids were all but obscured by wing dams that diverted flow to the canals. The aggregate energy used was about 10,000 horsepower, the maximum possible from the physical set up of canal and reservoir to run shaft and belt driven machinery. It wasn't enough. The need and greed for power then, as now, was insatiable. The stage was set for the electrification of

North America.

After the Civil War, land owners fenced the few remaining empty parcels blocking off views of the falls and charged tourists for use of peep holes. On the New York shore at least, tourism was secondary to profit from making things. But a gradual awakening to the importance of nature was gathering strength across America. It took fifteen years of lobbying and campaigning on the part of people seeking to establish permanent public access to the falls, but ultimately they triumphed. In 1883 the first state park in America was established at Niagara Falls to preserve and protect the natural beauty of the river and to allow New Yorkers to see it. When the New York State Reservation at Niagara Falls opened in 1885, it was with a declaration that Niagara Falls was "not property, but a shrine—a temple erected by the hand of the Almighty for all the children of men." Margaret Wooster points out in her book *Living Waters* that the park was a national precedent for the preservation of a natural area for the public good over private profit making activity.[1]

The combined cataracts of the American and the nearly ten times larger Canadian Horseshoe Falls don't make the official Seven Wonders of the World List. But an online list of "forgotten wonders of the world" includes them, and rightfully so. As you stare at the mesmerizing green glassy flow sliding over the lip of the falls, after a while you really do feel like climbing over the fence and jumping. People do it every year. Victorian novelist Anthony Trollope, described that hypnotic movement;

"The cool liquid green will run through your veins and the voice of

the cataract will be the expression of your own heart. You will fall as the bright waters fall, rushing down into your new world with no hesitation and with no dismay: and you will rise again as the spray rises, bright, beautiful and pure. Then you will flow away in your course to the uncompassed, distant and eternal ocean..."

The area also boasts other natural oddities besides the two great falls. Among the downstream gorge's claims to fame are the dwarf cliff hanging white cedar trees, some of them over a thousand years old, and the winter concentration of gulls who come to the ice free river to feed. The Niagara River has been called the best place in North America for birdwatchers to add a rare gull to their life lists with up to 18 species having been seen here. The birds are drawn in part by the dead and maimed fish that have passed through the turbines of the two giant hydro stations on each side of the gorge.

Those hydros total about 4500 MW capacity and are the direct descendants of North America's first large hydro electric plant built here in 1895 to send AC current to Buffalo. At that time Buffalo was a busy place. With a population of 255,000 it just missed being in the top ten American cities population-wise in 1890, and at one point no other place on earth shipped more grain than did this port at the eastern end of Lake Erie. Buffalo was the perfect place to consume all that potential power generated by the falls. But only if it could be transmitted to the city some 25 miles away. Once George Westinghouse and that tragic and fascinating genius, Nikola Tesla, along with other engineers figured out how to transmit polyphase AC over high voltage lines and then step it back down for use in the home or factory, electric power from the falls went to work moving trolley cars around the city and grain in and out of elevators at the port. Soon it also began doing work in people's homes.

The profound transformation of our world by electrification was (pardon the pun) truly shocking. One of its first uses was for lighting. No more coal gas, kerosene, oil or candles needed. The falls were first illuminated in 1879 by a 39 horsepower hydro powered DC generator that powered 16 arc lamps. (This was just three years after carbon lighting had been used to illuminate city streets in Paris.) There followed a long and at times tacky history of lighting up the falls and the gorge with various colored lights that continues to this day. The electrical era was truly the second great wave of industrialization. With it came a whole new range of industries, several of which pioneered their work at Niagara Falls with unfortunate consequences for the lake's human and non human residents alike.

The age of electricity converted Niagara Falls into a prosperous boom town. By 1914, 14,000 people were directly employed in the power generating industry on the U.S. side. The abundance of electricity and water fostered a concentration of electroplating and smelting businesses like the Pittsburgh Reduction Company, an aluminum producer that used electrolysis to create pure and then very costly aluminum metal. Other early industries attracted by inexpensive electrical power were the Carborundum Company, that used electric furnaces to produce very hard silicon carbide crystals used in abrasives, Union Carbide, Norton Abrasives and, in 1903, Hooker Chemical of Love Canal fame.

Hooker Chemical (later bought out by Occidental Petroleum) had all it needed in the Niagara area to build a successful business- abundant water, salt from nearby mines, and cheap power to make chlorine from salt brine by electrolysis. The chlorine was then used to create bleach and chlorinated lime for sanitation. Chlorine soon became a key component of various organochlorides such as polyvinyl chloride resins, vinyl plastics, and pesticides. After the war Hooker developed epoxy vinyl resins used to build fiberglass boats among other useful and profitable items. In the 1940s and 50s a number of chemical companies operated near the river. Some of them had contracts with the Atomic Energy Commission.

Hooker Chemical was not the only manufacturer contributing to future Superfund Sites in the area. A recent report from the Community Foundation For Greater Buffalo states that there are sixty six known active hazardous waste sites in Niagara County alone with another fifteen inactive sites. While Love Canal is far from the only one and may not be the worst one, it is certainly the best known thanks largely to Lois Gibbs a tireless former Niagara Falls resident. As a result of the Love Canal fracas, Congress passed the Comprehensive Environmental Response Compensation and Liability Act (CERCLA) in 1980 better known as "Superfund". This legislation taxed the chemical industry to establish a trust fund to clean up abandoned sites. It also attempted with some success to make polluters liable for the messes that previously the public had to pay for.

Love Canal is an example of a situation in which the community intruded upon the waste rather than the more usual situation of toxins escaping, spilling, or otherwise impacting a settlement. The canal itself was originally dug from the Niagara River by William Love to supply hydro electric generated DC power to a planned industrial settlement he called Model City. The project foundered, partly because of the success of that long distance AC transmission line to Buffalo that Westinghouse installed. But the section of abandoned canal he did finish proved to be a convenient place for the U.S. Army, the City of Niagara Falls and the Hooker Chemical Company to use for dumping wastes. (It's worth recalling that in 1950 this was and in some areas of the world still is, the standard method of dealing with toxic and radiological material. Find a nice rural area, usually good level farm land, and bury the stuff. Make it go away. Maybe somehow someday it will magically compost like orange peels and cardboard.)

The history of development in the Love Canal neighborhood of Niagara Falls in the 1950s when the baby boomers were moving out into the suburbs and when new homes and schools were going up all over the upstate countryside, is a depressing indictment of leadership failures at the local, state, and national levels. As residences and schools were built across a once rural upstate countryside of orchards, farm fields and old industrial sites, cutting corners and dismissing potential hazards and long term risks were the normal course of action in Niagara Falls and just about everywhere else.

Gibbs wrote; "Perhaps because they didn't understand the potential risks associated with Hooker's chemical wastes, the Board of Education began in 1954 to construct an elementary school on the canal property." Others have described a history of development here that suggests her assessment of the school board's grasp of the situation was highly charitable.[2] The Hooker Company actually put a statement in their property deed that warned of the presence of chemical wastes on the land. Yet written documentation shows the school board threatened to take the property by eminent domain if the company wouldn't sell.

Soon after the sale, the city had laid a sewer line through the middle of the repository allowing chemicals to leach out and follow the line through the neighborhood. Then more fill was scraped off the dump site during construction of the school. In 1968 the State Department of Transportation ripped into one section of the dump site while building an expressway. Then the school board sold off some of the land to various developers who put up housing.

By the late 1970s there were about 800 single family homes plus some low income apartment units in the area. No one showed the the new homeowners and renters the warnings on the deed to the original parcel sold to the school district for one dollar. But before long they were noticing odors and pools of liquid and an alarming amount of sickness in their households. In 1978 the New York Dept of Health conducted a study that found various toxic and carcinogenic contaminants. The home owners got organized, demanded help, and eventually most of them were moved, and their houses were bought up by the tax payers of New York. The worst of the dump site was "remediated" with drains to collect water that was then routed through charcoal filters to remove toxins before the leachate entered the Niagara River.

Today much of the mess is contained and monitoring for a variety of chemicals at the site is on going. This is more than you can say for some areas of the former Lake Ontario Ordinance Works. This particular nightmare is located just down the river from Niagara Falls and Love Canal in the countryside outside Lewiston. It resulted from military activity during World War II and in the early years of the Cold War. In 1941 the U.S. Government acquired 7500 acres of farmland about three miles from Lake Ontario and began making TNT for the war effort here. Later in the war, some of the Ordinance Works was set aside for rad waste from Manhattan Project work at a plant in Tonawanda where the abundant power from the falls was used for uranium enrichment.

Today assorted wastes from World War II and other secret military atomic energy projects remain buried underground out of sight and mostly out of mind. Among the leftovers here are the remains of some unfortunate lab animals that were exposed to high levels of radiation during experiments at the University of Rochester, along with plutonium and uranium that was extracted during efforts to recycle spent nuclear fuel at the Knolls Atomic Power Lab in Schenectady. Most of the material remains in a 195 acre site known as the Niagara Falls Storage Site (NFSS) that was taken over after the war by the federal predecessor to today's Department Of Energy. DOE still owns this portion of the property. Some of the radioactive materials stored there will remain hazardous to human health for thousands of years.

There are at least fifty buried containers of toxic material and figuring out what is in them has been a real challenge for the various government agencies charged with their stewardship. Wartime records were often sketchy to say the least. It's believed about 20,000 tons of material contaminated with low levels of radioactivity remain on site. A consultant wrote in 1982 "Waste disposal at LOOW was characterized by poor record keeping and general mismanagement with rad waste being buried, left on the surface in several areas and openly burned."

A report from 2001 by the Environmental Law Institute noted isotopes of uranium, radium, thorium and various toxic metals and organic compounds were known to be present at the property. Hot spots then contained radioactive emissions hundreds of times above 'safe' levels. A drainage ditch that moves water into Lake Ontario tributaries was reported to contain radium at 300 times New York State's recommended safe levels. The site is said to contain one of the largest known concentrations of radium 226, perhaps half of the world's supply. Most of the worst of this has since been 'cleaned up' and/ or contained. For the time being.

Part of the LOOW site is presently still being used as a chemical waste dump site (and is actively monitored under the terms of its permits). Adding to the original radioactive material and other government leftovers is a toxic stew of industrial pollution added after the feds sold land off in the early 1970s to private companies in the trash and toxic waste hauling business. Soon they were bringing PCB's, pesticides, solvents and a witches brew of industrial chemistry by the tanker load to the Niagara region for disposal. For years dirt contaminated with poorly described radiological material was pushed and shoved around by the landfill operator complicating later attempts to contain and clean up the worst contamination. There are some 'data gaps' as the consultants put it on the Chemical Waste Management portion of property, but we do know every day dozens of truckloads of toxic chemicals from all over the Northeast come to here a few miles from Lake Ontario to be put "away" in the ironically named Model City site. But where is "away"? How long do plastic liners remain water tight and how long before leachate collection systems fail?

Today the dump is the only site licensed to take hazardous waste in the northeastern U.S. It contains an unholy stew of industrial waste and radiological contaminants seasoned with those 'data gaps' and uncertainties. The NYS Department of Health has requested detailed surveys of radiation contamination at the surface, but Chemical Waste Management LLC, a company with a checkered past in its relationship with regulators and government, has dragged its feet. Small amounts of radioactive decay products of R 226 have been detected in the waters of one of the lagoons that discharges to the Niagara River.[3] And now the operator wants to expand the dump.

In 2008 an independent consultant, King Groundwater Science Inc, published a 232 page report *"The Community LOOW Project"* on the Ordinance Works site for the Niagara County Department of Health. One issue they noted is that of "fragmented jurisdictional oversight". This, the report says, has resulted in a "general lack of trust" between some members of the community and the government agencies overseeing the LOOW site. The Lake Ontario Ordinance Works Restoration Advisory Board (LOOWRAB) formed in 1999 and was made up of citizens and local elected officials. It worked with the main agency charged with clean up, the U.S. Army Corps of Engineers. A few years later, the Army Corps attempted to dissolve the Restoration Advisory Board, a move squelched by the NY Attorney General as being clearly outside the law. Under a Federal program called FUSRAP (Formerly Used Site Remedial Action Program) the Army Corps is charged with radiologic and chemical investigations here and at dozens of other sites around the country.

The advisory board has since been dissolved and another group has been put in its place by the Army Corps. Some of the old board re-organized as the Community Action Council and continues to communicate with the public and with the Army Corps as it works with government agencies on proposals to clean up the site and tries to obtain funding for doing so.

Several other agencies are also charged with responsibility for the property including the Department of Energy (formerly the Atomic Energy Commission), the EPA, the New York State Department of Environmental Conservation and the New York Department of Health. With overlapping and piecemeal responsibilities plus historic secrecy, it often happens that a given problem slips through the cracks and no one sees to a resolution of it. Such seems to have been the situation for much of the history of the LOOW, leading to some of the mistrust mentioned above.

A temporary repository now equipped with a liner and capped with clay contains much of the radium and other less radioactive soils and materials. This so called interim waste containment area was designed to last 25 years (or perhaps 50 years or maybe 200 years depending on whose model you use and the assumptions of same). It's been in place for 25 years, and there have been reports of high levels of uranium in several of the monitoring wells around the containment. The reports prompted the Army Corps to drill more test wells which to date have not detected movement of radioactive ground water off the site, according to Dr. Joeseph Gardella, a chemist, an expert on industrial pollution, and a member of the Community Action Council who has studied mapped and inventoried the materials and issues associated with the LOOW site for many years.

As of this writing the Army Corps was completing a feasibility study of various options for remedial action ranging from total clean up to doing nothing. Dr. Gardella and others in the Lewiston area are advocating for everything to be removed, but the elephant in the room is cost. It will not be cheap to excavate and transport thousands of tons of high and low level radioactive waste to more secure locations. As one activist put it these radiological clean ups are "gruesomely complex". And costly. This one could run two billion or more.

Nationwide efforts to 'clean up' cold war legacies of a nuclear nature have so far cost over 100 billion dollars. One estimate is that the ultimate tab will run over 300 billion. That's without the usual cost overruns. The Army Corps is is still a year or more away from a final decision on what should be done at the LOOW site as of this writing in 2015. Then, notes Dr. Gardella, the problem will be raising the money to do it. The Army Corps has no budget for this type of clean up. A special appropriation from Congress will be required. Gardella told me "Our (New York) federal elected officials get the issue really well." But can they convince other members of Congress to protect our Great

Lake?

* * *

As has been demonstrated many times trash attracts trash. New York state officials and local residents in the form of a "Siting Board" appointed by the governor in early 2015 were considering whether to grant a permit to Chemical Waste Management Inc. for expansion of its landfill, perilously close to the Canadian border and our shared water. Do we ever learn? The site is less than five kilometers from the Niagara River, already filled with so many chemicals that it's listed as an official area of concern by the International Joint Commission, the group that oversees the shared waters of Lake Ontario. According to an email from the Niagara Chapter of the Sierra Club member Charles Lamb, the permit application has been referred to a Siting Committee, presided over by an Administrative Judge. The group will review all the comments and hold meetings. Lawyers representing Niagara County, the Lewiston Porter School Board, and others will speak and bring expert witnesses. The Siting Board consists of five persons serving in state government and three local residents. Lamb wrote me in early 2015, "It seems clear to me that the testimony given in the earlier hearings was overpowering in its evidence against granting a permit, with the Niagara County Health Department, Lew Port School Board, Town of Lewiston, Village of Lewiston, Village of Youngstown, Sierra Club, and the Residents for Responsible Government, all speaking against the permit. Even the Department of Environmental Conservation said that an additional toxic waste landfill site is not needed."

He then concluded "Personal opinion only: if the permit is granted I think that our democratic system is not working very well." I would say that would be an understatement- but private profits at cost to the public who are left to clean the leftovers up is hardly unique to the Niagara area.

6. Pipelines, Unconventional Oil Plays and the Lake

On a calm sunny June morning we steered *Sara B* through a narrow channel into Burlington Bay. Two bridges loomed overhead, first a four lane lift bridge then the lofty fixed QEW Skyway arcing high above our two masts. Both of the huge steel structures were crowded with roaring rushing cars and trucks belching out copious amounts of green house gas and noise. *Sara B* and her crew had chugged into the industrial heart of the "Golden Horseshoe" of Canada, a heavily urbanized area that stretches from Niagara Falls to Canada's largest city, Toronto. Almost nine million people, more than a quarter of the entire nation's population, live mostly fast paced lives within the region. They work in heavy industries, at world class universities and research labs, at the Toronto Stock Exchange, in banking and finance, in government and tourism related jobs and in dozens of other industries. They make movies and publish books, cast lead keels for sailboats, build automobiles, write music, and create artwork. And though the heart of Ontario's once thriving industrial economy is now quieter than in years past, there is still plenty going on in the old blue collar town of Hamilton, home to over 700,000 people.

Our plan on this gentle summer day was to visit two of them, members of the Maccassa Bay Yacht Club who were the owners of a small wooden schooner that, like our own, was a classic Nova Scotia design. We had met the couple several years ago at a wooden boat fest and greatly enjoyed their company as we sat in their boat's cramped cabin sipping tea and swapping rot stories. We commiserated on owning old boats with obsolete out of production diesel engines that were impossible to find parts for, and we stayed in touch after the wooden boat meet. Now we wanted to re-unite our two little schooners for another gam. *Sara B* had made her way to the extreme west end of Lake Ontario to tie up for two nights as a guest at the hospitable boat club of Doug and Lois and their good little ship *Marina*.

As *Sara B* passed from the narrow channel into the bay, I studied the complex of buildings with associated research and Canadian Coast Guard vessels of various sizes off to starboard that made up one of the world's largest and most comprehensive centers for freshwater research, the Canada Centre for Inland Waters. Little did I know then that a few months after our visit, the conservative party controlled federal government would further slash lab funding already deeply cut the year before and would re-assign many of the researchers to the study of Alberta tar sands. (According to a CBC news story posted on line, the Harper administration eliminated 2000 scientific research positions nationwide between 2008 and 2013.) Nor did I know of the concern of Hamilton's various environmental advocates and city commissions for the future of their efforts to clean up their much abused waterfront after losing so much local academic capacity.[1]

As we ambled along a shoreline of concrete and steel bulkheads, giant tanks, immense warehouses and factory buildings, mysterious small mountains of gray and black material, tall chimneys emitting smudges of smoke and vent pipes spouting orange flames, I wondered how had Hamilton become the manufacturing center of Lake Ontario. How had a city that was once one of the greatest economic powerhouses in Canada grown up here? And how had Burlington Bay become one of the most polluted harbors on all the Great Lakes? What events had brought all this brawny gritty smokestack industry along with coke, coal tar, arsenic, mercury, and other toxins here?

Hamilton and the neighboring city of Burlington on the bay's north shore owe much of their early prosperity to their harbor and shipping. In 1824 construction of the Welland Canal for passage around Niagara Falls began. The next year a channel was cut and stabilized through the gravel bar that separated Lake Ontario from Burlington Bay. Suddenly the bay was the best natural harbor on the lake-big enough with its wide, deep, yet protected waters for a whole fleet of freighters. The permanent channel was an immediate economic boost to the region. Before long, fortunes were rapidly being made as Hamilton became a transportation crossroads and hub.

After the Welland Canal was completed, water dumped from the locks each time they lowered a boat down the Niagara escarpment to the lake was routed to millraces to power factory machinery. Before long, as at Niagara Falls New York, cheap hydro power from

Horseshoe Falls began attracting a variety of manufacturing enterprises. The area's importance as a transportation hub with its shipping connections increased even more after the Niagara Suspension Bridge was completed allowing a direct railroad connection to the bay from the U.S. and western Canada.

The earliest foundries in the 1830s used iron from upstate New York blast furnaces brought to Hamilton's harbor by schooners from Ogdensburg and Rochester as well as from more distant points. Before long, plows kettles and cookstoves were supplemented by other iron and steel products such as those of the R.M. Wanzer Sewing Machine Manufactory that cranked out 2000 sewing machines a week in its glory days. ("Of all the comforts of this life that there can ever be, there's nothing ever pleased my life like the improved Wanzer C".) Among the city's many manufacturing firsts were the first locomotive engine built in Canada, the first cut nail factory, the first saw maker, the first Canadian steel rolling mill, and the first matches made in Canada.

By the later part of the 19th century with the help of tariffs and other protection from competing U.S. industries, Hamilton was "the Birmingham of Canada" a smoky grimy industrial power house for all of Ontario. In 1911 a quarter of the city's population, 18,978 people, were employed in manufacturing. The city's industries then included rolling mills and plants producing products like nails, tacks, screws, wire, agricultural machinery, boilers, bridges, elevators, axles, wheels, and lots and lots of tin cans.

As in Niagara Falls New York, the early hydro electric plants launched a new wave of investment and industrial development including several steel mills, factories, and a Westinghouse plant that made railroad equipment. Hamilton's population nearly doubled in the first decade of the 20th century as the city promoted itself as "home to the cheapest hydro power in the entire world."

In the early 20th century even as finance and insurance shifted increasingly to Toronto's cleaner air and quieter streets, good rail connections port facilities and cheap electricity continued to build Hamilton's industrial might. Several smaller companies combined to form Hamilton Steel and Iron, forerunner of Stelco. Another huge enterprise was Internal Harvester, builder of the familiar little red tractor of my childhood, the Farmall Cub, and a dozen other models of Farmall tractors. International Harvester was then the largest agricultural machinery maker in the British Empire. By the mid 20th century more than 500 manufacturing plants were building elevators, Studebakers, railroad air brakes, washing machines, diesel trucks, railroad freight and passenger cars, tires, and more than a billion Lifesaver mint candies a year. And coal tar, oil, coke, PCB,'s, phenols, benzene, dioxins, mercury, arsenic, lead and a dozen other heavy metals and organic compounds poured into Burlington Bay and settled into its sediments.

By the 1950s the sadly abused waters of Hamilton Harbor were deemed unfit for any recreation and all the city's public beaches were officially closed. Ulcerated and cancerous fish were common, and sewage from the city nourished an abundance of green slime and rotting aquatic vegetation. A single location in the bay, Randle Reef located just offshore from the big Stelco mill, was declared the worst coal tar contaminated site in all Canada. An estimated million tons of sediment is slated for clean up from it at an almost surely optimistic cost estimate of 139 million dollars. In 1970s the IJC officially recognized Hamilton Harbor as one of the most "degraded" sites on all the Great Lakes.

But sometimes when rivers burn and harbors stink, people are moved to act. They dig deep into their pockets and begin the agonizingly slow and costly effort to at least partly restore things to some semblance of their previous condition. Since the 1960's various government entities and industries have spent about 800 million dollars on clean up of the harbor. The city of Hamilton has installed storage capacity to hold storm water runoff that formerly went straight to and through the city sewage plant causing raw sewage to enter the bay. The wetland area known as Cootes Paradise at the west end of the harbor has begun to show signs of returning health and life with cleaner water and re-established beds of submerged native vegetation. The number and variety of fish present in the harbor has increased. The lengthy and expensive containment and clean up of Randle Reef's coal tar deposits is finally beginning, and public access to the shoreline via a greenway and popular bike and hike path around the bay has been greatly improved. A non profit group that over sees the remediation effort estimates in its annual "report card" that the harbor clean up is about half way to its stated goals.[2]

In recent years the forces of globalization have helped the clean up by shutting down a number of Hamilton factories. The big Stelco plant was purchased by U.S. Steel a few years ago and went dark in late

2013. Another company, Dofasco, plans to shut down its 60 plus year old coke plant as tougher Canadian air quality standards are being phased in. Coke plants produce copious amounts of polycyclic aromatic hydrocarbons (PAH's) that are carcinogenic and also cause genetic mutations in lab animal studies and, it's suspected, in people.

Tens of thousands of jobs left Hamilton after NAFTA reduced or dropped tariffs on many of the goods coming into Canada from the U.S, Mexico, and elsewhere. Today, the city's largest employment sectors are health care and education. But the silver lining is that a lot less coke and coal tar is being dumped in the harbor these days, and the bay is definitely healing itself.

We spent several days in Hamilton at the yacht club and were chauffeured over to our friends' home for a spaghetti dinner and a short harp concert on our first night in port. Doug and Lois reside in an older neighborhood of big trees, tidy brick houses, well kept flowerbeds and craftsman style bungalows all equipped with porches. On this early summer evening we enjoyed the tree lined streets with mostly well tended lawns bordered by bright summer roses and pink peonies. This, we were told, was "Westdale" one of Canada's first planned communities, once a town well outside the city of Hamilton. It is bounded on one side by land owned by the Royal Botanical Gardens and the undeveloped marsh of Cootes Paradise (Thomas Cootes was a 18th century Naval Officer who spent his free time hunting the rich diversity of waterfowl that then resided in the wetland).

After dinner we walked with our genial hosts in the long June twilight to a nearby laundromat to take care of one of the tasks of cruising -restocking our supply of clean underwear. Black squirrels bustled about small lawns sprinkled with clover blossoms. I admired the tiny front yard vegetable gardens that used trellises raised beds and edible ground covers to squeeze maximum summer supplies of lettuce and beans out of a space the size of our two car parking area back home. The dog walkers smiled greetings as they passed us with our bags of laundry.

Robins sang evening vespers as our extended shadows stretched before us on the sidewalk. We felt a little like we were in a time warp walking through this sweet old neighborhood right out of 1930. Had we somehow wandered into Green Town, Illinois as portrayed in Ray Bradbury's *Dandelion Wine*? Westdale seemed to be a place of cheerful neighbors, banging screen doors, and children's laughter carried on soft summer air. We knew there was plenty of unemployment, sadness, accidents, sudden illnesses and other uncertainty here as there is in every city. We could hear the occasional siren screaming in the distance. But Hamilton with its gritty industrial waterfront, toxic harbor, empty mills, and closed factories, had another side to it on this summer evening. The middle class, including the owners of two small schooners, was still plugging along, hanging on for a few more years here on this block of Westdale.

Yet old problems remain, and new ones keep cropping up. Manufacturing at Hamilton and everywhere else around Lake Ontario runs on fossil fuel. Most of the natural gas that heats homes and fuels the remaining foundry furnaces at Hamilton gets there via a net work of pipelines. A dozen underground pipelines carrying gas and oil criss cross the city and surrounding region, and their presence was mostly ignored by the city's residents, government, and first responders until several recent events in the U.S and in Canada sparked a sudden interest in them.

About a week after *Sara B* departed Hamilton's harbor, 18 protesters were arrested. They included Hamilton residents and a number of Haudenosaunee (Iroquois) nationals from New York and Ontario. They had staged a six-day occupation at a pipeline pump station in Westover, a village northwest of Hamilton. They were not happy about a proposal to reverse the flow of oil in a pipeline that runs along the north side of Burlington Bay. "This is just starting, it is going to keep going and we'll keep fighting," a Tuscarora woman named Melissa Elliott was quoted in a news story. She told the news reporter that she and others were fighting the transport of tar sands crude through the area.

The group called themselves "Swamp Line 9". The area they were trying to protect is a forested wetland connected to Lake Ontario and is one of many such traversed by the pipeline. They wanted to swamp Line 9 because of the plan of a giant Canadian energy company, Edmonton-based Enbridge, to 're-purpose' its 38-year-old pipeline, originally built to move 240,000 barrels of conventional crude oil a day, for tar sands oil transport. Line 9 runs from Sarnia down to the Hamilton area and then along the north shore of Lake Ontario and the St. Lawrence ultimately to Montreal. According to the company website, the pipeline has 317 water crossings. According to Lake Ontario Waterkeeper it has just six safety shutoff valves along a 300 kilometer length. The protesters had some good reasons for their concerns as events in Michigan proved back in 2010. That's where the biggest inland oil spill to date took place from an Enbridge owned pipeline similar in age and construction to Line 9. That disastrous event involved tar sands crude.

For many years Line 9 carried imported oil from the East Coast via Montreal to the petrochemical plants and refineries on the south end of Lake Huron. But these days there is more potential profit in being able to move shale oil and or heavy tar sands oil from the west to eastern oil refineries. In the past, pipeline 're-purposing' had been done with a minimum of public scrutiny and governmental oversight. But not this time. Some members of Swamp Line 9, described by their detractors as "rabble rousers, anarchists, and useful idiots", chained themselves to a fence at the pump station to protest the planned transport of tar sands within the lake's watershed. And all along the route of Line 9 other groups of land owners, First Nation native tribes, farmers, environmental groups, and concerned citizens joined them in a chorus of protest.

Pipelines built to carry conventional crude oil, refined product or natural gas that have been converted to tar sands crude transport have a terrible track record. In 2010 a pipeline in Illinois broke and dumped 6000 barrels of "heavy crude" (said by environmentalists to be code words for tar sands dilbit). That same year Enbridge's Line 6 in Michigan that had been re-purposed to carry tar sands crude cracked, ruptured and spilled over 800,000 gallons of tar sands oil into a tributary of the Kalamazoo River in the watershed of Lake Michigan. About 35 miles of river were contaminated, and the spill clean up is still going on at a cost of a billion plus dollars spent so far. Another older re-purposed line owned by Exxon dumped 5000 barrels of tar sands goo on to the streets of Mayflower, Arkansas in 2013 and released a smaller amount of dilbit from another leak in Missouri near the town of Doniphan.

Tar sands crude has been called the dirtiest fuel on the planet. From extraction to transport and refining and on to its ultimate use it is viewed as a greenhouse gas disaster by anyone even remotely concerned about climate change. A gallon of oil from tar sands crude emits three to four times as much CO_2 as conventional oil from the process of extraction to when it's ultimately burned. Bill McKibben, professor of Environmental Studies at Middlebury College and climate change activist, says "Alberta's tar sands are the continent's biggest carbon bomb".

It's also having disastrous impacts on dwindling supplies of clean fresh water. Tar sands crude is a thick sticky goo that is either recovered from wells by injecting steam or, if deposits are shallow enough, by strip mining. In northern Alberta tens of thousands of acres of boreal forest have been destroyed during its extraction. The tar is separated from associated sand clay and other solids using hot water and agitation or other methods. It takes three barrels of water to produce one barrel of oil and 90% of that water is polluted beyond recovery. The contaminated water is too toxic to release and so is stored in huge lakes said to be visible from low earth orbit.

Well, it's just water. And the Athabasca River, Alberta's longest undammed river, has plenty to spare according to the industry.

However, the Canadian non profit Pembina Institute cites models that predict the combined impacts of tar sands water withdrawals plus climate change could reduce downstream flows by 30% within a few decades. Withdrawals during the winter when flows are low are especially likely to damage fish habitats and to adversely effect the large delta the river flows into. The Peace Athabasca delta, a huge wetland, is used by millions of birds and is one of the most important staging areas in North America for waterfowl.

Tar Sands crude is also more toxic than other forms of crude oil. In order to push it through a pipe, tar sands crude (also called bitumen or heavy oil) must be heated and mixed with thinners, themselves toxic, to make it flow. The treated bitumen is often referred to as dilbit. Photos of the dilbit spill in Arkansas clearly show chunks of solid material mixed in with the liquid. Because tar sands crude, like coal tar, contains high levels of carcinogenic PAH's and often contains heavy metals like mercury, lead, arsenic and cadmium, it is considerably more damaging to the environment when spilled than lighter crude oil grades. It is also so heavy that if it is spilled into water it often sinks, making it exceedingly difficult to clean up even in shallows. Four years and a billion dollars later they're still dredging the dilbit out of the river in Michigan and it's far from all cleaned up. Most people figure it never will be. It was the largest spill of crude to date into inland waters. A lot of people opposed to re-purposing Line 9 fear it won't be the last.

Tar Sands dilbit also poses special hazards to elderly steel pipes according to metallurgy experts because of its density and chemistry. It has to be moved at higher temperatures and pressures through pipelines. Although the industry denies it, some engineering studies suggest that it is more corrosive than regular crude because of its higher sulfur content and because it is moved at higher temperatures.[3]

Its high viscosity can stress old pipelines through large fluctuations of pressure as it moves through the line following the up and down contours of the terrain it travels through. Reversing flows in pipes, as is proposed for Line 9B, may aggravate existing corrosion and fatigue problems even further, because the pressure fluctuations of the traveling dilbit now hit in different previously "untested" areas of the pipe. An analysis of the Pegasus Line in Arkansas that dumped tar sands crude all over the streets of Mayflower, showed that manufacturing and welding methods used to produce the pipe left tiny "hook cracks" that may have been enlarged by the movement and corrosive chemistry of the dilbit.

Dilbit's impact on old pipes is enough of a concern that the U.S. regulatory agency the Pipeline and Hazardous Materials Safety Administration, (PHMSA) has contracted with the National Academy of Sciences to study the material's impact on pipelines. We can only hope this dilbit study number two will consist of more than a mere review of old and possibly outdated literature on the topic similar to the last such effort completed in 2011 that shed little new light on the issue.

There is intense economic pressure to re-purpose existing pipelines. It's quick and cheap, especially in a time of falling oil prices. Pipeline transport is a third cheaper than rail, and with a break even point of around $75 a barrel tar sands crude producers need to cut every corner they can to keep the stuff moving to market. Barge and rail transport are more costly and possibly more risky than pipeline transport. It's far cheaper and quicker to re-purpose an existing line by building a few new pump stations and installing some valves and other equipment along an existing line than to spend years and billions of dollars acquiring right of way access and build a new one like the Keystone line between Canada and the Gulf Coast or the proposed Energy East line that would run from Alberta to terminals and refineries in St. Johns New Brunswick. That project's cost is estimated at 12 billion dollars.

The tar sands oil fields as well as the shale oil from North Dakota's Bakken play are in the west while many potential consumers or export terminals are in the east. Increasing numbers of refineries on the Great Lakes and in the midwest and eastern part of North America are being re-configured to refine tar sands crude. Opposition to finishing Keystone for the export of dilbit to the Gulf Coast has helped push a sluggish flow tar sands crude toward the Great Lakes as companies put more old re-purposed lines into service. A network of more than 9000 miles of these lines encircles the Great Lakes region including one 60 year old Enbridge pipe that presently moves light crude oil under the Mackinac Straits. (Enbridge says it has no plans to re-purpose that line for dilbit transport. But plans can change.) About half the pipelines in Canada are over thirty years old.

An interesting regulatory loophole exists to promote dilbit transport via pipeline. Chunky thick tar sands bitumin is not defined as 'oil' so the pipeline operators don't have to pay into the clean up fund, called the oil spill liability trust fund. The IRS exempted tar sands crude from the eight cent a barrel fee in 2011. (The trust fund was established after the

Exxon Valdez spill.) Despite efforts to close the loophole in recent years it remains on the books. The Enbridge spill in a tributary of Lake Michigan has been said to cost 800 million to a billion dollars, however, the company's liability was capped at 350 million. We tax payers have been picking up the tab for the rest of the cost. Clean up costs for dilbit are estimated to run more than ten times the cost of conventional fuel. And within ten years we could be seeing 5 or 6 million barrels a day of dilbit moving around. That's a lot of potential trust fund underfunding.

A few months after our visit to Macassa Bay, Enbridge, quietly increased the capacity of another crude oil carrying line called Line 7 that runs right under the city by about 20% . Higher capacity means higher pressure and more potential for failure in a pipe that is 57 years old. Enbridge assured Hamiltonians they'd never notice capacity increase. We can only hope that they're right about that. According to a CBC news story the Hamilton area experienced 9 oil and gas pipeline "safety incidents" including spills and fires in ten years between 2000 and 2010, second only to the refinery heavy city of Sarnia.[4] And the number of pipeline failures has been increasing in recent years, possibly reflecting to some degree the corrosion and general age related deterioration of the pipes. Adding to the problem is that older pipes were grandfathered in after more rigorous safety standards were set in the 1970s. Out of sight and out of mind underground they age, but not always gracefully.

One group of people that has taken notice of all this re-purposing and increased pressurizing of old pipe lines is that of the aboriginal

First Nations whose reservation lands are crossed by Line 9. The Thames River Band of the Chippewas (Deshkaan Ziibing) appealed to the Canadian Federal Court of Appeals and were granted standing to challenge the National Energy Board approval of Line 9's reversal. The treaty right of 'aboriginal consultation' had been violated by Enbridge which did not inform the tribe of the planned reversal. Under the Canadian constitution the government has a duty to consult with the First Nations when a proposed project has potential to negatively impact their indigenous rights. In the case of Line 9 the tribe argued their right to use their land for foraging and fishing and their right to drink potable water from the Thames River was at issue.

The tribes press release stated; "First Nations are being drawn into pipeline discussions with Line 9B and Energy East projects. Chippewa is expressing concerns about the land and water but we find ourselves having to make assertions in areas covered by treaty. We want to help define what a new approach should be, as we prefer not be in the courts, and these matters should become standard practice". The reversal appeal was still tied up in the courts as of this writing.

Ironically, pipeline transport of oil first began because it was so much safer than overland transport. One of the earliest oil pipelines on the continent was built in the Great Lakes region, the birthplace of the inconceivably vast and incredibly profitable oil and gas industry. The very first oil boom in the U.S. took place just outside of Lake Erie's watershed in western Pennsylvania, and the nation's first natural gas well was in western New York, within the Great Lakes watershed. Back then oil was mostly used as as 'medicinal' substance or for lighting. One of the earliest attempts to transport oil via a pipeline took place about a hundred miles south of Hamilton as the gull flies near the shore of eastern Lake Erie back in 1861. At that time oil was being shipped in barrels by horse drawn wagon over all but impassable muddy roads or by flatboat on Oil Creek. Wrecks and spills were frequent. A four inch wooden pipe was proposed as a cheaper quicker way to send oil via gravity from the well field to Oil City, Pennsylvania.

Forty years before that a wooden pipe was used to transport natural gas from an excavated "burning spring" on Canadaway Creek to a nearby Inn near in Fredonia, N.Y. The city of Fredonia also used gas for street lighting and in 1823, gas was found bubbling up through cracks in a shale outcrop along the south shore of Lake Erie. It was captured and piped to the Barcelona Harbor lighthouse through hollowed out pine logs. This was the first lighthouse anywhere to use natural gas for illumination and was reported to be a great success by contemporary observers, though the keeper had a supply of whale oil on hand as his gas supply occasionally failed. (The stone lighthouse, though long since de-activated and now privately owned still stands today).

Pipes today are no longer made of wood and are far bigger than the leaky cast iron line that was the first commercial success in Pennsylvania. Today, more than two thirds of liquid petroleum products and crude oil moved around North America flow through pipelines. Enbridge alone oversees 50,000 miles of pipeline. The interstate lines that move petroleum products long distances are now 20 to 48 inches in diameter and transport trillions of cubic feet of natural gas and millions of barrels of crude oil a day. The Colonial line between Houston and

New York City, completed in 1963 after a disastrous strike by seafarers idled the U.S. tanker fleet, moves 600,000 barrels of liquid product a day. About 75 million barrels a month of refined products flow between the Gulf Coast and the East Coast states. A vast network of lines more than 2.5 million miles in length and mostly buried, now moves petroleum products around the North America and Great Lakes region. Pipes transport fossil fuels from well fields to refineries and from refineries to storage areas and ultimately to consumers. They are an utterly essential part of the vast infrastructure that supplies diesel fuel to *Sara B's* elderly engine, natural gas to heat the houses in town, and keeps our fossil fuel based economy chugging along.

Most of the time pipelines do their job without much incident. But, as we have seen, when they do rupture or blow a big leak, the results can be catastrophic. A lot of the lines were built and buried thirty, forty or even fifty years ago. They're made of steel and eventually they corrode or crack and ultimately fail. The big pipelines do have leak detection systems that, in theory, will prevent huge spills. But only if the alarms go off and if the control room operators monitoring them pay attention to the alarms, and only if they have shut off valves near the leak or rupture. None of those conditions is a given.

Most of the leak detection technology in use in North America is so called computational pipeline monitoring. It depends on software modeling and indirect detection through some secondary physical effect that can be caused by something besides a leak. These systems are prone to a relatively high number of false alarms. Because of the many false alarms, the control room operators sometimes ignore a 'real' leak or even disable the alarms. That may be one reason why so many pipeline leaks are discovered by people who happen to spot the problem in their backyard or neighborhood marsh. The indirect "internal" leak detection systems that rely on flow data and algorithms also detect relatively large leaks, one percent of daily flow through the pipe being a typical target. On a 36 inch pipeline that can amount to a loss of tens of thousands of gallons in a few hours.

According to a recent *Wall Street Journal* article there were 1,400 pipeline spills and accidents in the U.S. between 2010 and 2013. And four in every five pipeline accidents were discovered by local residents, or people who didn't work for the pipeline company.

Technology exists to make pipelines safer. Double wall pipe could be used in areas of critical environmental sensitivity such as wetlands or river crossings. Emergency shut off valves that can be closed remotely at water crossings are available. But they are not required in the U.S. or Canada. Building or retrofitting a line with more shut off valves and better leak detectors costs money. Unless they are required, no company is likely to install them and give its competitors a cost advantage by doing so. However, without them horrendously damaging spills will happen. In one instance a leak in an Enbridge line was detected and the flow was shut down took only 4 minutes. But 158,928 gallons of crude then spilled because the valves were so widely spaced. On that occasion more than 41 miles of the line drained into the environment.[5]

Newer technology can detect leaks more quickly and at smaller rates of loss than can so called 'internal' indirect detection systems. Some leak detectors use more reliable direct measurements that employ chemical or acoustic sensors or fiber optic sensors. Some of these systems can be retrofitted on preexisting pipes and often can detect even small leaks within seconds of their occurrence. But they cost more than the old indirect "internal" detector systems.

A good system in an ideal world would use redundant independent detection systems as is required by German regulators. But as a 2012 report by the consulting firm Kiefner and Associates for the PHMSA says 'there is a general reluctance' on the part of the industry to upgrade their systems and install external detection systems. Presently they're only required to use "computational pipeline monitoring".

A 2013 Bloomburg news story reported that the cost of fiber optic detectors on the proposed construction of Keystone in environmentally sensitive areas along about 141 miles of pipe would run 5000$ a mile. This sounds like a lot of money, but between 2001 and 2011 about 1.7 billion dollars in property damage was caused by various pipeline spills. At least some of that was paid for by the industry. If the dilbit-is-not-crude loophole was closed, even more of the cost would be an industry expense.

That loophole might be one reason the industry isn't rushing to install better safeguards on dilbit pipelines As long as tar sands bitumin is not defined as 'oil' and the pipeline operators don't have to pay into the oil spill liability trust fund for clean up, the tax payers will remain on the hook. IRS exempted tar sands crude from paying the fee in 2011. (The oil spill trust fund was established in 1990 after the Exxon Valdez spill.) Like Lake Ontario's nuclear power producers, dilbit pipeline owners let the tax payers take care of the insurance bills and clean up costs.

Unfortunately, pipeline companies, like other dividend paying profit making companies, tend to think short term, when it comes to laying out money for a leak detection upgrade even though it may greatly reduce the risks of a spill over the 50 year life of their pipe. The decision maker who opts not to install an upgrade may be long retired, maybe even dead when the pipe eventually is accidentally dug up or splits and dumps. It's easy to measure the upfront cost. It's not so easy to do the 'risk benefit' math though the Kiefner and Associates report done for PHMSA attempted to do so. They put the overall savings at 370,000 dollars a year over a potentially 50 year lifespan of a 400 mile long line if state of the art leak detection was installed.

However, without regulation the capitalist system does its own risk benefits analysis and inevitably concludes better to avoiding the upfront cost and worry about the spills later. Especially if somebody else is paying for part or all of the clean up. The real victims are Mother Nature and the general fishing, water drinking, tax paying public.

It is possible to reduce the risks of damage from leaks without putting the country back into the dark ages (which the pipeline operators and partnership stock holders might have you believe will be the result of additional government regulations.) The Germans seem to be managing, and their regulation and detection technology is cited by consultants as a model for how we could do it, too. It won't happen unless we tell Congress we want it to, though. A good place to start would be closing the spill liability loop hole for dilbit. After that, lets increase the budget and hire more inspectors for PHMSA (Pipeline and Hazardous Materials Safety Administration, the U.S. agency that oversees interstate pipelines) and its Canadian equivalent, the National Energy Board.

Barge Transport of Dilbit-Just Say No

ATB with refined product at Oswego steam station

During our brief stay in Hamilton we noticed shipping activity in the harbor was far lower than on a previous visit about ten years before. Then I had seen at least a half dozen freighters tied up in front of the factories and mills. On this cruise most of what cargo carrying we did observe was being done with barges. Utilitarian vaguely ship shaped barges pushed by a big burly tug in an "articulated tug barge" (ATB) arrangement where the tug is physically attached to a barge with a deeply notched stern now move much of the bulk cargo around Lake Ontario. Corn for the ethanol plant in Fulton on the canal, oil for electric power generation, asphalt tar for roads, powdered cement, and fertilizer are shifted in and out of Hamilton, Toronto, Oswego and other ports on the lake these days by barges. They're small enough to be efficient over short haul routes, reasonably sea worthy, and small enough to fit into ports with draft constraints that would keep the bigger bulk carriers out. They also need less manpower to operate than comparable bulk carrying freighters. As of 2015 double hulled oil barges were mandated on the lakes.

About six months after our cruise, a proposal to use barges to transport western shale oil and tar sands crude on the Great Lakes surfaced on the evening news. It was not well received. Rather it raised a storm of protests by various environmental watchdogs including Waterkeeper, Wisconsin Watch, The Blue Planet Project, and others. Liquid petroleum product is already being moved around the lake by barge. To date no crude has yet been shipped on Lake Ontario, though a tanker loaded with dilbit did go down the St. Lawrence river from Quebec headed for Italy in October 2014. (The dilbit was transported from Alberta via rail tank cars.) As others have pointed out, this may well be the camel's nose in the tent as far as tar sands shipments on the lakes goes.

Dilbit from Alberta poses unique problems should it find its way into a large deep body of water. There is no economical or practical way to clean it up if it ends up on the bottom 500 feet down. It will stay there once it sinks to the bottom of Lake Ontario or any of the other Great Lakes. Bakken Shale oil from North Dakota for which barge transport through the lakes has been suggested poses its own unique environmental issues. In early 2014 an oil barge in the Mississippi spilled 30,000 gallons of Bakken Shale oil into the river near New Orleans after colliding with another vessel. Estimates of the floating oil recovered there amounted to less than 1 percent (about 95 gallons).

Imagine the aftermath of a tar sands spill in deep water. Trying to collect heavy crude from the bottom of Lake Ontario, drinking water supply to 9 million people would truly be an adventure into the unknown. The Department of Homeland Security (which the Coast Guard operates under) has called the practice of recovering oil from underwater environments "a largely unexplored area of spill response". In plain English they have very little idea of how to go about it in a practical sense. The few prototype efforts that have tried to remove small scale spills using ROV's and dredging apparently were tested in shallower water than much of Lake Ontario and didn't do a very good job. Ironically, the Coast Guard research facility in Leonardo, New Jersey used to test and evaluate equipment and train responders to oil spills suffered serious damage from Storm Sandy, an event many scientists believe got a boost from global climate change linked to excessive use of fossil fuels.

At this point, it's safe to assume that any heavy crude that ends up on the bottom of Lake Ontario will stay there for a very long time, leaching toxins and carcinogenic mutagens into the drinking water of 9 million Canadians perhaps for hundreds of years. The U.S. Coast Guard doesn't recommend we ship it on deep freshwater. We should just say no to any barge movement on the Great Lakes of bitumin or grades of heavy crude that sink in water. The Council of Canadians has also called for an outright ban on shipping bitumin.

In late 2014 in response to the dispatch of that tanker from Quebec loaded with tar sands crude, Council of Canadians chairperson Maude Barlow wrote, "To protect the Great Lakes and the St. Lawrence River we must ban all transport of tar sands bitumen on, under and near the Great Lakes and St. Lawrence River." And the U.S. Coast Guard was quoted in a 2014 report from the Great Lakes Commission *"that adequate response methods and techniques do not currently exist for spills of heavy oils to open bodies of freshwater such as the Great Lakes."*

Bakken Shale oil also posed for barge transport, is a rather different sort of beast. It does float upon being mixed with water. But it also has some characteristics that make it more hazardous to transport than conventional crude. Bakken Shale oil maybe best known in the Great Lakes area for being involved with a lethal and spectacular train crash and fire in Quebec in 2013 that killed 47 people. It has also fueled other spectacular explosive train derailments around the U.S.

Shale oil is hydrofracked like gas, and some skeptics of its transport safety suspect the chemicals used in fracking may enhance its already volatile character compared to many grades of crude. It also contains a higher percentage of water soluble organic compounds similar to naphthalene, making it particularly toxic to aquatic life after it finds its way into a body of water. And its rapid dispersal makes it tough to recover after a spill.

Ships and oil barges may be statistically safer than trucks and trains when it comes to human lives and property damages, but, like pipelines, they have had their share of spills. Worldwide more than 7000 tons of oil was lost in 2013 alone. Closer to home some of us still remember the slick of '76 that occurred when a barge full of oil ran aground near Clayton in fog. According to Wikipedia after the first grounding holed the barge, the tug captain pulled it off and proceeded up the fog bound river leaking oil until he managed to hit another shoal. The barge eventually spilled 100,000 gallons. A number of other oil spills from barges have occurred more recently including one in the Chicago canal in 2005 that leaked after the barge exploded. (The cause was said to be using a propane torch to thaw a frozen pump). That time 600,000 gallons of spilled oil headed downstream to New Orleans. It could have happened on Lake Michigan or one of the other lakes, though.

Human error is the dominant cause of barge collisions, groundings and the other events that lead to oil spills afloat. A recent report on barge and tanker transport of oil from the Congressional Research Service (CRS) offered several suggestions for improving safety. They include strengthening the Coast Guard's inspection capabilities and putting limits on crew work schedules and hours of service similar to those applied to long haul trucking to help prevent fatigue related errors. (Crews typically work six on six off schedules during multi-day voyages.)

The CRS report cites an investigation of U. S. Coast Guard's Marine

Safety Office by the Inspector General of Homeland Security who reported that *"USCG has not developed and retained sufficient personnel, established a complete process with dedicated resources to address corrective actions, and provided adequate training to personnel on enforcement of marine accident reporting. As a result, the USCG may be delayed in identifying the causes of accidents; initiating corrective actions; and providing the findings and lessons learned to mariners, the public, and other government entities."* Both safety advocates and the barge owners being inspected have also complained about the Coast Guard's frequent re-assignment of ship inspectors who never had a chance to develop the familiarity and expertise needed to do their jobs.

There is growing recognition of the potential problems associated with unconventional oil production and barge transport of same. Barges are cheaper and safer than trains in many situations (there's a reason so many refineries are located on waterfront property) and more oil is being moved by barge. On some routes a lot more. According the Congressional Research Service report cited above, barge transport of oil increased ten fold on the Mississippi between 2009 and 2013. But when an oil spill occurs in an aquatic environment, the oil spreads rapidly and impacts far more species and habitats and a lot more drinking water than a land based spill usually does. It's also much harder to contain. And the effects may linger for decades. It's not easy to compare pipeline safety to barge safety. But it seems pretty clear that when oil is carried by barge or tanker ship and a spill occurs, the probability of water contamination is pretty much 100%.[6]

We should just say no to this one.

See the Last Word for some some specific actions we can take as individuals and as voters to protect our water from unconventional fuels transport.

7. Plastic Is Fantastic But Not In Food and Water

We departed Hamilton under power once again and by late morning were approaching Toronto chugging along over flat water on another windless blazing hot June morning. No sailing today. So far our cruise had been almost entirely fossil fuel powered. We were bored and there wasn't a lot to do except watch the city skyline grow taller and more detailed. We passed a large sheet of white plastic. Then another followed by a whole raft of smaller floating debris. Hey, let's get another sample for Sam, for sure there's gotta be plastic bits and microbeads in this water.

Chris rigged the boat hook outrigger up as Alice and I dug out the bottles sieves and clipboard, unlashed the stowed neuston net on the cabin top and tightened the two hose clamps of the plastic bottle collector onto it. Chris swung the net out lowered it into the water and called "Time". Alice checked her watch and wrote the time down, I attempted to throttle the Thornycroft back to two knots. *Sara B* was now in data collecting mode, doing citizen science for a study of plastic trash pollution in Lake Ontario.

As I watched the water flow through the net, I remembered my student days of collecting plankton on the Merrimack River estuary in 1974. My first samples featured an anonymous gray mass of detritus along with a few flounder eggs and copepods and a large number of mysterious tiny white objects. They were rounded and vaguely resembled eggs. I thought perhaps they were from some marine invertebrate. When viewed under the microscope, their identity became immediately obvious--styrofoam granules. Untold numbers of them, flowing down the river to the sea. I have wondered ever since about their impact on the marine food chain as they appeared perfectly sized for a larval fish to gulp down.

I'm 63 years old as I write this, slightly younger than the age of plastics and better living through chemistry. When I was a kid we still burned our mostly paper and cardboard trash in a fifty gallon steel drum. Mother still had a woven willow twig laundry basket, and our dishes were Blue Willow pattern ceramic ware. At school my cafeteria lunch milk came in a little re-useable glass bottle with a cardboard cap. There was nary a plastic fork or drinking straw or Tupperware dish in our house. I don't really remember them in grade school either though we did have plastic food trays by junior high. But at some point perhaps about when *Sara B's* cedar and oak hull was finished in far off

Nova Scotia around 1954 that lack of plastic in everyday life began to change.

A few years after *Sara B's* launch, dozens of models of fiberglass boats were in production in the U.S. and a cornucopia of pesticides, plastics, food additives and chemical preservatives was spilling into the marketplace. The busy laboratories of organic chemists everywhere were churning out a bewildering array of long chain polymers with bonds of ferocious tenacity. Styrofoam cups and dishes began to appear on the church dinner and picnic scene around 1957. The plastic milk jug arrived in the 1960s. Now we have plastic spoons and drinking straws that will be still be good as new 400 years from now and our beaches are littered with 'New Jersey sea shells' (a.k.a. tampon applicators). And our rivers are full of foam granules.

In January 1979 I took a trip as a volunteer worker aboard the *Anton Dohrn*, a beautifully kept German research vessel that was assisting in groundfish surveys off New England. My brief glimpse of the mid-winter continental shelf and Georges Bank environment was fascinating. Near zero Fahrenheit temperatures with ice fog and sea smoke, ten inches of ice on the foredeck, one honest winter gale and almost nightly multilingual gams fueled by lots of good cheap German beer and whiskey made lasting memories of my two weeks at sea. So did a calm ice free winter day off New York City.

Though no land was visible, I could just make out the unmistakable skyline of the Big Apple against the gray horizon, perhaps ten miles away. It was mild and clear though overcast, and the sea was calm. Our previously icy decks were now dry so I was out hiking around the "steel beach" forward of the wheelhouse for a bit of exercise. Over the side I saw a vast school of jellyfish. The surface waters around our ship were filled with hundreds of transparent and translucent ghostly forms as we drifted hove to doing physical measurements. I was entranced by the strange sight.

A crew member joined me to look over the side at the strange abundance of sea life. As I looked more closely I saw corners and squares and shredded shapes. Hey, that's *Plastic*! Yuk! A sea of plastic bags, untold numbers of them, filled the ocean around us. The German laughed and told me this is the city dumping ground. (At that time New York City barged its garbage out to sea to dispose of it.) I found it hard to believe there could be that many plastic bags in a barge load of trash.

But that afternoon our bottom trawl brought up a scant and depressing catch of a few hundred pounds of ulcerated hake, sculpin, and stunted four inch flounders with tumors and rotted stubs where their tail fins had once been. I guess he was right. Since then New York City has stopped ocean dumping. It now trucks its garbage upstate to a Canadian owned landfill in Lake Ontario's watershed about thirty miles inland from the lake's south shore. It's called Seneca Meadows. It's the largest active landfill in the state, affectionately known as Mount Trashmore by the neighbors. The garbage mountain is said to be a landmark visible for twenty miles or more. And while New York City's garbage no longer goes directly into the sea, plenty of other cities around the world do still send their plastic trash downstream to Mother Ocean.

Plastic production world wide is staggering. On average, 300 million tons of plastic are produced around the globe each year. Of this, 50% is made into disposable single use products such as packaging or medical gear like IV bags and tubing. Nearly all of this material comes from fossil fuel derived feedstock. Nearly a third of that hydrofracked natural gas that is currently impacting the Genesee River, Lake Ontario's largest tributary, is used to make chemical fertilizers and petrochemicals that go into everything from panty hose to fiberglass boats, while the website naturalgas.org states that nationwide 43% of the natural gas in this country is used to create various chemical fertilizer and plastic products.

Not much of that fossil fuel derived stuff gets recycled. Another website claims we've tossed a billion tons of plastic so far. That's a lot of trash mountains. In recent years perhaps 10% of the plastic produced has been recycled in the U.S., or more correctly downcycled to make things like parking lot car stops, plastic "Trex" decking or wheel chocks for airplanes.

While the giant Pacific garbage patch, often compared to the state of Texas (size-wise), has made headlines since at least 1999, the issue of plastic in drinking water supplies like the Great Lakes only recently surfaced. One day in 2011 a young chemistry professor, Dr. Sherri A. Mason who likes to go by 'Sam' was teaching an introductory environmental science methods course aboard the U.S. Brig *Niagara*, Pennsylvania's state ship, a replica of Commodore Perry's flagship of 1812 War fame, when she got the idea of sampling the Great Lakes for plastic with the help of some of her students. She was surprised, she told me, when a literature search turned up a nearly complete lack of freshwater plastic pollution studies. About twenty years before someone had surveyed Lake Erie for it, but no follow ups had ever been done.

She got a small grant from the Burning River Foundation to do one as part of the methods course aboard the *Niagara* the following year. She and several students took samples from Superior, Huron, and Erie, and then went back to the lab for the slow tedious sample work up of separating the small plastic bits from the natural debris and surface dwelling life forms that is inevitably captured at the same time. Her results got world wide coverage and were reported by the New York Times, National Geographic, the Buffalo and Toronto dailies, CBC and in many other media outlets.

What she found was a shockingly high concentration of tiny plastic particles as well as a largely unrecognized new form of pollution, the microbead. Microbeads are small bits of plastic about the size of a salt grain that are added to many facial scrubs and body washes as exfoliants. They go down the drain with the bathwater and right through the sewage treatment plant. Their presence in lake water is a pretty good surrogate for treated sewage inputs. Mason found tens of thousands of these particles of plastic in her survey of Lake Erie. One sample had 460,000 plastic particles per square kilometer of lake surface, with an average of 46,000 particles per square kilometer. These were counts far higher than the totals ever seen in any salt water trash surveys.

After I read about Mason's study, I sent her an e mail offering *Sara B's* services as a sampling platform for Lake Ontario during our round the lake cruise. She hustled up a spare neuston net and a case of sample bottles and a couple of fine meshed brass sieves and sent them along via UPS with directions for how to collect "plastic plankton". We eventually did eight tows and delivered the results to her lab. She herself along with three students also sampled Lake Ontario a month or so after our cruise using the 72 foot yacht *Sea Dragon* owned by the Pangaea Foundation. Their track ran along the north shore of the lake between Montreal and Toronto while most of our samples were taken within three miles of shore on the south shore of the lake.

Each tow lasted a half hour with start and end GPS positions noted down. Most were done under power, though a couple were done under sail. Chris worked out a technique using the boat hook as an outrigger to keep the neuston net out away from the boat and her bow wave turbulence. Tows were for a half hour followed by about another half hour of wash down and sample transfer. That was the most tedious part of the whole process. We certainly did see some plastic. We also saw woody detritus, lots of cottonwood fluff, insects and many many midge pupa cases, and a brownish sort of slime which I suspected was some form of one celled algae or diatoms smaller than the .333 mm mesh we used. The results of our samples were not pretty we learned a few months later after Sam's students had worked them up in the lab. Lake Ontario, recipient of upstream pollutants from the other lakes plus sewage and runoff from its own populations, took the prize for containing the most plastic pollution- up to 1.1 million bits of plastic per square kilometer in one sample. Mason's team of researchers along with other scientists on salt water, continue to study how plastic moves through the system, how much ends up in sediments or inside a fish or bird and what the effects of that may be.

Plastic trash is stable and slow to break down in the environment but that does not mean it is necessarily benign. A number of lab studies as well as evidence from the field have already documented harmful effects of plastic trash on fish and aquatic bird life. Plastic microbeads probably aren't too good for some zooplankton either. When plastic is ingested by an animal it may physically block the digestive system sometimes with fatal results. In the open Pacific ocean far from shore one study have found 9% of the pelagic fishes had plastic in their stomach or gut. Dr. Mason has done a small preliminary survey of Lake Erie's food web and has found plastic inside at least some of the individual fish of all 18 species sampled so far (including species of fish like salmon and trout that people eat). At lower levels in the food chain 75 to 100% of the fish had ingested plastic. She also found plastic inside double crested cormorants from a Lake Erie island. She told me, "We tend to see lower amounts at lower trophic levels, perhaps a tenth as much in a minnow as in a bird, but without further analysis we can't say for certain if this is due to biomagnification. It could simply be that the bird is bigger and so takes in more material. But we have established without a doubt the plastics are making it into the food chain of the Great Lakes."

If plastic is so prevalent in forage fish it seems highly likely it's also present in at least some of the lake's zoo plankton. Such inedible material might easily interfere with digestion and nutrient uptake. And chemicals associated with the plastic could be entering into the bodies of the animals.

A couple years ago a popular sailing magazine published some spectacular and gruesome photos of dead sea birds whose decayed remains were stuffed with plastic. They were taken by an award winning photographer named Chris Jordan who understands the impact of visual images in educating the public about environmental issues. He produced a documentary on his expedition to Midway Island in the Pacific Ocean that showed the deaths of thousands of albatross chicks fed plastic trash by their surface feeding parents. The adult albatrosses thought they were capturing edible food for their young as they mistook plastic lighters and spoons for small squids and fish.

Even if Lake Ontario's fish and birds aren't physically stuffed with indigestible objects like those baby birds, they may well be suffering from other more subtle impacts of the plastic soup they are swimming and feeding in. The tiny plastic particles such as Dr. Mason documented in such abundance in the lake adsorb various toxins from the water and can leach plasticizers into the water. When they are eaten, these associated toxins can be moved into the bloodstream and cause liver damage, or scramble the hormone systems of the hapless fish or bird. BPA is a plasticizer that has been banned in Europe for use in some food containers. It and other chemicals associated with plastic bits in the water are known endocrine disruptors. These are compounds that impact animal health and metabolism at incredibly tiny concentrations in the environment.

Sherri Mason is first and foremost a teacher. But she is firmly committed to advocating sustainability (she is, after all, also a mother).

She does not hesitate to use her research results as an opportunity to urge seeking solutions to pollution. As she tells her students "The world is an interconnected system. This is not just about aquatic animals; it is a significant concern to human health as well."

Her work builds on that of earlier researchers who were more concerned with outright acute poisoning or carcinogenic actions of toxic substances being dumped in the lake or leaching from places like Love Canal. Toxins like mirex, PCB's and dioxins led to fish consumption advisories limiting the amount of Lake Ontario fish humans could safely eat back in the 1970s. Since then toxin levels have dropped in the lake and in its food chain, and consumption advisories have been relaxed some. However, they still remain in place. New York's advisory states that children under 15 and women of child bearing age are still advised to eat no fish from Lake Ontario.[1]

We also now know there are more subtle dangers associated with seemingly harmless chemicals that we live with in our food water and in our homes. When I had lunch with Dr. Mason after dropping our samples off, I looked at my glass of ice water and asked if there were microbeads in it. She assured me that the municipal water treatment plants did a good job of removing solids. But they don't remove all the chemicals that now enhance our lake water.

Endocrine disruptors are chemicals that interfere with the hormones that regulate vertebrate development in the egg or womb and subsequent growth and metabolism after birth. The differentiation of tissues in the womb that determines an individual's life long destiny is an incredibly intricate and sensitive process dating back to the dawn of life on earth. It is still not fully understood. Hormones may act in concentrations of parts per trillion or even less. This system is based on organic molecules much like those found in synthetic compounds derived from petrochemicals. It can be derailed or jammed by those molecules that resemble hormone molecular structure.

If the endocrine system fails to work properly during embryo development, results include a weakened or disordered immune system, autism, diabetes, cancer, and most famously, all sorts of gender scrambling. In some tributaries of the Chesapeake Bay's heavily populated watershed, 75% of the small mouth bass show both male and female reproductive cells in their gonads. "Intersex" white perch have been collected from Hamilton Harbor and from the Bay of Quinte.

Man made hormone mimics only became widely recognized about 25 years ago after a ground breaking study of transgenerational health impacts of chemicals in Great Lakes animals by Dr. Theo Colborn. Her book *Our Stolen Future* published in 1996 with two co-authors, helped open a new area of research on chemicals in the environment.[2] (See appendix for a brief bio and information on her interdisciplinary approach to science.) Colborn went on to research many aspects of how tiny amounts of chemicals can sabotage of our endocrine systems including health effects of air and water pollution from oil and gas well fracking on nearby populations. She wrote shortly before her own passing in December 2014 that endocrine disruptors *"dehumanize the human race by stealing the ability to love, socialize, enjoy each other, and sit down to converse with others in order to solve problems."*

When I first went to a scientific conference on toxins in the lake around 1980, lab equipment able to detect these substances at parts per trillion concentrations was just becoming widely available to researchers. We now know plastics are not inert in the environment. However, long term low dose exposure studies are tricky to do. One problem at least in studying human health effects is that there is no large population of humans on earth that hasn't been exposed to some amount of plastic who can serve as an experimental control group. (One U.S. study found 96% of the pregnant woman who were tested had BPA in their systems.) The best summary of health effects that a group of experts convened by the FDA could come up with was; "*BPA at concentrations found in the human body is associated with organizational changes in the prostate, breast, testis, mammary glands, body size, brain structure and chemistry, and behavior of laboratory animals.*"

As the quote suggests there have been studies that showed adverse health effects of plastic on animals. BPA was banned by the FDA as a component of plastic baby bottles because of possible interference with the growth and development of infant humans a few years ago, but it is still used to line cans for processed foods. And dozens if not hundreds of other synthetic chemicals are also capable of scrambling the endocrine system's intricate workings as it directs embryonic development.

Plastic bits leach other substances besides BPA and also attract and concentrate any toxins and heavy metals present in the water. These adsorb onto the surface of the particles. In one lab study minnows were fed a diet 10% of which was plastic bits collected from San Diego Bay.

The fish showed liver abnormalities and damage after two months. One fish developed a tumor that took over 25% of its liver. Another group of fish that were fed "clean" plastic bits as 10% of their diet also showed abnormalities but to a statistically significant lesser extent. The researchers suspect that both chemicals from the plastic and other compounds adsorbed from the water including carcinogenic PAH's (polycyclic aromatic hydrocarbons) and fire retardants caused the damage.

Tiny pieces of plastic are not the only source of harmful chemicals in the Great Lakes. A witch's brew of pollutants of "emerging concern" pours into the lake with sewage, from upstream sources over Niagara Falls, from storm water runoff and farm fields, and even from the air with rain and dry deposition. Pharmaceutical drugs routinely fed to farm animals, used and excreted by humans, or tossed into landfills and flushed down toilets, are one such pollutant. Various fire retardants are another. An antibacterial substance called triclosan widely used in soaps now resides in nearly every waterway in North America. It is extremely toxic to some types of algae, the base of most aquatic food chains, and appears to be another hormone mimic. Herbicides and pesticides wash into the lake from lawns golf courses and agricultural land. Approximately 84,000 chemicals including those fragrances and dyes in your shampoo and laundry soap are in routine use today, only about two hundred of which have been tested for human health effects.

Along with the microbeads and the well known legacy chemicals like the PCB's, mirex, dioxins and PAH's lodged in our sediments and incorporated in our body tissues, now we must cope with these "new" potentially harmful compounds. Fire retardants are especially pervasive. They've been found in honey from Brazil, Antarctic penguins and Arctic orcas, in the blood of 97% of Americans in one study, and in Lake Ontario. According to recent EPA survey Lake Ontario once again took honors as the most polluted great lake, this time for fire retardants. It boasted the highest concentrations of two different classes of flame retardants known as PBDEs and OPEs. Both are known carcinogens. and are widely used in furniture upholstery foam and other materials to the tune of nearly 5 billion pounds sold world wide each year.

The fire retardant story is an interesting one as it illustrates how science can be overridden by industry self-interest, effective lobbying, and profits. It's not unlike the story of big tobacco and its defense of cigarette sales and profits using distorted research half truths and outright fabrications. Some of the most vocal and militant groups now fighting for bans on these ineffective and toxic compounds are made up of city firefighters who are organizing to lobby state legislatures. The San Francisco Firefighters Cancer Prevention Association has noted an alarming rate of Parkinson's among its members along with a seeming epidemic of cancer. A National Institute for Occupational Safety and Health study that evaluated the health of nearly 30,000 firefighters in San Francisco, Chicago and Philadelphia found higher rates of prostate cancer, kidney cancer, multiple melanoma, and other cancers in firefighters compared with the general population.

Evidence against the usefulness of fire retardants continues to accumulate, even as more regulations are passed to include them in consumer products for our "safety". Recently California moved to lift a requirement for their use in furniture foams. We can only hope other states will follow.

* * *

So faced with thousands of potentially harmful chemicals in our air, soil and water, what are we to do? Short of wearing fur, sitting on logs and sleeping on the floor, eating a paleo diet, and avoiding soap how can we reduce the amount of this plastic and chemical stew in our bodies, environment and in our Great Lake?

As individual consumers our options are limited. We can certainly avoid body lotions with microbeads and spurious uses of antibiotics and other antibacterial products, and opt for organic foods where ever possible. And Dr. Mason reminds us all to minimize single use plastic wherever possible in our lives. Hold the drinking water straw. And the plastic water bottle! And of course, we can take our reusable bag to the grocery store and put the blue box out every week, though probably some of that plastic is headed for the landfill. It's pretty hard to eliminate all plastic petrochemical products from our lives, though. While individuals can attempt to balance risk, convenience and environmental costs as best they can, we need government oversight and regulation, too.

One thing we can do as individuals is demand that at least some constraints be placed on this rush to better living and corporate profits through Chemistry. Thanks in considerable part to the work by Sherri Mason and her colleagues, over 100 mayors from cities along the Great Lakes and the St. Lawrence Seaway are now calling on regulators and manufacturers to stop the use of micro plastics in personal care items. A bi national coalition of local officials called the Great Lakes and St. Lawrence Cities Initiative (GLSLI) is reaching out to their constituents and businesses to raise awareness of the threat of micro plastics and trying to head off any new introduction of micro plastics to the Great Lakes. The Cities Initiative has also contacted the leading producers of microplastics which include companies like Beiersdorf, Bath and Body Works, Johnson & Johnson, Proctor & Gamble, Reckitt-Benckiser and Unilever.

Illinois has already banned the sale of soap with microbeads after 2017, and after an industry led effort defeated a ban by one vote in California, the legislation there is being re-introduced. Other states are also attempting to pass bans but until they do, the health conscious bather should be on the look out for "polyethylene" on the ingredient list on the label of your toothpaste or body lotion cleansers as it is an indicator for plastic microbeads. As of this writing the bead had not yet been banned in New York State or Ontario though legislation is under consideration in both areas and needs popular support.

The scattered halting efforts to regulate plastic microbeads at the state and provincial level point out the need for federal action. Manufacturers don't want to deal with fifty different sets of regulations (and have previously beaten back some state laws dealing with food and product safety by claiming in court that they interfere with interstate commerce, a federal jurisdiction.). Broader oversight is required and one way to achieve that is to update the Toxic Substances Control Act (TSCA) written back in 1976.

In the U. S. chemicals are presumed innocent until proven guilty. The burden of proving a given chemical as unsafe falls upon the EPA and the general public. Only after people start getting sick or we see obvious environmental issues like feminized and sterile fish does a chemical get a second look from the regulators. Sometimes it's then withdrawn and replaced with a 'safer' new one. More often than not the new untested chemical is just as bad or worse. Making it even harder to track health effects, are many manufacturer claims that their mixtures of chemicals are "trade secrets".

When the TSCA was passed, most concern was about chemicals that were known carcinogens or could cause mutations in the DNA that would pass to offspring. We now know that compounds that interfere with hormone metabolism can have a host of subtle but harmful health effects. A huge rise in various 'diseases' and disorders ranging from asthma to rheumatoid arthritis that are associated with immune system impairments is one suspected consequence of our failure to regulate endocrine disrupting chemicals.

Current federal legislation does not mandate any safety testing for newly introduced chemicals. And it poses huge obstacles to timely action when the EPA has to prove "unreasonable risk" of health dangers exists. The peer reviewed newsletter "Health Affairs" cites a ten year risk assessment study of asbestos by the EPA that included collecting thousands of pages of published studies. After all this, when asbestos regulations were finally issued, the manufacturers challenged them successfully in court as having failed to prove 'unreasonable risk' existed.[3]

Europe does it differently. Chemical manufacturers must submit safety testing data for both new and existing chemicals in the EU. And importers have to meet the same standards. This, plus a growing number of state based laws led to an attempt to update the TSCA with new legislation in Congress in 2010. Not too surprisingly, that legislation has gotten nowhere. And it won't go anywhere unless the public demands passage of a strong effective honest set of regulations. Unfortunately, right now it looks like everyone will keep fighting their own private brush fire, be it BPA in baby food containers or fire retardants in couches or triclosan in diaper cream. Somehow, we need to make overhaul of the TSCA an exciting glamorous cause so millions of Americans will demand it for the good of the lakes as well as their own health. Maybe some high profile celebrity will get behind it. And the overhaul must not be another watered down industry friendly version that pre-empts stricter state regulation that environmental activists were describing was the case for the Vitter-Udall proposed update that was in committee in the Senate in early 2015.

Until that happens our best hope may be good old American ingenuity in the form of new 'greener' products. We already have biodegradable substitutes for microbeads in body soaps for those grimy people who feel they need to 'exfoliate' and don't want to flush plastic down the shower drain. And several mattress and furniture upholstery makers have developed effective fire resistant physical barriers and fabrics made of non flammable materials like glass fiber to help reduce the spread of flames once a cushion fabric or mattress catches fire.

The most interesting innovators are those who have embraced the total life cycle 'cradle to cradle' concepts of recycling promoted by William McDonough, John Todd and others. They are coming up with some truly green products that can be effortlessly recycled by nature. The Ooho edible container made of a gelatin like material derived from brown algae, may not save the world, but it's a noteworthy effort to substitute for all those zillions of plastic juice bottles that litter our beaches. There's even a YouTube video for a DIY version, although I don't see anyway to put a cap on it if you only want to drink part of the liquid.

An outfit called WikiFoods makes an edible covering that can substitute for foil or plastic wrappers and another company in England is developing a biodegradable film that protects meat from microbial action. If they succeed in scaling up production of these products, a whole lot of annoying foam and vacuum package plastic could be eliminated. And as a bonus some of the edible films are a good source of dietary fiber. Other innovators are working on biodegradable plastic drinking glasses that come in various flavors, packaging made from agricultural waste and mushroom mycelium, and 'green' construction materials ranging from recycled steel to thatched roofs and straw bale walls, wool insulation, and plant based rigid foam board.

There are more alternatives to plastic out there all the time. One that is receiving considerable interest is a material called Chitosan. Chitosan is a completely bio degradable "biopolymere" derived from crab and shrimp shells that are made of chiten. Chiten is to insects and other arthropods as cellulose is to trees- a complex polysccharide. Chiten makes up the sturdy wing covers of that pesky Asian lady bug trying to go for a swim in your coffee cup during fall migration and the gossamer wings of the mayfly spinning over the water beside your anchored boat on a quiet summer morning.

Chitosan been used for several years in the medical business. Recently a group of Harvard researchers at the Wyss Institute for Biologically Inspired Engineering came up with a different formulation process to create a pliable transparent material that can be cast or injection molded like regular plastic. The researchers are now working to scale up production of the material. Their version of chitosan can be pigmented, and the dyes can be recovered when the plastic is recycled.

It would seem ideal for many of the single use plastic products that are now so incredibly pervasive in our world, assuming a sustainable supply of feedstock material exists. Perhaps we can establish factory farms to raise zillions of giant Madagascar cockroaches fed on household and institutional kitchen food waste to provide chiten supplies. Our current medical establishment uses and disposes of a staggering amount of single use plastic. Hopefully in the not too distant future truly biodegradable materials like chitosan may replace the PET plastic of bottles and containers and the petrochemical derivatives in all those IV bags that get tossed by the ton across America.

An outfit in Germany called Heppe has been working with chitosan to make products for the pharmaceutical and medical industry for several years (it has a natural antimicrobial action against a broad array of bacteria and fungi and has been used for wound dressings for some time.) Several companies sell chitosan coated fiber for weaving into textiles for the health care industry. And now you can purchase antimicrobial underwear and odor free socks thanks to chitosan.

Our best hope is to turn loose the innovative power of industrial designers, chemists, CEOs and back yard and table top tinkerers with sustained funding for their research. An often cited example of how an industrial process can be 'greened' is that of publicly traded Interface Global's carpet tile business whose founder Ray Anderson embraced sustainability in 1997. He wrote then, "If we're successful, we'll spend the rest of our days harvesting yester-year's carpets and other petrochemically derived products, and recycling them into new materials with zero scrap going to the landfill and zero emissions into the ecosystem. And we'll be doing well, very well ... by doing good..."

The company has made significant progress towards that vision. According to its website it has a factory in the Netherlands that is running on 100 % renewable energy and sending no scrap to landfills. By reducing its waste and its use of water, the company has saved hundreds of millions of dollars since 1997.

Interface has even launched a program called Networks that works with a supplier of nylon carpet fiber to recycle monofilament gill nets cleaned up from beaches or pulled out of the sea where they had been drifting as trash 'ghost nets' killing marine life. The initial Networks programs in West Africa and the Philippines benefited participants by paying them cash for the cleaned up baled nets. The villagers then used some of their windfall to start micro-lending programs so they could diversify their own local economies away from unsustainable levels of fishing.

The Interface website refers to the company's twenty year

sustainability 'journey', a voyage that is ongoing. Every journey begins with a single step and for the sake of our lake we can only hope more individuals and policy makers will soon begin their own commitments to "Mission Zero" running their businesses and homes on 100% renewable energy supplies.[4] Carefully crafted federal regulations and standards that recognize the true costs of pollution would go a long ways towards helping this happen. But in order for that to happen we'll have to start putting the pressure on for some leadership and integrity down there in DC.

8. The Great Atomic Lake Down In The Dumps

About two hours after our departure from Whitby we were again under power when the rain began. First, a few heavy drops splatted on deck and plunked into the water around us. Then with a rush of sound came the deluge, straight down thankfully. No wind and no need to call all hands on deck for this one. The lake stayed flat. The sail covers stayed on. The curtain of rain swept over us and water poured flowed and puddled underfoot and pooled overhead in the sail cover, the excess periodically spilling out onto my head and down my neck as we chugged along. The rest of the crew stayed below and dry. Another wet day on what was turning out to be one of the soggiest cruises I'd seen in thirty years of sailing Lake Ontario.

Many climate change models predict more extreme weather events with intense downpours, droughts, and hot and cold records. This month was certainly living up to it. By the end of June my rain gauge at home had measured over seven inches, more than twice the long term average and close to a record for our area. At least we weren't in Florida where not too long ago the panhandle got nearly two feet of rain in less than twenty four hours. Or in Colorado where my in-laws got a year's worth of rain in a day a couple years ago.

It rained hard for two hours that afternoon, with just enough lightning to worry the crew of a sailboat with two wet wooden forty foot lightning rods and attached wire rigging. At last, the clouds drifted slowly off taking the rain with them as a deluge dwindled to a drizzle and then faded away into memory. Land and a large cubical white factory building emerged from the mist off to port. I recognized the distinctive structure and nearby jetties immediately as those of the City of Port Hope, home to Cameco Fuel Services, formerly known as El Dorado, the world's oldest continuously operating nuclear facility. As I studied the building I wondered can nuclear power save us from the relentlessly rising atmospheric CO_2 levels now powering our increasingly weird weather?

Port Hope in the rain

El Dorado was built back in 1932 to extract radium from uranium ore. Today the refinery still hums away at the heart of the town that radiates friendliness according to an old Chamber of Commerce slogan. It now makes fuel grade uranium dioxide for the CANDU reactors of Canada and uranium hexafluoride used in light water reactors around the world. Port Hope is also home to Canada's largest collection by volume of low level radioactive waste.

If nuclear power might be part of the answer to the global climate change problem, then Lake Ontario is a good place to consider the possibility. Nowhere is the industry more in evidence than here. Along with the Cameco plant, it has fourteen operating nuclear reactors powering the electrical grid, two of which are among the oldest in North America, plus two more mothballed units, a couple small research reactors, a tritium recovery facility, and several legacy radioactive dumps, including the massive rad waste collection at the Lake Ontario Ordinance Works site near Lewiston. Plus Port Hope's deposits.

Lake Ontario's atomic age began early on both shores. During World War II, while El Dorado hummed away to supply material from Canadian ore for the Manhattan project, Linde Air Products of Tonawanda on the Niagara River used some of that abundant supply of electricity generated by the falls to extract uranium for the first atomic bombs from ore shipped in from the Congo. Linde was chosen because of the company's past experience with uranium employed to create ceramic glaze colors (remember those orange-red Fiesta Ware plates from the 1930s?) The secret operation's code name for the Linde refinery was "The Ceramics Plant". Refining operations ceased after the war on the U.S. side of the lake, though not before thousands of tons of ore tailings and various radioactive byproducts were dumped flushed or otherwise hastily disposed of on the U.S. shore at a top secret site.

About 8000 tons of the rad waste ended up in three locations near the Linde plant in Tonawanda. Some of the residues were dumped on the ground in a layer 1 to 5 feet thick at the property now known as Ashland 1. Liquid wastes containing small amounts of radium and uranium were sent down the sewer or injected into wells that sometimes over flowed. Another 20,500 tons of high-radium-content residues from processing extremely radioactive pitchblende ores from the Congo were stashed at the Lake Ontario Ordnance Works in an area called the Niagara Falls Storage Site near Lewiston. Perhaps half of all the known radium in the world lies here approximately two miles from the Niagara River.

Much of the waste dumped in Tonawanda is radioactive enough to be considered "source" material. This is radioactive material that is dangerous to the general public and is supposed to be closely monitored and controlled. But it wasn't. The government sold the dump site in 1960 to Ashland Oil for 56,000 dollars. The group FACTS of Western NY on their website calls this an "abandonment of regulatory responsibilities by both the federal government and later by the state government."

In the frantic get her done at any cost time of an all out war effort perhaps the careless disposal of material from a secret project that would remain deadly for 100,000 years is understandable. But to continue the culture of secrecy and sloppy custodial care for twenty years after World War II's end seems unforgivable to the residents of the Niagara Falls area, some of whom worked with the lethal material in the Linde plant and died of cancer years later. A study done by the New York Department of Health in 2001 at the request of area residents found the people living near the Tonawanda Linde plant site had about

10 % more cancers of various types than would have been expected in that population, a statistically significant difference. Cancers associated with radiation exposure included colorectal cancers in men and women plus thyroid and breast cancers in women. Some of those cancers occurred with far more than expected frequency. Thyroid cancers in women, for example, were 81% more frequent and bladder cancer in women was 26% above expected incidence.

Black dust from uranium contaminated the Tonawanda factory for years after the war ended. A *USA Today* newspaper account from 2003 quoted workers recalling the powder sometimes sifted down from "the rafters" and covered work surfaces in the 1970s. The various parts of the plant were de-contaminated several times after the war, yet radiation was still found in high enough levels to pose a health hazard in 1976. The *USA Today* story quoted a worker, "We began to get a funny feeling in the early '70s, when the company started monitoring us (for illnesses) and telling us not to eat in the buildings."

Some of the older Linde Plant workers attempted to file for "special exposure cohort status" a condition that would strengthen their claim for compensation from the federal government. Congresswoman Louise Slaughter is quoted on the FACTS of Western NY website as saying "The Atomic Energy Workers at Linde were robbed of their health while working to defend and secure America for future generations. It is simply disgraceful that these brave men and women have had to wait so long for the compensation they deserve." Eventually those who had been at the facility during and shortly after the war were given compensation. However, workers that were hired after 1953 to work in the contaminated factory were deemed ineligible.

Subsequent petitions were submitted on behalf of Linde plant workers to the government and the National Institute for Occupational Safety and Health (NIOSH) conceded that residual contamination remained in some areas until 1995. Only after New York's two Senators and Congresswoman Slaughter intervened in 2008, did the government officially recognize the health impairments from radiation exposures to people who worked at the plant as recently as 1969.[1]

Today the plant operates as a research and technology center for Praxair. Since 2000 the Army Corps has removed 360,000 tons of contaminated soil from the site and replaced it with 'clean' fill. The Army Corps of Engineers has signed off on remediation, stating "this property complies with Federal standards and there is no threat to the surrounding area."

* * *

Just upstream from Lake Ontario perhaps fifty miles from the lake's west end as the gull flies lies another nuclear nightmare, the West Valley New York mess in Lake Erie's watershed. This is one of the worst nuclear legacy waste sites in the Northeast. Three named streams run through the property near Buttermilk Creek, a tributary of Cattaraugus Creek that drains into Lake Erie. All of them are actively eroding the dump site. In 1992 a plume of radioactive groundwater containing strontium 90 was discovered moving off site. Efforts to contain it to date have not been entirely successful, though the DOE website states that a underground wall of clay has "achieved remedial action objectives" (an approximately 90% reduction of the amount of

Strontium 90 moving off site). For the time being, anyway.

The West Valley site entered the nuclear age in 1961 when New York acquired 3,345 acres of land in the town of Ashford, New York for the Western New York Nuclear Service Center. The next year a private company called Davison Chemical established Nuclear Fuels Services, Inc. (NFS) to reprocess fuel rods from commercial power plants. NFS developed 200 acres of the land and operated from 1966 to 1972 "processing" 640 metric tons of spent reactor fuel. During this time 660,000 gallons of highly radioactive liquid waste were generated. The liquid waste was stored in an underground waste tank. NFS also used two unlined areas for the disposal of radioactive waste from commercial waste generators. In 1976 NFS decided the costs and regulatory requirements of reprocessing made the venture unprofitable and departed after its lease expired on December 31, 1980. This left the state's taxpayers on the hook for taking care of the mess in yet another example of the privatization of profit while leaving the ecological debts for society to clean up. The Department Of Energy eventually got involved as the job was beyond the ability of the New York's taxpayers to fund it. But only after a determined group of local residents formed the West Valley Coalition and took the feds to court. Several times.

Between 1984 and 2002 the worst of the liquid wastes were solidified into a glass like material in a process called vitrification. As the DOE history of the site put it, *"This highly successful project resulted in 275 stainless steel canisters of solidified high-level waste, safe in storage and ready for transport to a disposal facility."* If only there were a disposal facility somewhere around ready and willing to take it.

As of 2014 about two hundred contractors were busy moving gravel, dirt, concrete, tanks, the virtrification melter and other radioactive objects around, shifting glass logs of solidified waste to steel casks for storage above ground on site, and preparing to demolish contaminated structures. Monitoring for radiation on and off site was on going. A report from the contractor in late 2014 noted that *"as of August 11, 2014 one million safe work hours had been achieved without a lost time work accident. The West Valley Demonstration Project is among the safest in the DOE complex."* If only it would be equally safe for its neighbors and Lake Ontario water drinkers in the centuries to come.

photo supplied by Joanne Hameister

Estimates of the amount of money spent so far on all that 'clean up' are not easy to come by. One I saw from 2010 was five billion dollars so far and counting. This is more than half of an estimated total 9 billion dollar cost for complete removal of wastes that was published in 2008. Is the job half done yet?

It appears to some observers that DOE is inclined to leave the rest of the stuff presently buried right where it is even as more studies are commissioned. Long time West Valley watcher and tireless activist Joanne Hameister sent along a photo via email showing the original "disposal" of barrels and boxes of waste, stacked in a dirt trench on what appears to be a wet surface. She wrote, "From the Coalition on West Valley Nuclear Waste's jaundiced view, we have felt that DOE and NYSERDA keep on doing study after study, hoping against hope that the numbers change, to justify leaving the 'stuff' on site....For some reason, the decision makers refuse to give any serious concern, except word service, to the effects of Climate Disruption and the highly erodible burial grounds, which are plain dug trenches, unlined and unengineered."

In 1987 a paper by a Canada Centre for Inland Waters scientist described the detection of plutonium from West Valley in sediments of the bar at the mouth of the Niagara River. The sediment core suggested that deposition probably took place around 1970 when Nuclear Services was busy "processing" spent fuel rods at the site. We can only hope the lake continues to lay uncontaminated sediments down over this marker of idiocy, and that we don't forget what still remains buried out of sight out of mind at West Valley on the eroding banks of

Buttermilk Creek lest it, too, end up in Lake Ontario.[2]

* * *

The Lake Ontario Ordinance Works (LOOW) at the west end of Lake Ontario near Lewiston has already been discussed in Chapter Three. Because the deposits in it are older and were dumped during wartime and during the Cold War days that followed, less was known about the contents of this dump than those of West Valley. We do know there is still a lot of deadly radioactive material there. An article published in 2008 in Buffalo's alternative media on the area quoted John Shannon, an engineer of the Knolls Atomic Power Laboratory in Schenectady, an institution that apparently sent wastes to LOOW in the 1950s, *"Aside from Hanford, Washington, the Niagara* (area) *contamination is probably the worst in the country."*

Another article on line written by Jeffrey Hastings posted at the website terrain.org suggested some the difficulty in getting information on the site by quoting from an Army Corp document, *"We are interviewing workers and residents because written records are incomplete."* Dr. Gardella of the State University at Buffalo has worked on mapping and describing the many toxic legacies of the area including LOOW for ten years or more. Hopefully, the Army Corps has managed by now to get a reasonable idea of the site contents. The big problem, is going to be getting someone to pay for the clean up.

Ironically, a legacy of waste on and near Lake Ontario that will remain deadly for ten thousand years, appears to have already been largely forgotten after scarcely half a century. Few people living along the south shore outside of the Niagara area have ever heard of the Lake

Ontario Ordinance Works. I suspect even fewer Canadians have heard about it.

It has been pointed out repeatedly that the Lake Ontario Ordinance Works, Port Hope, the Tonawanda sites, and West Valley's repository are on about the least suitable land for long term storage of radioactive material that you could find anywhere. This material should not be left in tanks and drums or covered with concrete and left in the ground buried a few yards from eroding stream banks that relentlessly cut back closer and closer to the stash. The best guesses on West Valley's future are that some of the radioactive areas could be eroded within 200 years and that may not account for recent projected increases in extreme precipitation events from climate change. Modeling suggests nearly all the buried wastes on site would be washed downstream by erosion in a thousand years. Some observers wonder given the current rate of funding, if the clean up will be done by the time we hit that 200 year mark.

What do you do with nuclear waste? Right now, nothing. Or maybe cover it up and forget about it (the so-called kitty litter box approach suggested by the U.S. Department of Energy for the West Valley mess and by the Port Hope Area Initiative for the lower level rad waste at Grandby.) The Coalition on West Valley Nuclear Wastes and other observers suggest the best interim approach is to stabilize the stuff and store it above ground in a monitored site where it could be retrieved if and when a safe long term solution to disposal presents itself. They don't advocate moving it until there is a reasonable assurance of such a long term storage place or solution. But clearly it shouldn't stay buried in ground a few yards from the banks of actively eroding waterways upstream from the drinking water of ten million plus people.

It should not be left for a thousand years out of sight in a populated area where it inevitably will be disturbed by construction or other activity in a century or two. If it stays where a busy human population keeps moving stuff around, perhaps encased in concrete, buried and eventually forgotten, those deposits will be accidentally excavated and spread around causing future exposures and cancers and general human misery. The consultants call for "maintaining institutional controls" over the stuff. The problem is we have to do this essentially forever for some materials.

Even keeping track of it for a mere thousand years would seem an "improbability" as one report puts it. There is only one nation on earth (Iceland) that can be said to have maintained a constant government and language for a thousand years. For that matter, even if the language is still English, today's reports are likely to be totally intelligible to English speakers of the year 3015 even as we now find the epic of Beowulf incomprehensible and the 600 year old English of Chaucer's day heavy going. And that assumes the media those reports are recorded on will still exist in a readable condition somewhere. Perhaps we should be carving some of this information on stone. I don't have a computer anymore that can read stories on five inch floppies that I wrote twenty years ago.

As I corresponded with the women of the West Valley Coalition, I wondered what keeps this tiny band of people going? How have they manged to keep a cause alive for over forty years? (And to get an unresponsive government to eventually spend five billion dollars on stabilizing and cleaning up at least some of it).What has fueled their dogged determination to attend meetings and hearings, do presentations and power points, write letters and make phone calls in what must seem at times like a hopeless effort? Surely their courage must falter at times. Yet they plod on. Like a Quebec license plate, they can say, Je Me Souviens. I remember. For how many more years must they remember?

* * *

Port Hope entered the Atomic Age about ten years before Lewiston with the Lake Ontario Ordinance Works, when the Labine brothers of Eldorado Gold Mines Ltd. established a radium refinery on the shores of Lake Ontario. In 1930 a prospector named Gilbert LaBine who was looking for gold discovered high grade pitchblende and silver ore on the east end of Great Bear Lake in the Northwest Territories. The El Dorado endeavor immediately switched its focus to radium, then the rarest and most valuable mineral known. It was worth far more than gold. Prices for one gram ranged in 1930 currency from 50,000 to 70,000 dollars (roughly half to three quarters of a million dollars today). It was so valuable that bags of ore were actually shipped by air to the railhead in Alberta by way of the Radium Silver Express, a small airplane equipped with floats.

Purified radium is a white silvery metal that quickly oxidizes to become black. It has a dark history, too. As Wikipeda puts it, radium "is not necessary for life". Indeed, while radium can and does serve humans, all too often it has turned on them. The isotope radium 226 is intensely radioactive- more than 2 million times more than the same amount of naturally occurring uranium. One of the products of its decay is the lethal gas radon which collects in basements and closed rooms and when inhaled causes lung cancer. Radon is believed to be the second most common cause of lung cancer after smoking.

Radium occurs in tiny quantities in uranium ore, only about one gram per eight tons of the Great Bear Lake stuff. And because it emits deadly gamma radiation, it was costly and dangerous to isolate and purify. In 1918 just 13 grams were produced worldwide according to Wikipedia. (After nuclear reactors came on line it became easier to obtain radium as it was a byproduct of their operation.) Its scarcity and known effects on living tissue provided much of its allure in the early twentieth century when El Dorado was ramping up production on Lake Ontario. First isolated by Marie and Pierre Curie from ore excavated from silver mines in Austria, radium is generally thought to have killed Marie by damaging her bone marrow cells. Austria's monopoly on it until discoveries in Colorado and Canada kept supplies scant.

Ironically, this lethal element was once thought to have healing powers. Bizarre radium "cures" and tonics reached their peak of popularity in the U.S. in the 1920s. Radium, it was claimed, would cure constipation, arthritis, female troubles, goiters, and revive one's libido. Radium spiked water was touted as a cure "for the living dead" (the insane and profoundly retarded). Radon gas was actually sold in inhalers as a tonic to treat over two dozen different illnesses.

Radium and radon gas were also used as cancer treatments in the 1920s and 30s. We now know some of the patients died from the treatment rather than the disease. Wikipedia has an entry on Howard

Kelly a pioneer in gynecology, inventor of the Kelly Clamp (hemostatic forceps used to restrict bleeding during surgery) and one of the Johns Hopkins Hospital founders. He used capsules of radium to treat various tumors and cancers. He treated his own aunt with radium and both the tumor and the patient succumbed.

Radium water as a cure all for everything began to lose popularity in the U.S. after a steel tycoon in Pittsburgh named Eben Beyers drank 1400 bottles of the stuff. Portions of his mouth and jaw were surgically removed before he died in 1931 of cancer. His gruesome high profile demise, noted on the front page of the *New York Times*, was the beginning of the end of the popular radium water cures and also of the radium bubble. As a contemporary news account of the poisoning noted "Persistent swallowers of radium will do well, however, to consult a competent physician immediately, to be tested for accumulated radioactivity..."

More awareness of the element's danger arose after the Radium Girls made news with their lawsuit against a maker of military watches. Their fight was well publicized probably in part because of the inherent gender biases and unstated social tensions involved. The workers were paid 1.5 cents per painted watch dial and were encouraged to keep the production rate up by shaping their camel hair brush points with their tongues. Wikipedia says some of the young women also painted their teeth and nails with the glow in the dark paint.

Eventually the dial painters developed "radium jaw" and an assortment of other serious ills. The defense contractor declared their various cancers and anemias were the result of syphilis, and it took a worker named Grace Fryer two years to find a lawyer willing to take on the corporation on behalf of a "bad girl". Eventually four more workers joined her and won their case in 1928. Today it is viewed as a landmark decision for advancing worker safety regulation.

Belief dies hard though. In the early 1930s El Dorado Mines published a 24 page pamphlet (available on line) called *The Romance of Canadian Radium* in which the author wrote;

"Belief in magic minerals is as old as history.... the magical mineral must be propitiated, conjured cajoled -that an ounce be gleaned from ten thousand tons. It is called radium. Radium cures cancer. Furthermore, radium cures by touch. Stranger still, it touches without direct contact. Nothing is observed to happen when radium is brought close to a cancerous growth. But a few days later the growth begins to shrivel; eventually it disappears without a scar and terribly disfigured parts become normal... Radium is more than a magic mineral. It is a talisman."

The booklet author also wrote, *"Belief in magic minerals is as old as history.... the truth is stranger than myth."* He had that right.

El Dorado operated from 1933 to about 1940 providing radium to various markets before World War II disrupted the trade and shut it down. The refinery then re-opened in 1942 to supply material for the Manhattan Project and luminous paint for aircraft instrumentation for the war effort. It has been cranking away ever since.

Typically a ton of pitchblende ore from the deposits in northern Canada produced considerably less than a gram of radium. According to a website on the early history of Canada's nuclear industry the Port

Hope refinery produced 2.8 g of radium in 1934, 8.5 g in 1935, 15.5 g in 1936 and 23.8 g in 1937. It went through thousands of tons of uranium ore to do so. Most of the mildly radioactive tailings ended up sitting around Port Hope or nearby Port Granby in various piles and deposits. Some of it found its way into the Ganaraska River. Some of it ended up in the harbor. A lot of it ended up underfoot as it was used for construction fill for road base material or other purposes. The tailings contained uranium, arsenic, other heavy metals and some nasty residues from the refining process.

After high levels of radon gas were detected in 1975 in an elementary school built atop radioactive fill, clean up of the worst radioactivity began. From 1976 to 1981 about 100,000 tons of contaminated soil and fill was transported to the Chalk River facility on the shores of the Ottawa River for storage. This reduced much of the really acute contamination in homes schools and other locations throughout town. Just a bit late to the game in 1982 the Canadian Government also started trying to keep what was left in Port Hope from being spread around by new home construction and other human activity.

This was done by establishing a Task Force to find a secure storage facility for the stuff. For the next eight years the Siting Task Force invited various municipalities to take Port Hope's radioactive waste. Strangely enough, no one wanted it. In 1997 Port Hope began working on a plan for long term storage and in 2001 the Port Hope Area Initiative hereafter known as the PHAI, got underway. This was a legal agreement between town and Canadian Government to proceed with long term "management" of the stuff.

For seven more years assessments were done, meetings were held, and reports written and we assume a fair number of trees were sacrificed for the paperwork. In phase two beginning in 2012, 1.28 billion Canadian dollars were committed to actual clean up activity. The current plan is to excavate a little over a million cubic meters of contaminated soil and pile it up in a secure facility with restricted access. According to the city's website; "The facility will have the capacity to safely manage the historic waste now located within the Municipality of Port Hope for hundreds of years". (Bear in mind some of this material will remain potentially hazardous for far longer than the 1600 year half life of radium-226). Some of the material, about 450,000 cubic meters of it, will be excavated from a site that sits directly on the shore of Lake Ontario just west of Port Hope known as the Port Grandby dump that is now eroding into the lake. It will be moved about a half mile inland to a 50 hectare site for "long term" storage.

According to the PHAI website, the finished mound of low level rad waste would be shaped "to resemble a natural landform and tilted to mimic existing drumlins in the area." The excavated lake shore "will be restored and returned to a natural state", and the 175 hectares of land, now owned by the Government of Canada, "could be managed by a land trust or alliance organization". One wonders about the durability of that possible future management. And about what surprises await the unborn who might decide to build houses with lake views upon this shoreline "drumlin" in the year 2350. And if our current average erosion rate of one to two feet a year continues, some still radioactive material may again be washing into the lake around 1600 years from now.

Other radioactive and toxic hotspots containing radium 226, uranium, arsenic, and other heavy metals remain within Port Hope's city limits. The slow clean up of homes and properties continues. In 2011 the *Toronto Star* reported about 450 homes had been tested and or de-contaminated while ultimately about 5000 residences and properties were to be evaluated. All this testing and precautionary action takes place against a background of blithe assurances that a Port Hope resident on average receives smaller yearly radiation dose than someone living in Toronto. Certainly anyone buying or selling a home here would prefer to ignore the whole issue. Yet if the exposures and health effects are so trivial, why is the Canadian Government spending over a billion dollars to clean the place up?

Epidemiological studies are costly and difficult to do when evaluating prolonged exposures to low levels of radiation. It takes decades for the effects to appear. It is not easy to tease out the small number of cancers caused by radon gas exposure in the home, for example, from other factors over a thirty year period. One study by the Canadian government did show a higher than expected number of lung cancer cases among women in Port Hope between 1992 and 2007. This, the government study asserted, could be explained by a higher incidence of cigarette smoking among the population. But in a 2009 report for the non profit group Canadian Association of Physicians for the Environment two independent experts, Dr. Linda Harvey, and Dr. Cathy Vakil commented that if this were the case, other smoking related cancers of the liver stomach and bladder should also have been elevated among the women. And they weren't. The experts suggested some testing for radon gas levels within residences might provide clues as to the causes.[3] I haven't found results of such testing for radon or any follow up studies on line to date.

When concerned Port Hope citizens sought independent testing of their water soil and the urine of a small number of residents a few years ago, their results were debunked and condemned by many both outside and in the community. A columnist for the National Post of Toronto wrote *"Take, for example, the water running in to Lake Ontario from a Cameco effluent pipe. Local activists took a sample, and found traces of arsenic and uranium. Ms. Todd [one of the activists] said the arsenic level was "five times higher than Ontario guidelines" and the uranium 49.2 times. What she did not say is that the guidelines are Ontario tap drinking water standards. Nobody drinks effluent. The effluent levels are, according to Cameco, within the company's limits under its government license..."*

It is true no one knowingly drinks effluent directly from a pipe, but they certainly do drink Lake Ontario. The often cited "dilution is the solution" argument does have its limits especially with all the other nuclear facilities on the lake each of which is also emitting "insignificant" and legally permissible levels of radiation plus upstream facilities on the other lakes also contributing radiation. A chronic (and valid) complaint about various impact statements is that they ignore cumulative effects. At what point do we admit that human activity has raised "background" radiation to new levels?

Here's what the Canadian Physicians for the Environment had to say about it in their 2009 report Health Implications of The Nuclear Energy Industry; *"From an ecological point of view, humans in the past have succeeded in polluting huge volumes of the earth's water, air and soil, by considering each small (or large) release of a contaminant as "safe" or trivial. There is certainly risk that repeated releases of small amounts of a carcinogenic, mutagenic and teratogenic substance such as tritium into the drinking water of a large population, will have some deleterious health effects."*

9. Great Atomic Lake Power and Light and Heavy Water

A week after passing up Port Hope's harbor, *Sara B* set out from Main Duck Island to cross the lake on her return to her home port. In the distance off to port a white plume of vapor from the Nine Mile Unit 2 cooling tower rose into the blue sky, a guiding beacon back to our homeland. Staring at it as we motored along I thought of my stint as a firewatch twenty some years ago at another Lake Ontario nuke, the R.E. Ginna plant, the smallest and one of the oldest nuclear reactors in the U.S., in the lee of Smoky Point about a mile north of my mother's home near Ontario, NY.

I have long been a nuclear skeptic. Yet I shoved my scruples to the back shelf and took a job at the plant in the fall of 1990 after a lag in the writing income and the need to pay some imminent winter heating bills of a large essentially uninsulated house led to a search for some quick money. I was then working several nights a week at various mindless tasks as a "temp" in a law book publisher's factory. As I collated, packed, and glued end papers for $5.50 an hour, I watched the giant high speed presses and the clattering cutters and binders and daydreamed of writing a book that would be created in just such a place as this.

One night while chatting with the other temps on the mail line, I learned of a temporary worker's haven, the power plant right at the end of my road. "Surely only nuclear physicists and highly specialized technicians and engineers work there," I said. "Oh no - there's lots of temp work. There's janitor work and d con work and firewatch. ANYBODY can be a firewatch," my informant told me.

Since this was coming from a source who, like myself, had been putting tax manual updates inside large manila envelopes for three nights, I figured his assessment of the qualifications needed to be a "firewatch" was probably pretty trustworthy. I drove to a grimy residential area on the west side of Rochester near the county incinerator plant. There in a two story house with heavily barred windows I found an outfit that mostly signed up janitorial workers for big manufacturing companies and applied for a position as firewatch. The job description sounded so improbable I decided to check it out from sheer curiosity. Besides, I could walk to work, and it paid a lofty 6 dollars an hour with a guaranteed 20 to 30 hours of overtime during the "outage".

After finger printing, drug testing, and my three day training where I learned that we never sweep we always mop inside nuclear plants and prudent workers never step in puddles under dripping valves, (due to possible radioactive water) I was a full fledged firewatch. Despite the hazards of nuclear fleas, zoomies, and the remote and trifling chance of getting "crapped up" (the industry's technical term for being contaminated by radioactivity while on the job), I decided I would give it a try. I was a highly educated and intelligent writer. I figured I could judge for myself how safe this place was. I have since become less complacent.

During that long, quiet winter on second shift pursuing what must be among the top ten boring jobs ever devised by man, I had ample time to consider the bizarre phenomenon of using controlled fission, one of the most complex and potentially dangerous technologies ever devised by man, to boil water. And though the constant monitoring and carefully regulated operation of the station were reassuring, little hints that all was not quite as controlled as it seemed still occasionally penetrated even my state of denial.

My temporary vocation was invented when the NRC decided nuclear power plants needed human smoke detector backups after a couple of diligent atomic industry workers looking for air leaks around a penetration managed to ignite some insulation with a candle at the Brown's Ferry power plant. (As Dave Berry would say, honest, I'm not making this up.) Subsequently the assorted commercial nukes around the country hired housewives, retirees, truck drivers, laid off landscapers, former servicemen, and free lance writers to be firewatches.

At that time the firewatch basically roamed around the less

radioactive areas of the nuclear plant checking on places where for some reason the fire detection or the suppression system like the sprinklers was inoperable or a fire barrier of some sort had been breached. (This could be something no more ominous than a broken latch on a fire door). When people were welding or engaged in other activity that could cause a fire, someone assigned as firewatch stood nearby with an extinguisher, ever vigilant for sparks landing in oily rags, a surprisingly common occurrence during the annual maintenance period known as the "outage".

Most active maintenance and repair work in a nuclear power plant occurs during the outage when the reactor is shut down and refueled. The rest of the year the firewatch usually wasn't very busy and mostly hiked around the station and grounds sort of like a low level night watchman. Occasionally, when an alarm and a fire barrier were both impaired in some fashion, a firewatch was assigned to "sit post" gazing steadily at the offending area lest it spontaneously burst into flames. These periods of serving as a human heat and smoke detector were a great time to plan the next writing project.

Firewatch, at least between 5 PM and 5 AM during normal plant operation, was a pretty good job for a writer. It involved a good deal of sitting and staring. Such a contemplative occupation was ideal for authors since that's mostly what they do anyway. But here no telephones rang, no one knocked on the door, nor did a pesky cat ever walk across the keyboard to disturb one's meditations. I also had ample time when making my rounds to consider the bizarre juxtaposition of the power plant's subtle but constant sense of safety first and extreme hazard.

The armed guards in their cement bunkers and watch towers looking out over the lake, the double security fence with cameras and motion sensors, the lofty light poles with their clusters of huge flood lights, and the ubiquitous yellow and magenta radiation hazard warning signs reminded you constantly that this was no ordinary power station. Yet things soon fell into the same dull unvarying routine that had prevailed at the book factory. Night after night all winter long I entered the guardhouse, picked up my badge and TLD (a radiation monitor that workers always wore while on site), passed through the metal detector, and retrieved my x-rayed lunch to begin another eight hour shift inside a warm peaceful power plant. It was easy to accept it all as a perfectly normal way to make electricity and money and to not ask questions. Still, I wondered about the body counts of the worms that crawled across the sidewalk on rainy nights when my wet shoes set off the radiation monitor and of the pigeons that hung out on top of the containment dome next to the big pipes that vented air and short lived radiation from the plant. And my nightly hikes across the catwalk over the spent fuel pool linger in memory.

There was nothing normal about that part of the plant. The spent fuel pool was a deep, water filled pit where hundreds of used fuel rods were stored. The water kept them cool and acted as a protective shield. These used rods were intensely radioactive and produced a blue glow of Cherenkov radiation that has been characterized by others as eerie or hellish to look upon. I found it strangely compelling. This fierce frightening beauty was the only visible sign I ever saw of actual radiation. I was haunted by its soft blue light. It was wondrous strange and also deeply troubling knowing that without the water's protection I would receive an imperceptible but lethal dose of ionizing radiation in minutes as I stood upon the catwalk.

Nuclear power has been called the safest form of generating electricity ever deployed by mankind, the large stack of barrels stuffed with disposable booties, gloves, and protective suits stashed in one of Ginna's storage areas in the spent fuel pool building not withstanding. The federal governments (that is the U.S. and Canadian tax payers) provide "insurance" to the industry on Lake Ontario because the potential staggering losses after a meltdown would require such high premiums that the business wouldn't exist if it had to pay them. The Japanese disaster has cost over 500 billion in U.S. dollars so far and it's far from over. So there is good reason for the obsession with safety. And for the industry's markedly reticent attitude towards releasing information about incidents and accidents.

Lake Ontario, the great atomic lake, is home to 9000 MW of nuclear generating capacity, a fact that most of its shoreline residents are blissfully unaware of. Perhaps it's just as well. Four of the six operating nuclear plants in New York State and twelve of Ontario Province's twenty reactors are located on the smallest Great Lake. (Most of Canada's nuclear power production takes place in Ontario Province at plants situated on the Great Lakes.) There is also a small reactor at McMaster University used for research and the production of isotopic material for medical use as well as another little one in Kingston at the Military College. Only Lake Michigan with six U.S. plants comes anywhere close to matching the amount of fissile material parked on our shores.

Nuclear power according to the World Nuclear Association provides 19% of America's energy mix. Although 99 reactors currently operate nationwide, few new ones have been built in recent years because of the daunting costs of construction. Commercial nuclear power in the U.S. has always been closely tied to government subsidies, partly because, as one environmental activist put it, the industry and the defense business have been joined at the hip since day one. Our existing commercial reactors create plutonium, a key part of nuclear bombs, though used "reactor grade" fuel from power plants is not presently reprocessed for weapons making.

By far the biggest subsidy that the industry receives is the already mentioned exemption from paying for private liability insurance for damages in the event of a serious accident. Most nuclear critics believe there would be no commercial nuclear power industry without this exemption given the horrendous and on going costs we have seen for the clean ups of the Chernobyl and Fukushima meltdowns. Many if not most of the commercial plant control room operators in the U.S. receive tax payer supported training in the nuclear navy. And as yet, the industry has not had to deal with the costs of long term storage of nuclear waste or the full costs of decommissioning the power plants.

The power plant operators do pay into a trust fund for decommissioning of reactors, a pot of money that nuclear critics (and some accountants) believe is seriously underfunded. It took 15 years and 600 million dollars to decommission the Yankee Station in

Massachusetts a plant that took three years to build. And the plant owner still has to monitor and provide security for the deadly spent fuel stashed in dry casks on site at a cost of about 8 million a year. There is no permanent repository for nuclear waste presently in the U.S., and one wonders if there ever will be one.

Lake Ontario is home to two of the oldest operating reactors in the U.S. 'fleet', the 581 MW Ginna plant, a pressurized water reactor similar in design to those used in nuclear submarines, and Nine Mile Point Unit One east of Oswego a 600 MW boiling water reactor. They went into service in in 1970 and 1969 respectively. Both these old timers along with the four geriatric CANDUs at Pickering's A unit, have issues related to their age.

The U.S. plants were originally licensed for forty years and all have gotten twenty year extensions. The operating units of Pickering recently got a shorter extension through August 2018. Critics of the boiling water reactor (BWR) designs like Nine Mile One and the Fukushima plants in Japan say the containment system and torus used as a heat sink for steam in an emergency, are less robust than the systems used at Ginna. They also don't like the above ground storage of the spent fuel pool at the BWR plants. They fear these storage areas for intensely radioactive spent fuel may be more vulnerable to earthquake damage or to the aftermaths of other disturbances such as a general failure of the electrical grid perhaps from a electro- magnetic pulse associated with a severe solar storm or an attack by hostile forces. After the Fukushima plants lost on site power, at least one spent fuel storage area boiled dry and released large amounts of radioactivity.

Another age related issue associated with the pressurized water reactors like Ginna is the embrittlement of the stainless steel reactor vessel. The welds of older plants gradually are affected over time by the intense radiation and become less able to withstand sudden temperature changes. If a plant's emergency cooling system were called upon to flood the reactor vessel weakened by embrittlement, it could fracture possibly leading to a meltdown. The reactor vessels are monitored and tested periodically and at least one plant, the Palisades Station on Lake Michigan that went into service in 1971 may have to shut down by 2017 due to such weakening.

Critics of nuclear power also point to the greater economic pressures that the plant operators now deal with in a partially de-regulated market place for electricity. This, they say, makes it harder to justify spending money on the old clunkers until something gives out. Obviously, the industry and the government regulators don't agree with this viewpoint. But the Union of Concerned Scientists website page summarizing past issues at Nine Mile Point Unit One isn't very re-assuring. As far back as 1988 the plant was suffering from corrosion in its torus, a key part of its emergency cooling system, wall and floor cracks, and various deficiencies in emergency procedures and instrumentation. While all those problems have presumably been rectified, new ones keep cropping up.

Another New York reactor, the FitzPatrick Plant, on Nine Mile Point east of Oswego, is also showing signs of age. In 2012 The Alliance For A Green Economy and several other groups petitioned the NRC with an "emergency enforcement petition" against Entergy, the owner of

FitzPatrick for failing to meet the Nuclear Regulatory Commission's financial strength requirements. (The need for adequate liquidity on the part of a nuclear power plant operator should be fairly obvious. A less than adequate cash and credit cushion is all too likely to lead to some corner cutting.) The petition noted along with staff layoffs, a trend of increasingly frequent unplanned outages and emergency shutdowns at the plant. They and another watchdog group, the Union of Concerned Scientists, called for replacement of the plant's steam generator by the 2014 maintenance shutdown. The steam generator is a key part of the plant and is crucial to safe operation. It is also a big ticket item to replace- perhaps something on the order of a new engine or a tranny in your old car. Entergy did replace all the tubes, but only after their plant's tube failures accounted for nearly a third of all such failures in the entire U.S. nuclear 'fleet' over a ten year period. It's future remains in doubt as of this writing. Another nuclear plant operator out in California declined to replace its steam generators at San Onofre's units 2 and 3 in 2013 after unexpected steam tube wear was detected. Instead it decided to decommission part of the plant (at an estimated cost of 4.4 billion dollars according to Wikipedia).

 Several other old nukes have also been shut down in recent years because they cost too much to operate. The Ginna plant, according to the Alliance For A Green Economy produces power at a cost of 48$ per megawatt (MW) hour while the average wholesale market price for the area was 37.45$ per MWh in 2013. Ironically, much of the problem for Lake Ontario's old clunkers stems from cheaper production of power from gas fired plants benefiting from all that Pennsylvania hydrofracking.[1]

The situation is much the same on the Canadian side of the lake at the Pickering Station just east of Toronto. Pickering consists of a cluster of eight reactors lined up along the lake shore like gray puffballs on either side of a common "vacuum building" which is supposed to contain any radiation releases. The four oldest ones having been built 1966 are the oldest commercial reactors in Canada. Two of them are out of service and have had their fuel removed. Greenpeace Canada and other groups have called for a shut down of the entire plant citing the risks to a large nearby population and the lack of demand for power. They point to the fact that Ontario Province is currently exporting excess power to the U.S.

All the Canadian reactors on the lake are of a design known as the CANDU and use U 235 as a fuel and heavy water as a moderator. One expert, Arnold Gunderson, a nuclear engineer who submitted comments during the hearings to extend the Pickering Station's license, pointed out the inherent drawbacks of the design include a complex plumbing system of fuel channels and pressure tubes. He stated that as the reactor ages it becomes increasingly difficult to monitor the condition of the various components leading to uncertainty about the safety of the plant. The eight reactors also share one containment building, unlike the station I worked in which had its own containment dome as a back up to the reactor vessel itself. This lack of redundancy in a heavily populated area quite naturally leads to some unease among the nuclear skeptics as the Pickering plant ages. It has already suffered from several blown pressure tubes.

Passing Pickering on a calm day

According to Dr. F.R. Greening, a Canadian chemist and former Ontario Hydro researcher quoted by Gunderson in his comments on re-licensing, *"the CANDU reactor design incorporates a number of intricately engineered and highly complex systems that require an inordinate amount of skilled manpower to operate, inspect and repair. Many components are difficult to access, or are located in areas of high radiation fields adding to the problems..."*

Gunderson concluded that the plant, built back when slide rules were used for engineering calculations for the CANDU design, should not be re- licensed. There are simply too many uncertainties, he wrote. The Canadian Nuclear Safety Commission, the country's regulatory agency, authorized operation of the plant for another five years in 2013.

All nuclear power plants release radiation while operating. The official position is that what they vent and release into the water is short lived, harmless and insignificant in the overall scheme of things. But the routine release of one form of radiation, tritium, has received attention from both environmental groups and health officials. Tritium is an unstable isotope of hydrogen and is weakly radioactive. U.S. pressurized and boiling water plants release tritium but in far lesser amounts than the CANDUs at Picking and Darlington (which also has a tritium extraction facility. This removes some of the radioactive tritium from water that is then sold for use in luminous instrumentation and in airport runway lights. However, it releases some tritium as gas while operating.) Dr. Ian Fairlie in a report for Greenpeace writes that the CANDUs are collectively the world's largest single emitter of tritium.

Although it emits a less powerful dose of radiation than radium or some other radioactive materials, tritium is a carcinogen, a mutagen and a teratogen (a substance that causes birth defects). It has been linked to testicular and ovarian tumors, chromosome breaks and aberrations, fetal death and malformations, and mental retardation. Though it is weakly radioactive, it is also unique in that our bodies use it as ordinary hydrogen. Tritium as a part of a water molecule is incorporated potentially every tissue and cell and may even end up in the DNA molecule itself. When in close proximity to the cell's genetic material it can cause damage to the host organism and its offspring.

Presently the acceptable level of tritium in drinking water in Canada is 7000 Bq per litre, almost ten times the U.S. drinking water limit of 740 Bq per litre. In Europe the limit is 100 and the public health goal in California is 15 Bq per litre. Canadian drinking water limits for regulated toxic chemicals are based on a 70 year exposure and attempt to limit the excess of deaths to 1 in a million. Yet tritium exposure limits assume people only drink tritiated water for one year and the overall death rate is set at five times that for regulated chemicals. According to Fairlie's report *"The current Canadian Federal limit for tritium corresponds to a risk of 350 excess fatal cancers per million people. On the other hand, the Canadian Federal drinking water objectives for chemicals are set at levels that provide a lifetime risk of 1–10 excess fatal cancers per million people."*

This curious double standard for risks associated with radiation is not unique to Canada. It is a "privileged pollutant" in the U.S. as well.[2]

In 1992 a spill from Pickering was tracked by the municipal water authority as it passed outlets from Oshawa to Hamilton. Over 20,000 gallons highly contaminated with two trillion becquerels of tritium ended up in the lake. A reading of 195 Bq/l was seen at a Toronto water intake, well below the Canadian limit but nearly twice the European limit. Another intake reading peaked at over 600 Bl/liter. "Dilution was the solution" once again, but with a half life of 12 years and with more coming in than is removed by flow down the St. Lawrence, the overall amount of tritium in the lake appears to be slowly increasing. In 1998 the level in Lake Superior (with no nukes on its shores) was 2 bq/liter. In Lake Ontario that year it was just over 7 Bq/liter. That was nearly twenty years ago. One wonders how close the lake is to California's 15 Bq limit now.[3]

The Ontario Drinking Water Advisory Council (ODWAC) a group made up of engineers public health researchers, chemists and other professionals with expertise in drinking water treatment and safety standards issued a formal report in May 2009 in response to a request by the Minister of the Environment on the tritium standards. They concluded that the Ontario Drinking Water Quality Standard for tritium should be revised from the current 7,000 Bq/L level to a new, (much!) lower 20 Bq/L level. However, the proposed revision was turned down.

A scientific paper published in the Journal *Dose-Response* by four authors in the Department of Medical Physics and Applied Radiation Sciences at McMaster University, and coauthor Dr. D. R. Boreham, an employee of Bruce Power, operator of a big nuke station up on Lake Huron stated; *"...scientific research from leading authorities on the carcinogenic health effects of tritium exposure supports the notion that the current standard of 7,000 Bq/L (annual dose of 0.1 mSv) is a safe standard for human health."* So much for the precautionary principal. Canada's standard remains unchanged.

It's hard to know how much of a threat tritium poses to Lake Ontario water drinkers. But having a drinking water standard for tritium that is 70 times higher than Europe's doesn't make me feel real warm and fuzzy. Fairlie's report published by Greenpeace in 2007 noted that the required epidemiological studies to prove health effects from low dose exposures are expensive and time consuming. Fairlie is an independent consultant and former member of the Committee on Examining Radiation Risks From Internal Emitters, a body of specialists formed by the British Government to study the risks of exposure to ingested radioactive materials like tritium. To date, he wrote, no effort has yet been made to tease out the effects of radiation from all the other variables the population around Pickering and Darlington and the rest of the Lake Ontario water drinkers are exposed to.

As with so many of the chemicals in the air and water, we simply don't know what the negative effects are. They may not be immediately life threatening (at least for healthy adults), but we can be pretty certain that this stuff isn't good for us. Using the precautionary approach that prevails in Europe for risk management would seem to make sense here, too.[4]

It has been suggested that the power plant operators could hold their tritiated water in long term decay tanks to reduce its radioactivity before releasing it into the lake. Another quicker way to reduce tritium in the lake would be to shut the old Pickering reactors down. This might also reduce the odds of a Fukushima/Chernobyl type incident that could render the water supply for millions of people unusable. But will we then be left sitting in the dark on long winter nights without enough electricity to run our heaters, computers and dvd players? Given the harsh realities of climate change, what else besides nuclear power can we use for reliable continuous base load production of electricity? Without getting tangled up in the life cycle analysis of nuclear plants and their green house gas emissions (which include the emissions associated with mining, processing and transport of fuel, as well as all the zillions of cubic yards of concrete used to build a nuke) there is still that rad waste issue. Even the next generation 'safe' nukes still have that problem.

How else can we keep the electrons flowing? In the short run while we're waiting for cold fusion, efficiency in the form of rigorous building codes, smart grids, and distributed generation may be our best bet. And improvements to the grid would also give renewables and distributed generation a considerable price advantage over the present market place values. Dr. Mark Diesendorf of the University of New South Wales (Australia) has modeled electricity supply and demand and states that the inability of renewable generation to supply reliable constant "base load" power is a myth. He puts forth a model of power generation that uses wind, photovoltaics, thermal solar, biomass, hydro, and gas turbines (which could be partially fueled by biogas from those "base load" dairy cows that produce manure 24/7) that supplies all needs. However, his model assumes an electrical grid that is far more interconnected and able to shift power around the country than the present North American infrastructure is able to do.[5]

Another intriguing way to add base load capacity to intermittent renewable energy sources is being demonstrated in a small scale project in Toronto by a company called Hydrostor. Their early proof of concept was installed next to the Toronto Sewage Plant by Leslie Head Spit. They then put a small power plant on one of the Toronto Islands near the airport. Hydrostor is using a modification of an old idea of pumped storage plants to even out supply and demand. Pumped storage plants like the Lewiston Pump-Generating plant at Niagara Falls use electricity during low demand periods to pump water up to a reservoir. Then when electricity demand peaks, the operators run the water downhill through turbines to produce power to feed into the grid. Hydrostor proposes to use wind or solar power to store compressed air in large balloons or bladders tethered underwater. The pressurized air is then used to turn air turbines when demand peaks. It's an interesting variation on the pumped storage plan that also uses gravity to "fill up" an energy reservoir of sorts.

According to an article in the Financial Post published in January 2015, Hydrostor had signed a contract to build a plant in Aruba where the steady trade winds will drive a 30 MW wind farm to "charge" the underwater batteries or compressed air. The company website states that the technology is 'scalable' and could be used to produce local power or for large centralized power production.

There are ways to reduce our dependence on aged leaky nuclear power plants and to stop making more radwaste. But the transition to renewables will be not quick painless or cheap. However, the alternative of business as usual is looking increasingly grim. We will re-visit the topic of giving renewables a chance to increase their contribution to the mix in Chapter Eleven on climate change and the lake.

10. Reweaving The Lake's Web of Life

Since European settlement a wave of extinctions perhaps even more extreme than the Cretaceous-Tertiary event that wiped out the dinosaurs has overwhelmed Lake Ontario's native species and completely rewoven its web of life. Lake Ontario is not alone in experiencing severe biodiversity losses. All over the world freshwater ecosystems are in trouble. Lakes and rivers cover less than one percent of the world's surface, yet harbor 10% of its animal species. Environmental stresses are causing massive changes in those systems leading to rapid biodiversity loss. Many of the world's most endangered animals are aquatic freshwater species with general extinction rates of four to six times that of marine or terrestrial ecosystems. Freshwater mussels in the Great Lakes are among them. More than 70% of North America's mussels are either extinct or on the edge of disappearing. Half the crayfish species in North America are either gone or about to go. And nearly all of Lake Ontario's once predominant native open water fishes including a local strain of lake trout, the kiyi, shortnose, and blackfin ciscoes, blue pike, whitefish, Atlantic salmon, lake sturgeon, and even the once ubiquitous American eel of inshore waters, have either completely vanished or are hanging on at very low numbers.

Declining biodiversity, defined as the variety of organisms in an ecosystem, is an under reported issue little understood by the general public. However, it has direct impacts on human well being. Simplified degraded ecosystems are less stable and robust and often offer lower qualities of production than more varied and diverse ones. In Lake

Ontario historically a group of a half dozen or more forage fishes fed top level predators. Those fish have been largely replaced by a single species, the alewife. If a new disease of some sort were to reach the lake and eliminate or greatly reduce alewife populations, the lake's multi-million dollar open water trophy fishery would be severely disrupted.

A few years ago an Ebola like disease devastated populations of some of the lake's fishes. In the Bay of Quinte more than a hundred metric tons of freshwater drum were killed. VHS (viral hemorrhagic septicemia) was not previously known to have been present in the lake. Some researchers suspect it came to the region in ballast water as so many other invaders have. The genetics of the Great Lakes virus resembled those of marine East Coast VHS populations. Like other nonnative species, it could possibly have been transmitted by ship, perhaps being picked up during a ballast water exchange offshore though it is not yet known for certain if the virus could survive that long in a ballast tank. Various species of microorganisms including the cholera bacterium and viruses have been transmitted around the world's waters via ballast water.

Today the leading cause of extinction is habitat destruction. But a close second to that is competition from introduced non native species. In recent years the rapid worldwide loss of species has given rise to the term the "anthropocene era" defined as the time of man's shaping every aspect of the world environment, even its climate. Humans with their constant movement of goods and themselves also transport microbes, fungi, seeds, snakes, plants, crabs, earthworms and other life forms to places where they have never before been. Often the new organisms find opportunity, especially in an environment like that of Lake Ontario that has already been disturbed and disrupted by human activity. Sometimes they then crowd out other already stressed native plants and animals. Some fear that if plankton eating Asian carp now present in the Mississippi drainage become widespread here, Lake Ontario could reach a tipping point in its food web that might lead to a general collapse of the open water food chain and its much valued salmon and trout fishery.

The Great Lakes watershed, overfished and polluted for two hundred years, is now home to more than 180 nonnative invasive species, the alewife, smelt, and round goby among them. The poster child for aquatic invasive animals everywhere in the U.S. in recent years has been the *Dreissena* sisters- the zebra mussel and the closely related quagga mussel, two little shellfish that are still re-weaving the web of life in Lake Ontario in ways not yet fully understood. They have been called ecosystem engineers because they literally have re-engineered the lake's physical and chemical systems. Their arrival sparked the passage of federal legislation called The National Invasive Species Act in 1996 and helped expand a whole new field of biological study. By feeding on phytoplankton, the lowest level of the lake's food chain, they continue to propagate shifts in energy flows throughout the lake's ecosystem.

During *Sara B's* cruise we stopped at two places where nonnative plants and animals were thriving. Though contrasts were sharp between Main Duck Island, the lake's most remote island surrounded by the least polluted water remaining here, and Leslie Street Spit, a peninsula reaching out into the lake next door to Toronto's sewage plant, they nonetheless have both been extensively colonized by invasive plants and animals.

Sara B spent two nights anchored in a peaceful sheltered lagoon filled with moored yachts a few yards from one of North America's largest cormorant colonies. Our mooring provided by the decidedly proletarian and hospitable Aquatic Park Sailing Club was protected from the open lake by the long narrow peninsula created by fill and rubble from city construction. The spit continued to grow even during our visit as a steady procession of dump trunks trundled down the narrow road to its end to tip their loads of concrete dirt and wood.

I rowed around the anchorage to examine the peculiar mix of hardy native and non native plants and animals that had colonized this barren man made strip of dirt and fill. This, I thought, is probably the future of nature everywhere. It had a certain strange charm, and the unmanicured spaces of the spit (officially known as Tommy Thompson Park) draw urban cyclists, joggers, bird watchers and kayakers by the score on weekends. *Sara B* visited during the week when the park was less busy. On our forays ashore to this little wilderness of scrub, tall reeds, cottonwoods and alder thickets we several times encountered a lone pedestrian. He was a sturdy muscular man, middle aged, with the round face, stocky build and long straight raven hair of the aboriginal Canadian. He was usually walking along the main gravel road or drifting down one of the numerous foot trails that wandered through the scrub. I felt no menace from him when we crossed paths as we hiked to the bus stop. Rather, there seemed a gentle melancholy about the man. He sometimes gave a slight nod of acknowledgment, but never spoke when we passed.

A yacht club member assured us the homeless man was harmless. I wondered if this lost soul far from his native village had washed up on the lakeshore after an unfortunate encounter with drugs or booze. Perhaps he had been drawn to the city in search of work or opportunity. Now had he come here to find shelter in the healing quiet of this small enclave of nature?

The spit is an odd mix of ecology. Native mallards, beavers, foxes, great egrets, and cottontails share it with feral cats, Norway rats, and exotic mute swans escaped perhaps from the nearby Park Islands. The shuttle bus driver, a college student who had done a study project on the cormorant colony, told us they had heard "brush wolves" (hybrid blends of wolf-dog-coyote) howling here at night. He also told us that the cormorant colony was doing well, though the birds did have to contend with a healthy population of fire ants. Masses of fire ants crawl up the trees to attack and devour nestling birds, he explained.

"Charming ecosystem," said my spouse later as we looked over at the guano streaked dying trees. "No wonder the birds don't nest on the ground."

The cormorant story is an interesting one of comebacks and controversy. Controversy centers on the question of the birds' status. Are they natives? The EPA website and many fish and game managers say no, other ecologists and naturalists say yes. The question is controversial because if they are another example of an invasive species, then it is easier to justify killing them off. And a lot of people want them killed. There is a marvelous quote from Steinbeck's "Sea of Cortez" cited on several websites about cormorants in which he sums up the prevailing attitude in Baja Mexico towards these "evil" black goose sized fish eating birds. "Everyone hates them", he wrote. Pretty much everyone up here hates them, too. As Steinbeck said, here and in Baja, they're considered subversive forces against the Perfect Balance i.e. that all the fish in the sea and in the great lakes, too, were created exclusively for human use. So Steinbeck wrote, like all radicals and subversives the birds should be slaughtered.

I'm not crazy about cleaning up a large smelly splat of subversive cormorant guano off *Sara B's* poop deck, something now and then I have to do in the fall when the birds leave their island rookeries and start heading south. But you have to admire the cormorant's fishing talents and the way they handle themselves in the water. And because they are sensitive indicators of toxins in the Lake Ontario environment, we can take some comfort in their impressive comeback from the 1970s when the "devil bird" as the anglers sometimes refer to it, was all but extinct on the Great Lakes thanks to pesticides in the food chain.

They've been on the lake since the 1930s if not a lot longer. Farley Mowat, the famous Canadian author and naturalist, wrote of banding cormorants on an island in the lake when he was a kid. But by the 1950s and 60s they were a rare sight. Unlike the hardy gulls, they were far more sensitive to the effects of organochlorides in the environment. Photos of deformed eyeless Great Lakes cormorant chicks with distorted twisted bills helped mobilize support for laws to restrict point source pollution. Once levels of PCB's mirex, and other toxins began to drop in the 1980's the birds began to thrive once again. On Lake Erie the number of cormorant nests on five major nesting islands increased from 87 in 1979 to 12,973 in 2004.

The first time I saw the colony of fish eating birds on Little Galloo Island around 1998 when it included hundreds of Caspian terns, thousands of ringbill gulls, and countless cormorants, I was thrilled by the throngs of birds. They were such a powerful manifestation of life, tangible proof that the lake still had a food web. They were proof of resilience and hope here. Their clamor (and smell) was stunning.

Cormorants themselves reduce biodiversity on the islands on which they nest. They crowd out neighboring birds like the black crowned night heron and various other native fish eaters. Their guano kills trees and plants eventually transforming once green islands into barren bits of land. The current thinking seems to be some culling of the birds is in order, and now and then unsanctioned vigilante control efforts occur here as in Baja.[1]

Humans have eradicated cormorant colonies before, and could certainly do so again, but there's little chance of human control of the lake's most recent high profile invaders, the zebra and quagga mussels. They first arrived in the Great Lakes Basin around 1988 as passengers aboard sea going freighters from the Caspian Sea area. The hardy shellfish, like a number of other organisms ranging from cholera bacteria to Chinese mitten crabs and the round goby are able to survive in the water ballast tanks of ships traveling to the lakes. Once they arrived, the shellfish, having no natural predators or controls here, were able spread rapidly throughout the Great Lakes. A single adult mussel can produce a million eggs a year. Within a couple of years they had carpeted the bottom of Lake Erie and much of Lake Ontario's depths and were clogging power plant and city water intakes.

Up to 700,000 mussels have been found in a square yard of hard surface. Shortly after their invasion of Lake Ontario we found windrows of inch long white shells three and four feet high on the beaches of Main Duck. Since each mussel can filter up to a liter of water a day while feeding on tiny one celled phytoplankton, it's easy to see how they could impact the food chain. One model suggested that zebra mussels along with some of the larger invasive zooplankton could reduce whole lake phytoplankton production by 70%. The hardy little shellfish are picky about their diet. They seem to prefer more nutritious diatoms and certain single cell green algae over other species of algae and selectively filter and reject some strains of toxic blue green cyanobacteria. When billions of them do so they can change the composition of the phytoplankton species of large areas of the lake in short order. Researchers suspect this selective feeding has helped fuel more frequent toxic blue green blooms as the cyanobacteria have less competition from other algae.[2]

The mussels also transfer vast amounts of energy from the open water food chain to the bottom of the lake to the detriment of some of the lake's offshore fish like the salmon and trout. Overall supplies of phytoplankton have decreased 60% in spring in Lake Erie since the mussels' arrival according to some studies. A Lake Michigan study author calculated the mussel population in one portion of Saginaw Bay was sufficient to filter the entire water column in twelve days.

Vast beds of shellfish now compete with various zooplankton and the little shrimp- like *Mysis* that are vital foods for many of the lake's larval and juvenile fishes. Small water fleas of the order Cladocera that feed on one celled algae and protozoans in the lake have historically been a major food item for juvenile bait fish. But lab experiments showed zebra mussels out competing them for food as well as filtering and consuming just hatched cladocerans. All of this filtering leaves us with a nice clear lake and lot less nourishment for young fishes. The zebra and quagga mussels are also suspected of playing a role in the increase of botulism poisoning in Lake Ontario as discussed in Chapter Three thanks in part to that nice clear water.

Some fish that feed on or near the bottom like the freshwater drum, lake sturgeon and lake trout do eat mussels. But unfortunately, the mussels' quality as a food source is second rate. They're less nutritious than native foods, as the fish must use metabolic energy to crush breakdown and eliminate the mussel shells. To make matters worse, the mussels also appear to have displaced a far richer more nutritious food source on the lake bottom, that of a small shrimp like crustacean called Diporeia. This bottom dweller was a key part of food chain for a number of the lake's native fishes including the once commercially important whitefish and lake trout. It appears to have been impacted by decrease of up to 90% in its food supply of spring diatoms along with other foods thanks to busy mussel filters. Today, it is virtually extinct on Lake Ontario's bottom. We can't rule out toxins in the sediments or other changes in the lake's environment as a contributor, but this particular localized extinction may well be another example of displacement by a successful invader.

* * *

Sara B's last stop before returning to home port was Main Duck island. As we approached we saw the island on the horizon as a thin dark line of land. It is the lake's most remote island and is invisible to most mainland residents so few people visit here these days. It is mostly known to fishermen and cruisers, and was privately owned for years. Once John Foster Dulles, Secretary of State under Eisenhower, used it as a resort and getaway. After he died, I was told, his caretaker

Bob Hart bought it from the estate perhaps with the intention of making money from rentals to hunting and fishing parties. Instead, according to the story I heard, a Canadian boating magazine editor started a campaign for her country to reclaim its lost island. Ottawa eventually did so in the late 1970s, and Main Duck is now an undeveloped and largely untended park island open to all who come by boat (with proper paperwork in hand if they're not Canadian).

In precolonial times it was forested, and the shallows around it teemed with life. Vast flocks of ducks visited the island to feed on fish and invertebrate life in its extensive shallows. Huge schools of gleaming silver fish swarmed over the ledges. When Rene La Force dropped anchor off the island in 1758 and sent his weary ship's company ashore to forage, he wrote that they killed wild pigeons and some small birds and found "cabbages" and wild garlic to put in their cooking pots, a welcome change from their usual ration of dried peas salt pork and hard tack.

Those stony ledges that supported so much life also caused a number of shipwrecks. There are yet unmarked graves hidden away in thickets of scrub on the island. On a quiet summer afternoon of calm water and light wind Main Duck is a peaceful retreat from reality. But the overgrown ruins of several cottages and tangible traces of past human mishaps lend a mild melancholy to the scene even on a tranquil day.

Like Leslie Street Spit, the Main Duck landscape shows ample evidence of human usage. Much of its forest is gone leaving patches of an odd savannah-like landscape where once Claude Cole's bison herd roamed. A thin layer of topsoil overlies its limestone bedrock and patches of grassland and flower filled meadow flourish. Areas of alvar barrens show outcrops of pavement like limestone, with deep cracks and mysterious minature caves. In the early 1980s I visited in late summer and found the island swarming with thousands of migrating monarch butterflies. The insects had been grounded by strong headwinds and were waiting out the southerlies. They were fueling up, feeding on abundant goldenrod flowers before attempting the thirty plus miles of open water before them. But now an invasive weed called dog strangling vine (swallowwort) has overrun large areas of the island. It has choked out much of the butterfly friendly milkweed and goldenrod and is doing its best to muscle out the poison ivy.

In the little harbor where *Sara B* rested at anchor I peered down at the sunlit mud bottom through six feet of limpid water. Here I saw countless fingerling sized round gobies- a dozen or more in a square foot of bottom. We amused ourselves for awhile by dropping crumbs over the side and watching them slowly descend through the clear water. The moment a bit of food hit bottom an instant scrimmage of one to two inch gobies surrounded it tussling, writhing, pushing, shoving and snatching at the morsel in a miniature but fierce feeding frenzy.

A few yards away on this June day hordes of big brawny carp were thrashing around in the shallows at the head of the anchorage. They were broadcasting eggs and sperm to create the next generation of carp. Carp, originally introduced to North America in the 1830s for pond culture, have been in the lake longer than gobies and have done well here. Both ashore and afloat during our visit, it seemed, Main Duck's surviving natives were slugging it out for survival with a varied AIS (alien invasive species) crowd. And this year no bobolinks perched on small cedars and sang over the grasses. The black and white and yellow males were conspicuous by their absence.

The round goby, like the invasive alewife before it, has reshaped a large part of the lake's ecosystem and energy flow. Unlike the alewife that spends most of its life in the open lake, gobies are easily observed in their summertime inshore habitat. They are nondescript little fish that spend lots of time resting on the bottom. I think they're rather cute with their froggy little upward looking eyes and puffy "cheeks". They rarely get much over six inches or so, and human anglers generally despise the little bait stealers. But cormorants bass and Main Duck water snakes gobble them up. On Lake Erie a subspecies of the common watersnake *Nerodia sipedon* once listed as a threatened species now depends heavily on gobies and has made a bit of a comeback. The little fish now account for up to 90% of the snake's diet. As the lake's web of life continues to be re-woven, it will be interesting to watch how the goby fits in.

We already have seen that they seem to have played a role in the botulism outbreaks. Gobies are from the same part of the world (the Black and Caspian Sea) as the zebra mussel, and adults feed readily on shellfish. But unlike many of the lake's other inshore fishes, they feed both day and night allowing them to out compete many of our native fish species. Gobies also eat fish eggs, including those of the various sunfishes and important game fish like the bass that they share the inshore shallows with. However, adult bass eat gobies as do a number of other important game fishes. The ultimate role of the little immigrants in Lake Ontario's intricate dance of life remains as yet undefined by science. Another experiment in modified ecosystems is well underway, however.

Lake Ontario's open water fishery now consists almost entirely of nonnative species. The hatchery raised West Coast salmon and trout feed mainly on non native alewives and bring anglers to the lake in search of 40 pound fish. The big late summer fishing derbies still bring in hundreds of anglers from across the state and from Connecticut, Pennsylvania, New Jersey and Massachusetts. Though some salmon and steelhead do reproduce on their own in Lake Ontario tributaries, this valuable recreational fishery is largely supported by artificial propagation.

Efforts have been made for years to restore self sustaining populations of one of the lake's native top predator fishes, the lake trout. Unfortunately, it seems to be especially sensitive to thiaminase, an enzyme that destroys B1 that is found in alewives or possibly in bacteria associated with the alewives. In a hatchery, B vitamins can be added to the water to assure survival of eggs and fry. But not in the open lake. Historically, lake trout would have had a variety of prey fish to eat, some of which would have contained sufficient B vitamins to keep them healthy. Lake trout that eat mostly alewives are reproducing with limited success partly because of the vitamin deficiency which kills the just hatched fry as they begin to absorb their yolk sacs. There are some suggestions that the trout may also be feeding now on gobies that move offshore into deep water in the fall. This could be a positive influence on their reproductive health.

The history of the Lake Ontario's large native fishes including the sturgeon, Atlantic salmon and the whitefish is a repeat of the same dreary pattern seen almost everywhere-that of overfishing a stock until it collapses and then moving on to the next thing and fishing it down to zero. By the 1960's there was nothing left to fish for commercially in the open lake except smelt. By the 1980s about the only profitable commercial fishery was that for the American eel. (not to be confused with the lamprey eel, a very different fish that some believe is also a recent invader.) Most of the eel catch went over to Europe, often as live fish by air freight.

The lake's inshore fish community has been hit hard by the goby, by the alewife that eats the larvae of other natives when it moves inshore to spawn, and by other invasive species, the deliberately introduced carp among them. And a key player in the inshore web of life has gone missing. The American eel was once one of the most abundant fishes in the lake's shallows and bays. One estimate holds that a third or more of the total biomass of the inshore fish community consisted of eels. Now they are nearly gone. It appears that habitat destruction rather than invasive species is responsible for this local near extinction.

Eels have a complex and still somewhat mysterious life history. All of Lake Ontario's eels make their way here as young from the Sargasso Sea. They take several years to arrive via the St. Lawrence and the fish ladder around the power dam. Once they make it to the lake, they are long lived fish and may stay in freshwater for thirty years or more before they make their one and only spawning run. And it's a major one. When it is time to reproduce, the adult eels must run back down the river to the sea and then travel to their saltwater spawning ground, a distance of 3700 miles or more. Since all the flow of the St. Lawrence river goes through the turbines of the big hydro dam, so, too, must all the eels.

About thirty five years after the St Lawrence power dam was built, the population crashed suddenly and dramatically. In the early 1980s when I was sailing the lake solo and dodging the eel trot line floats around Main Duck, there was a thriving fishery and 20,000 young eels a day were climbing the fish ladder around the dam during their ascent of the river. Ten years later the number of eels was down 90%. Today the eel watchers are lucky to see a few eels a week ascend the ladder.

The Great Lakes Fish Commission website sums up some of the issues. Management is difficult because at least twenty-five state, provincial, and federal governments must work together in a highly coordinated fashion to protect the eel. A major challenge has been simply to get these governments to agree that there is a problem. Canada now designates the eel as an endangered species. Despite a law suit by the Council for Endangered Species Act Reliability, the U.S. Fish and Wildlife Service has refused to declare eels endangered.

There are at least a half dozen theories as to why the eel population crashed- global climate change has shifted ocean currents, parasites are weakening the fish, the degraded toxic environment is killing them being a few suggestions. But the power dam is a prime suspect.

In 1985 more than a million elvers climbed the dam's fish ladder at its north end. Fifteen years later virtually no baby eels appeared there.

The speed of the collapse stunned the scientific community. Studies suggest that up to 40% of the eels running downstream to the sea were being killed outright as they passed through the dam's power turbines. Unfortunately, the biggest most fecund fish were also most likely not to make it through. And no one knows how many eels were injured but still able to swim away. Even a slight wound would almost certainly impact an eel's chances of completing her long grueling journey to the Sargasso. Studies of eels moving to the sea in Maine suggest power dam turbines there kill up to 90% of them.

In 2003 at a conference in Quebec, scientists from 18 countries drafted a "Declaration of Concern" regarding the embattled eels. Among other things it said "recruitment of the Lake Ontario population has virtually ceased". The number of baby eels coming into the system was less than 1% of the 1970 numbers seen. "Time was running out" for the lake's eels the researchers concluded.

Even as various scientific conferences urged action to no avail, two brothers on the East Coast launched a citizens' petition in late 2004 requesting that the eel be listed under the Endangered Species Act. Theirs was a true jousting at windmills as they took on the vast federal fisheries bureaucracy. The effort gained national press coverage (perhaps because of its human interest angle- what kind of odd balls could possibly care about slimy nasty eels). Three years later, in 2007, after reams of paper work, tens of thousands of words, much foot dragging and finally a lawsuit filed on behalf of the brothers to prod the feds into action, the Fish and Wildlife Service declared an endangered listing for the eel was 'not warranted'. The finding still stands as of this writing.

Canada has been making an effort to restore the eel. Between 2006 and 2009 3.8 million elvers and glass eels were stocked in the Bay of Quinte and upper St Lawrence area. Small eels were seen in the streams surveyed and some of the little eels dispersed hundreds of kilometers from their stocking site. A few thousand adult eels have been transported around the power dam and released downstream in an experimental program. But trap and transport isn't viable long term without a large lake population.

There is no physical downstream bypass for the dam. Some power dam operators on the coast have shut their turbines down during the eel migration to allow safe passage for the fish, but on the St. Lawrence the downstream movement historically took place over a long period. Spilling water over the dam likewise sacrifices a lot of revenue. Perhaps there is some way to re-design the turbine passages to make them less lethal, but at this point there appear to be few good options for bringing back what was once one of the lake's most abundant native fishes. Stocking small elvers and glass eels might stave off extinction here, but it is a distinctly stop gap measure. As one recent Ontario Ministry of Natural Resources report put it, "the future of the American eel in Ontario waters is uncertain."

However, there has recently been a glimmer of hope for the lake's most mysterious and amazing fish. Within the last year or two against long odds, some populations of eels in North America and Europe have appeared to stabilize or even increase slightly. Possibly the tough little fish may yet be climbing the slippery slope up from the pit of extinction.[3]

* * *

Another Lake Ontario native, the lake sturgeon, nearly extinct here thirty years ago, appears to be getting a second chance. Because of its great size, long life and rare status the sturgeon seems almost a mythical fish today in Lake Ontario. But once 200 pounders were common. The sturgeon is an ancient species, among the most primitive of all the lake's piscine community. Its skeleton is largely made up of cartilage, and the young fish wear a prominent bony armor of plates called scutes. Lake sturgeon are slow growing and female fish typically don't reproduce until their late teen years. On Lake Ontario a female sturgeon may reproduce only once in four or five years. This slow growth made them highly vulnerable to over fishing. Historically the rich oily meat was often smoked and the swim bladders were used to make a gelatin called isinglass that was, among other things, used to clarify beer and wine. Today prime sturgeon caviar may fetch 2500 dollars a pound and the smoked flesh has recently been priced at 65 dollars a pound. There is no season for sturgeon on the lake, but poaching for fish worth a couple thousand dollars apiece is an understandable temptation. Small wonder then that in a recent report on sturgeon restoration in the St. Lawrence River the author hedged on the exact location of the spawning grounds. Sturgeon prefer to spawn in rivers over clean gravel but they can and once did spawn over clean wave washed ledges like those around Main Duck and Galloo Island.

When I was six or seven my mother hauled me off to a lake shore neighbor's house on a cool and breezy May afternoon for a woman's church group picnic. Bored by the proceedings at the lunch table, I wandered over to the edge of the low bluff to look at the water. Below in the light surf washing over a wide shoal rock shelf, I saw a dozen huge brown fish. They were thrashing and flailing and lunging to and fro in the surf. I stared at the fishy Pelee in a mix of fascination and fear. These monsters were way bigger than I was! What were they doing? Were they trying to crawl out of the lake? Perhaps they were dying. I ran back to the picnic table hollering about the big fish.

"Oh, they're sturgeon, they're just laying their eggs, they come here every year," the hostess reassured me. Alas, they don't come now. They haven't been seen for years. Yet a remnant population has managed to hang on in the lake, and recently has even made a bit of a come back with some human assistance. Sturgeon still spawn over the Niagara River bar, and they have been re-introduced to the Genesee and Oswego Rivers. In recent years small number of fish have gathered at the mouth of the Black River to spawn, and sightings and reports of the big fish appear to be on the increase.

Bottom feeding sturgeon feed low on the food chain. Like eels, they are also generalists and can survive on a variety of foods. Insect larvae, zebra mussels, gobies, amphipods, even plant material and in the old days, grain spilled from harbor elevators, have been found inside sturgeon. This varied diet along with their long lives has helped keep them around. They have managed to hang on through tough times, enduring, until now when they are starting to get a little help from the species that brought them to the brink of extinction in Lake Ontario.

Over the last ten years more than 85,000 six to ten inch hatchery raised fish have been stocked at various locations around the lake and St Lawrence River. The Genesee River fish have shown good growth and survival. Young sturgeon weighing nine or ten pounds have been seen with an estimated 2 to 300 young fish in the river. An artificial spawning bed was established below the Moses Saunders Power Dam in the tailrace, and fish have been seen using it. Just hatched fish were collected from the area indicating successful spawning. Net surveys suggest that several thousand sturgeon may spawn in the Niagara River area. Juvenile fish have turned up in the surveys, so they are having at least some success in sustaining themselves. There may be guarded hope for the largest and longest lived of the lake's fishes.

* * *

Ecosystems can and sometimes do adjust and rebalance to co-exist with invasives. Possibly with some help in the form of reduced nutrient inputs, careful biological control of invasives, and a general clean up of the lake some of our natives like the enduring sturgeon, might hang on here for a few more years. But sometimes the impacts of the new plant or animal are so profound that we never can return the system to its original condition. Will the lake reach that tipping point? If anything can push our inshore food web over the edge it may be the Asian Carp.

There are three species of these filter feeding carp knocking at the door of the Great Lakes that have a lot of fishery management folk biting their nails. These carp are so fast growing and efficient in exploiting the plankton at the bottom of the food chain that they have displaced up to 97% of the native fishes in some sections of the Mississippi. One species, the bighead can grow to 100 pounds. They are river spawners and may be able to use many tributaries of Lake Ontario. On my first trip to Toronto with our 32 footer we visited Chinatown where in a fish market tank I saw live bighead carp for sale. That was before a 2005 law was passed forbidding their import as live fish. However, a 2014 Congressional Research Report states that as recently as 2012 shipments of now outlawed live bigheads bound for Toronto were intercepted at the border. One would not find it surprising if they're still being imported.

A vast amount of energy and money has been expended on keeping the carp from entering Lake Michigan via the Chicago Sanitary Canal. But they may well find their way into the lakes by other routes such as fishermen's bait buckets or even deliberate introductions. There are reports of ethnic customs designed to propitiate the gods of good fortune that involve the release of live fish. This may account for the discovery of a bighead carp in a Toronto fountain a few years ago. And Wikipedia says a live bighead was seen in the Don River in 2003. If a well meaning but ignorant petitioner seeking wealth and good luck were to release a male and female bighead into Lake Ontario, the results could be very far reaching. And unfortunate for the lake's remaining natives.

Humans may never again see the relatively diverse and highly productive ecosystem the lake once had. In recent years more environmental stressors like climate change, eutrophication of inshore waters, wetland losses, and lost forest cover in the watershed have hit the already simplified ecosystem here. Each new invader, it sometimes seems, does more damage to the still surviving natives and further stresses the survivor populations. Today the lake is more vulnerable than ever to invasions by alien species like the faucet snail (which carries a parasite deadly to native ducks that feed on it) and the plankton eating Asian carp. Even though we now mandate ship ballast water exchanges at sea to flush any unwanted freshwater organisms out of the tanks before they reach the lakes, new creatures keep showing up to exploit the damaged system.

Recently, efforts have been made to diversify the bait fish supply in the open lake, now almost completely consisting of alewives, by introducing two species of native Great Lakes fish, the lake herring and the deepwater cisco. Eggs were obtained from Lake Michigan stocks and hatchery raised fry were released in the hope is that future Lake Ontario populations will re-establish now that the competing alewife's abundance is at least somewhat controlled by stocked salmon. It will be a few years before we know if the program is successful, but other natives to the Great Lakes ecosystem like the osprey, the bald eagle, the sturgeon, and, on Lake Erie, even some of the native clams and mussels hit hard by the *Dreissina* sisters have made comebacks of varying success. Some natives have survived with human help, and some have made it on their own. Even a badly damaged ecosystem has a surprising ability to at least partially repair itself. Sometimes it does so with surprising speed.

I live on former field and orchard land that was abandoned by the farm family in the 1920s. It is now covered with second growth hardwoods. You wouldn't mistake these wooded acres for virgin forest lands yet, but a forest is on its way, slowly recovering its diversity and productivity. The lake's tattered food web may yet re-weave itself, if we can keep those Asian carp out. Possibly the key food item *Diporeia* will persist in the deepest areas of the lake, ready to re-claim its historic range. A little bottom fish, the deepwater sculpin thought to be extinct in Lake Ontario, was re-discovered in 1996. A limited amount of natural reproduction of Atlantic salmon, a species that once abounded in the lake, has been seen in New York tributaries. And a bird that I never saw on the lake back in the 1970's, the osprey, is now a regular sight each summer on *Sara B's* home waters of Fair Haven.

There are limits to the piecemeal approach to restoring an ecosystem's integrity, and we have made plenty of mistakes in the past when we have tried to "improve" things. (The common carp comes to mind as one such effort in the lake along with those pesky multiflora rose bushes DEC told us to plant for wildlife back in the 70's.) Yet people have restored and healed natural places in the past. There is even an emerging field of science called restoration ecology that seeks to expand such efforts. Given that extinction rates are now perhaps 10,000 times faster than at anytime in the past, the need is obvious.

There is also a growing recognition of the need to 'manage' fisheries and other natural resources differently. In the recent past the lake has been viewed as an "open access resource" owned by no one and available to all to exploit. This quite naturally has led to a 'use it or lose it' mentality. As we shall see in the last chapter, an older and much longer lived notion, that of the lake as a commons owned by everyone and managed for the benefit of humans present, those yet unborn, and for non human life is gaining traction

* * *

After two peaceful days in Main Duck's harbor we cast off the dock lines and chugged off to New York State and the end of our journey. As we set out across the lake, I looked back at the bit of land receding into the distance astern and thought about the turtle. We had noticed its dark shape approaching the boat through the clear water the day before. The snapper lumbered along just under the surface, paddling purposefully towards the boat. He surfaced a few inches from us, raised his massive head and gazed up at us intent and unblinking. After a bit, he slowly paddled along *Sara B's* waterline still looking up. His shell was perhaps a foot or so in diameter, not huge by Main Duck standards. But he looked old. His wrinkled neck head and jaws large and strong, and his shell and tapered knobby tail were furred with long strands of blueish green filamentous algae.

The turtle returned to where we sat in the boat's cockpit and hung motionless in the water looking at us with unblinking reptilian eyes set in an ancient wrinkled face. Small wonder aboriginal Great Lakes region peoples like the Haudenosaunee considered turtle to be an animal of great wisdom. Turtle, they say, bore the weight of the world on her back.

We were baffled by the snapper's behavior. "He's begging," I said. I remembered seeing snappers pan handling in the harbor at Main Duck on other visits. But when we dropped two bits of ham beside him, the turtle never took his eyes off us. He wasn't here for food. He seemed to be searching, seeking. He swam to the stern, then slowly returned and again looked up at us as he floated. A few minutes later we left the boat to go ashore. The snapper still floated beside *Sara B's* gazing solemnly up at the boat.

What was he seeking as he looked so long and steady at the three jabbering humans perched above him? I have read that snappers can recognize individual humans and that turtles can live as long as we do. It was downright unnerving to return his fixed gaze. That turtle wanted something. He expected something from us. It wasn't food. Was it perhaps a partnership to preserve his world?

11. The Lake and Climate Change

After *Sara B's* cruise around the lake Alice went home to her farm, and we spent the remaining summer days sailing on short excursions with friends and family until October haul out. While *Sara B* hibernated under her winter cover, my husband and I drove cross country to arid populous southern California and back. Enroute we detoured to Lake Mead. We had long fancied the idea of going boating in the desert. The whole surreal environment of a colossal man made lake dammed up to grow alfalfa in California's central valley and light up the casinos of Las Vegas begged for exploration by boat. We also felt that we should do this while there was still some lake to go boating on.

The infamous white bathtub ring was very much in evidence on Lake Mead in early 2014. At that time the lake was near all time lows. It had dropped over 130 feet since 2000. After we found a marina that was still open and paid for a three hour rental of a runabout, we walked out a long extension to the floating docks. The marina and lake itself were very quiet. It was, after all, "winter" though on this sunny calm afternoon we were in shirt sleeves. I asked the marina worker when their busy season was- "Summer when it's 112 and everyone wants to go swimming," he told me. We saw perhaps four boats during our brief voyage down Virgin Canyon.

The exhilarating novelty of roaring along at 30 mph in a speedboat wore off pretty fast. We idled at *Sara B* speed into a rock lined cove and shut the outboard off. Stillness surrounded us. No redwing blackbirds bullfrogs or marsh wrens called. No green rushes or cattails swayed or whispered at the water's edge. No glittering dragonflies skimmed by and no caddisflies danced over the water surface. The cold clear still lake and the sunbaked rock cliffs seemed sterile and lifeless to an upstate New Yorker accustomed to abundant biomass everywhere when afloat on a boat in a quiet anchorage. I knew Lake Mead had a recreational fishery. I'd seen at least a couple of striped bass along with a school of giant carp under the floating docks where we'd boarded the speedboat. But here in the cove this artificial lake felt just that. Artificial.

Lake Mead-note white band marking past highwater

Some observers think climate change may provide a very rude shock to the regional economy that Lake Mead and the other big Colorado River reservoirs are propping up. It might happen as soon as 2021. One study predicted fifty-fifty odds that Lake Mead would hit 'dead pool' (the level at which no water can flow out past Hoover Dam unless it's pumped) by then. If that were to happen, perhaps the only permanent fix would be to dynamite the concrete plugs that now block tunnels by passing the dam. Tree growth ring information suggests that the drought over the last decade in the western U.S. represents the driest conditions in 800 years.

Climate change models predict increased evaporation rates from the reservoirs and soil alike of the Southwest. One model holds that if evaporation increases 2% and precipitation remains constant then runoff volume will decline by 14%. Impose a decades long 'mega drought' on top of already lower river lows and it's all but certain we'll see many more abandoned citrus groves of dead trees and more of those carefully graded flat lifeless fields flanked by long straight dry ditches in New Mexico. Almost certainly more stretches of Interstate 8 will be shrouded by clouds of blowing dust where cotton once grew.

A study that used 17 different models to predict climate change impacts was published in a peer reviewed journal in early 2015. It suggested a greater than 80 percent chance that much of the central and western United States will have a 35-year-or-longer mega drought later this century.[1] Maybe we'll see some abandoned cities along with the farms. And if the Midwest 'corn belt' does get hit by the worst drought in a thousand years, this will have huge impacts on our nation's food chain. One of the study authors called the projections "a bit bleak". They wrote in the online journal *Science Advances*; "Our results point to a remarkably drier future that falls far outside the contemporary experience of natural and human systems in Western North America, conditions that may present a substantial challenge to adaptation."

The central plains are well within the realm of possibility for a water diversion from the Great Lakes via the Chicago canal. I'd be willing to bet some the humans out there will try to "adapt" by yet another huge irrigation project. People have been moving water around for at least 3000 years. It's worked before. For awhile anyway.

Some climate change models also suggest hotter summers, increased evaporation, drier soils, less tributary flow and lower water levels ahead for the Great Lakes region as well. In 1998, a dry warm year, lake levels dropped an average of 60 cm (about 23 inches) throughout the basin. One projection suggested St. Lawrence River outflows could drop 40%.[2] Summers in Buffalo could feel like those presently experienced in southern Florida according to Climate Central's blog that cited peer reviewed models. More ticks and Lyme disease coming soon to a field near you?

However, these predictions contain a huge amount of uncertainty. Most of the older climate models assume reduced ice cover on the lakes due to milder winters. But if the recent pattern of weaker winter polar jet winds that meander (possibly connected to arctic warming) and arctic air outbreaks producing colder winters in the Great Lakes basin continues, we might not see those mild winters. Other climate models predict when rain does come, it will come hard and fast resulting in more flash floods and runoff. The overall precipitation in the Great Lakes region may change more in how it comes down rather than in the total amount that comes down. At this point we don't have enough data to make good predictions.

We do know this, though. Only about one percent of Lake Ontario's volume is renewed each year. If more than that is removed, lake levels will drop. If things get really arid out in the central plains and the southwestern U.S. will we see political pressure for diversions intensify? It's been said that water can flow up hill if that's where the money is. And large water transfers between watersheds have been done before in North America. During that dry summer of 1998 mentioned above, an effort was made to divert water from Lake Michigan into the Mississippi via the Chicago Sanitary Canal to keep the barges moving. Fortunately, the lawyers and the courts prevented it from happening that time.

Around 2007 the Great Lakes states got together with Ontario and Quebec to write a legally binding agreement called the Great Lakes Compact. This was designed to keep the Great Lakes water in the Great Lakes. It became law in Dec 2008 after the states and the U.S. Congress approved it. Most legal experts feel it's reasonably well designed for doing so, but there are a couple of loopholes in the Compact that worry some people. One is called the bottled water loophole. Because several of the Great Lakes states had sizable bottled water businesses, they pushed for an exemption for withdrawals from the lakes if the individual containers were less than 21.6 liters (5.7 gallons). Presently the entire amount of water being taken from Great Lakes tributaries, springs or groundwater by the bottled water business is a fraction of the amount diverted into the Mississippi via the Chicago Canal. The concern, though, is that allowing water removals by the bottlers sets a precedent of treating water as a commodity.

Legal Scholar Noah Hall wrote in 2008 on his blog *"Nor does the so-called "bottled water loophole" implicitly turn the Great Lakes into a product or commodity as some have suggested. The "bottled water loophole" (section 4.12.10) has nothing to do with the definition of a "product" under the compact, but rather relates to the prohibition on diversions. It specifies that removal of water from the Great Lakes basin in containers greater than 5.7 gallons is prohibited as a diversion. ... this provision does nothing to turn the Great Lakes into a product or commodity."*

That is a legal opinion. Is he right? At least one legislator, Congressman Bart Stupak of Michigan, had his doubts. And so did Jim Olson, another expert in water law. Here are a few words from the honorable Mr. Stupak taken from the Congressional record Sept 23, 2008; *"I am deeply concerned that this compact would allow Great Lakes water to be defined as a ``product." By allowing water to be defined as a ``product," the compact could subject the Great Lakes to international trade agreements such as the North American Free Trade Agreement, NAFTA; or the World Trade Organization, WTO."*

The Congressman also said, *"There is also no language in the compact that recognizes that Great Lakes water is held in public trust. The public owns the waters of the Great Lakes, and anything Congress passes should preserve this principle."*

Mr. Olson, the lawyer, says the definition of water as a 'product' is key. He believes that under NAFTA, once water is "produced"—and that can mean pumped from the ground, lake, or a stream or labeled a "product"—or becomes a product that enters into commerce, it is then treated as a commodity that would be covered by NAFTA. To me, that sounds like water sent through municipal plants and to people's water meters might be considered a "product". Possibly, we won't know which one of these contrasting legal opinions will prevail until the matter gets into court before a judge or judges.

Could the federal government override the Great Lakes Compact between itself and the states and provinces at a later date (if California or other points south and west got thirsty enough)? One lawyer told me he didn't think the feds would arbitrarily negate an agreement between states, but that they could go to court to have the agreement declared unconstitutional, (action which he thought would probably drag on forever). However various legal sources point out that the U.S. President has executive powers for use in emergency situations. In times of emergency, the president can override Congress and issue executive orders with almost limitless power. Abraham Lincoln used an executive order to fight the Civil War, Woodrow Wilson issued one in order to arm the United States just before it entered World War I, and Franklin Roosevelt approved Japanese internment camps during World War II with an executive order.

There was a proposal floating around a few years ago to suck water out of the western end of Lake Superior and send it west via a pipeline system. At the time it was considered technologically possible but "prohibitively" expensive. As others have noted, "legal obstacles can be overcome." And treaties have been broken in the past. Water is already being shipped around by tanker. As climate change intensifies, images of the Aral Sea, sucked nearly dry in just thirty years come to mind. Could Lake Erie look like that in 2055?

Imagine, if you will, a day twenty years from now when a drought like no other visits the west. Corn seedlings and bean plants shrivel and whither. The earth dries and cracks and once again the dust begins to blow. The dirty thirties drought lasted nearly ten years in some areas. Experts suggest it was a kitten compared to the climate change enhanced tiger of a dry spell that may be coming soon to a farm near you.

What will happen then to food prices? Corn is an ingredient in an astonishing array of processed foods. Some estimates are that three quarters of the food items on the supermarket shelf contain corn in some form. Corn oil, corn starch, corn sugars of one sort or another, or the actual grain are components of soda pop, dog food, snack crackers, cereal, salad dressings and even some kinds of beer. Corn and soybeans are a major component of the feed for egg laying and meat producing poultry, for factory farm raised bacon, and for dairy cows that provide milk and butterfat for a multitude of foods. Is it so difficult to imagine food prices going through the roof if such a drought were to occur? What will America do if their Buffalo chicken wings cost five dollars apiece? Could America see social unrest or even riots as did Mexico and other countries did a few years back when corn prices doubled and tripled in large response to the market distortions of the Energy Independence (corn for ethanol fuel) Act? Would a president then choose to exercise his emergency powers to divert Great Lakes water south and west to the fields of Iowa and Minnesota? No one knows how we would react, should the climate change model predictions become reality. But we do know if we take more than the tiny volume of annually renewed water from the Great Lakes, their levels like those of Lake Mead will begin to drop.

* * *

I did not know when *Sara B* began her cruise that twenty percent of America's water supplies are currently used by coal, gas, oil, or nuclear fueled power plants for cooling. Only agriculture in the U.S. is more dependent on large amounts of water. For every gallon of residential water used in the average U.S. household kitchen and bathroom, five times more is needed to provide that home with electricity. And more power production takes place on Lake Ontario than on any of the other Great Lakes. Eight large thermoelectric power generation sites including all those nukes, the least water efficient thermoelectric plant type, depend on Lake Ontario for water needed to produce power, while two of North America's biggest hydro power installations lie at either end of the lake. Together the U.S. and Canadian hydros at Niagara Falls plus the jointly owned St. Lawrence River power dam produce almost four times as much electricity as Hoover Dam's peak potential output. Niagara Falls is the largest single location for hydro electric power in North America.

Hydro stations don't consume water, but they rely on its flow and will be affected by climate change if it leads to more extreme weather events that cause flooding or very low flows. And New York State gets almost 20% of its electricity from hydros, the lion's share of that being from the Niagara and St. Lawrence stations. Thermoelectric plants with once through cooling systems like the older nukes and fossil fuel stations on Lake Ontario withdraw water, heat it up, and then discharge it back into the lake. They "borrow" the water and actually consume very little of it. Some of the newer plants that have cooling towers do consume water. They withdraw less water than the once through plants and recirculate it, but they also send some of it off into the air and potentially out of the watershed as vapor while cooling that water. The once through stations that use the water and then dump it back in the lake at elevated temperatures also have impacts. All the plankton larval fish and other life contained in the water get cooked by the process to the general detriment of the lake's food chain. And too much warm water can adversely affect larger fish, too.

Climate change is predicted to reduce power output at stations throughout the Northeast. In the next few years lower river flows and higher river temperatures could cut overall power production considerably even as peak summer temperatures rise. Summer power demand typically surges to supply air conditioning even as the cooling capacity of the water supply used by the power plant decreases. Power plant operating licenses usually limit how much heat the plants can dump into rivers and lakes to avoid fish kills. Operators can't legally dump as much heat when the water temperatures are high, so they have to cut power. Cuts in power production have already occurred during droughts in the southern U.S. In July 2012 U.S. nuclear fueled electrical outputs dropped to their lowest level in nine years after generators from Ohio to Vermont were forced to cut power because of low water supplies.

Most climate change models for the Lake Ontario region predict more uneven patterns of rain fall and more extreme precipitation events with record rainfalls leading to increased farm field erosion nutrient runoff and more stormwater discharges. The last fifty years have already seen this happening with the largest increases in heavy rains occurring in the Northeast. That region including the Lake Ontario basin has seen a 78% increase of precipitation received during intense downpours since 1958. The once a century storms and floods may soon be occurring every twenty years here.

More runoff and nutrients fuel more plant growth. When algae or rooted plants in shallows and bays die, they rot. This is expected to increase oxygen depletion in near shore waters and bays leading to more frequent botulism outbreaks. Type E botulism outbreaks were virtually unknown in the lakes back in the 1960s when I was pushing dead alewives aside so I could go for a swim. But since 1999 outbreaks have increased in frequency on Lakes Michigan, Erie and Ontario. The goby and the zebra mussel may be part of the cause as we have seen. Climate change-induced heavy rains, warm temperatures and nutrient runoff may also play a part in the increase.

Making things worse is the fact that warm water holds less oxygen at saturation than colder water, even as the need for oxygen increases at higher temperatures for cold blooded invertebrates and fish. Simple oxygen depletion has been the cause of numerous fish kills in eutrophic waters in the past even without any heated water discharges from power plants. Low oxygen levels also stress aquatic animals even if they don't die. Stress makes fish more vulnerable to disease or parasites and reduces their growth rates.

Many researchers expect more frequent toxic blue green blooms because of heavy rains washing more nutrients into the lake and because some of the algae themselves are favored by warm water temperatures. Already cyanobacteria and other types of algae seem to be producing more frequent hazardous and toxic blooms on the Great Lakes and at locations around the world. One type of cyanobacteria that often produces toxins favors high temperatures and also seems to thrive in somewhat turbid water. It reproduces most rapidly at around 89 degrees F (32 degrees C). Unfortunately, hot spells heavy rains and silty runoff into the lakes as we saw during *Sara B's* cruise seem to be getting more frequent.

It's impossible to guess today how climate change will impact the surviving native animals and plants of Lake Ontario in the near future. Since many evolved in a cool nutrient poor oligotrophic lake and are now living in a warmer increasingly nutrient rich lake at least near shore, it seems likely they will not do very well with it. Quite possibly we won't be either, as we may find ourselves dealing with mobs of climate change refugees from coastal cities flooded by sea level rises and the burned up dried up Southwest. At the least we can expect local taxes and the cost of food and housing here to go up along with perhaps a surge of Lyme disease and other illnesses associated with pathogens spread by insect vectors. The only way to head off all the possible nightmare scenarios is to get serious about countering climate change.

Water and energy are intimately connected with each other as we have seen here on the lake. Power producers need water. But pushing water around also takes energy as any farmer irrigating his fields can tell you. One study by researchers at the University of Texas at Austin determined that about 12% of the total U.S. electricity use was employed to move water and sewage through municipal systems. Water and energy are also closely coupled with food production and distribution. Our current industrial agricultural system is heavily dependent on fossil fuel to fertilize fields to produce the food and to transport it to distribution centers and markets that in turn use more energy. As the well known food writer Michael Pollan pointed out in a 2008 article in the New York Times magazine, each time we take a bite of food we're also eating oil. He wrote in that in 1940, when manure was the fertilizer of favor, it took 1 calorie of fossil fuel to produce 2.3 calories of food. Today the ratio is 10 to one.[3]

Food production in the U.S. is also increasingly dependent on irrigation (which itself uses a huge amount of fossil fueled energy to move water around). A vast share of the U.S. fruit and vegetable supply nationwide is grown in California mostly on irrigated land. For example, according to California Food and Agriculture Department publications, 83% of the nation's fresh broccoli and 90% of the leaf lettuce is trucked in from California's irrigated fields.

Surprisingly, even here in the Great Lakes region blessed with abundant summer rainfall, I've seen over the last decade or so, an increasing number of farm fields with center pivot irrigation rigs like those of the high plains out west. Between 1970 and 1998 irrigated acreage in the Southeast tripled. Hotter summers that reduce soil moisture will only aggravate the trend. As perhaps will the 'Energy Independence' Act that continues to prop up prices with its subsidies for the production of corn for ethanol.

Serious green house gas reduction must happen and happen soon for the sake of the lake and that of western civilization, too. Possibly, the growing movement towards local foods will help save our climate and our lake. Sixty years ago the lake shore region in New York and Ontario Province with its water moderated climate produced a wide variety of fruits and vegetables. Some were canned, some were frozen, and some consumed fresh. Tomatoes, carrots, spinach, snap beans, corn and pickles were all canned by local businesses near my home when I was a kid. The canneries were also a mainstay of summer income for high school and college students. On the other shore of the lake, Prince Edward County was once the "garden county" of Ontario and was home to one of the earliest commercial canneries in Canada.

Nearly all of that diverse agriculture has vanished in upstate New York. Even the tart cherry orchards are being pushed out now. The plum, peach, apricot and sweet cherry trees that once bloomed along the lake shore are mostly memory. The mucklands that grew lettuce and celery are now either growing brush or perhaps corn. A few potato and onion fields remain in production, often planted year after year with the same crop. And we do still have the apple business. The Interstate highway system and cheap energy are partly to blame for the demise of the state's diverse agriculture by small producers along with other Government policies like subsidized crop insurance that favors farm consolidation. But thanks to the 'locavore' movement a bit of a revival in less energy intensive regional production of fruits and vegetables is now under way.

Farmers markets featuring fresh seasonal produce are blossoming across the land like red runner bean vine flowers in July. Community gardens are popping up around the lake and in some rustbelt region cities there are even commercial urban farms producing year around food from roof top hydroponic green houses. An Ohio State University researcher, Parwinder Grewal, believes that Cleveland could become essentially self sufficient in food production if it were to fully use all current vacant lands available along with commercial roof tops within the city and about ten percent of the land now devoted to residential lawns. And it would taste better than that iceberg lettuce that spent five days aboard a truck making its way from Yuma, Arizona to the upstate New York supermarket where I shop.

Professor Grewal says nationwide, food now travels an average of 1500 miles to get from the field to the consumer's plate. Fresh food requires plenty of diesel fuel for transport and refrigeration as it moves across the country. *"Just like the organic food movement, where it was about five to six years ago, the local food movement is gaining a similar type of momentum right now, and every city has the potential to at least increase its local self-sufficiency and resilience by producing its own food,"* Grewal wrote in a report posted at the Ohio Ag Research and Development Center website.

Within Lake Ontario's watershed several entrepreneurs have launched greenhouse based efforts to grow year around vegetables and herbs. One of the bigger ones is Finger Lakes Fresh that grows hydroponic lettuce. It is now run by a non profit called Challenge that provides people with disabilities meaningful work and income. Finger Lakes Fresh sells high quality fresh lettuce throughout a six state region. A smaller scale effort by a friend of mine attempted to produce hydroponic greens and tomatoes year around for local restaurants. She did so for several years before a combination of labor shortages and health problems hobbled the endeavor. But greenhouses heated by geothermal, biogas, compost and even by heaters burning wood pellets or waste cooking oil are producing food year around in cold climates. A neighbor of mine has grown spinach and kale through the winter for personal use in an unheated small greenhouse for six or seven years now. She and her husband dug down about four feet, then built a north wall of cement block, bermed the dug up earth up behind it and closed in the south side with old patio and storm windows. Enough heat resides in the earth and in the thermal mass of the concrete wall to keep the beds of soil from freezing even on sub zero winter nights.

One lawn garden and greenhouse at a time, we could reclaim some of the food 'self sufficiency' we previously enjoyed here. Since the global agricultural industry is believed to contribute perhaps 30% of our total greenhouse gas output, self sufficiency using organic techniques could make a significant contribution to reducing the CO_2 increases.

During *Sara B's* stay in Hamilton we took a hike one morning down to the doughnut shop. We passed through a neighborhood of modest bungalows and small houses, and the image of one front yard remains in my memory. Every square inch of it was in production on a late June morning. Bean and squash vines climbed a trellis at each end of the front yard. Raised beds of lettuce, carrots, and spinach flourished. Pea vines were nearing the end of their season. Undoubtedly, they would be pulled up and something else planted in their place. There was even a dwarf fruit tree of some sort in once corner of the yard. It was an interesting example of intensive food production in a very small space.

What besides eating local (and cutting back on meat consumption) can we do to help stave off climate change? Growing our own food would help. Many individual actions add up. While one backyard garden is not a significant force for reducing greenhouse emissions, hundreds, thousands and millions of them would be. Hamilton, like Cleveland, could be largely self sufficient at least seasonally.

Trees also are an excellent carbon 'sink' as they grow throughout the summer transforming CO_2 and water into sugars and cellulose. The old lake port of Oswego now has an active program underway to restore its "urban forests". City trees help reduce storm water runoff and reduce the urban 'heat island' effect. Their shade in summer and action as windbreaks in winter are a significant source of savings in energy use as the trees themselves "sequester" carbon dioxide in their woody structure. (There is a stunning graphic representation of the huge seasonal uptake of carbon dioxide by plants during the northern hemisphere growing season on the Internet at NASA's Scientific Visualization Studio. (Find "watching the earth breathe" posted at **http://svs.gsfc.nasa.gov**). And, as a number of peer reviewed medical studies have shown, urban trees improve human health and well being. There is good reason for the higher property values of homes located in green spaces with a diversity of trees and plants.

Efficiency is a big part of the rapid response that we badly need to reduce fossil fuel use. The net zero house and other high efficiency building construction is gaining ground both in Lake Ontario's watershed and elsewhere. Recently, New York City pledged to reduce its fossil fuel use 30% by 2030. Since about 75% of the city's energy is used in residences and commercial structures, a lot of the reduction is being done through building efficiency. Similar uniform state or nationwide building codes that promote such efficiency would go a long way to help standardize the construction and reduce costs of high efficiency construction.

In 2004 a statewide effort to increase the share of renewable electricity production in New York's energy mix got underway. It lacked a few vital elements such as long term fixed price contracts for small power producers and grid connection assistance as we have seen at the Patterson Dairy power house, but it was at least lip service to the need for reducing green house gases. That goal, tweaked three years ago, now seeks production of about 10.4 million megawatt-hours of energy from hydro, wind, solar, biomass and landfill gas annually by 2015. In 2013 the state was about half way to that goal, mostly thanks to the water flowing through Lake Ontario's two big hydro installations. Only about 4% of the rest of our power production was coming from wind, biomass, or other renewable sources. As many have commented, the crucial factors here for increasing that percentage are developing markets through incentives and providing some stability in pricing of electricity for new projects.

***

We can ride our bikes to the store and resist turning on *Sara B's* diesel when the wind dies and sign up for wind power with our electric utility, but for state wide and the big nationwide global scale change that's needed we must have Big Government involvement. And all too often that involvement has been heavily influenced by Big Money fossil fuel interests. Tom Friedman in his book *Hot Flat and Crowded* quotes an oil producer as saying the 'stone age didn't end because they ran out of stones.' Rather, it was technology shifts that rendered those flint knives obsolete. Likewise, renewable technology could push aside old dirty fossil fuels as an energy source right now. But it won't happen without some help to build needed infrastructure and to overcome years of subsidies and institutional inertia.

There is an ongoing need for government funding of basic research. Ultimately, innovation stems from science. Unfortunately, federal support of science in many areas has been flat or declining over the last decade or so in the U.S. as well as in Canada. There's also need for government subsidies to build up the infrastructure that's part of the energy revolution. That includes things like hydrogen fuel pumps or charging outlets for 'green' electric cars or a 'smart grid' that can handle many small distributed power generators like those roof top solar arrays and dairy farm digesters feeding into it. Our basic current electrical power system grid design dates back to the early days of rural electrification. It is not well suited to dealing with many small sources of power or for transmission of 'intermittent' power sources such as solar and wind energy.

Congress has not approved major energy legislation since 2007. Though the Senate did formally acknowledge that climate change is real and not a hoax recently, the politicians came up a vote short from stating it was due to human actions. We need action from the government to work on this one. Only the people in Washington DC and Ottawa have the power to shape markets and encourage innovation on the scale and time frame that's needed. A sensible energy policy to head off the worst effects of climate change will include both taxation and regulation.

Most prices of goods do not now include "external costs", like those unrecognized and unpriced burdens on society that pollution imposes. Under our present economic system what is not priced is not valued. We must change that lack of direct cost to the polluter. Eventually, Mother Nature submits an invoice in the form of an additional case of cancer or immune dysfunction or fish kill or other health issues. But she often does so many years and many miles away from the original act of pollution. By then the CEO of that company has retired to his private island in the Med. This needs to change. We must make polluters accountable. Companies and consumers must pay the prices upfront, rather than shifting it to others and deferring it to the next generation.

An interesting effort to make governments accountable for taking action to protect their citizens from climate change under the doctrine of public trust is beginning to work through courts in the U.S. and elsewhere. As this book went to press an organization was suing the Dutch government for knowingly endangering its citizens by failing to prevent dangerous climate change. The Urgenda Foundation says this is the first case in the world in which human rights are used as a legal basis to protect citizens against climate change. Another case in the U.S. got all the way to the Supreme Court in 2014 which declined to hear it. The press release for Our Children's Trust noted that the Supreme Court typically hears only 75 to 80 cases a year while it has requests for 10,000 or more. However, Our Children's Trust and other groups will continue to seek an extension of the public trust doctrine to protect resources essential to human life including the atmosphere and climate. Law is evolutionary. It changes over time. And an increasing number of legal experts around the world have come to believe that the lack of action on climate change represents a gross violation of the rights of those who will suffer the consequences including the unborn children of the future.

We can get by for a while using our ecological natural resources credit card account with Mother Nature. But she may already be starting to call in some of those debts. In years to come she will tighten the squeeze. Our bodies are largely made of water. There's a reason the computer software workers refer to 'wetware'. Our brain is 75% water. If our ecosystem and atmosphere aren't healthy our water isn't healthy. And if our water is unhealthy than will we not be healthy.

Friedman writes in his book *Hot Flat and Crowded* that "That which is not priced is not valued." An unlimited unrestricted resource like clean air or water that belongs to no one is free for the taking (or polluting). If the market fails to price these resources into the costs of goods and services, human health and national security suffer. It then becomes the job of the government for the sake of the greater good "shape the market to correct that failure". In the last chapter we will explore a possible way for the greater good to be empowered and change the practices that have resulted in so many of Lake Ontario's impairments.

12. Commons Comeback Could It Be Our Last Chance?

Shortly before we set out around the lake with *Sara B*, I received an email from someone named Paul Baines, a Toronto based lake watcher and creator of a website called The Great Lakes Commons collaborative map. Since I often feel isolated and alone in my writing about Lake Ontario, I was intrigued that someone else shared my interest in our sweet water sea, so I spent an hour or two exploring the site. We corresponded back and forth, and eventually I sent a post to the website about *Sara B's* plastic sampling citizen science venture during the trip. This was the first I had heard of the concept of a Great Lakes Commons. It seemed at the time rather vague and hopelessly Utopian. But I have since come to think otherwise.

Back in the 1970s my fisheries science indoctrination included mention of "the tragedy of the commons" in reference to fish stock management. The idea is that a given population of free roaming fish belongs to no one and there is no incentive to 'save' the fish for another day as someone else will come along and catch them if you don't. The inevitable result is that the stock is overfished in a general 'gold rush' grab for resources until it collapses. Reference to the commons in connection with Lake Ontario mystified me. How could this "tragic" idea possibly help the lake?

I now know that a few facts were overlooked in my freshwater fisheries textbook published in 1970. In truth, a number of fisheries have been successfully managed as commons by the people exploiting them for hundreds of years. The key, it seems, was that those people felt they owned the fish, and they had the ability to keep others from exploiting their fish. When people had local control over a given commons resource, they often managed it sustainably and equitably for generations. In many areas of the world absolute private ownership of land is a relatively recent concept. Even today in Europe there are places like the alpine pastures of Switzerland that are managed by commoners.

As a number of recent scholars have pointed out, the commons and associated 'commoners' have been around for tens of thousands of years, and the concept remains firmly a part of First Nation peoples' culture around the Great Lakes. Some writers have gone so far as to characterize the phrase "tragedy of the commons" as a smear campaign against a perfectly legitimate form of property control. A commons is not the same as an open access resource. The latter is a fish stock that is not under the control of local users. Rather, the fish are available to everyone and owned by no one. In that situation the boat with the biggest net makes short work of the resource. It may well be that the long standing failure in academic and economic circles to distinguish between a locally controlled commons and an open source resource was at least partly political. Over the years the British upper class expropriated grazing lands that had been used by villagers for centuries. Their justification for "enclosure" of the commons for private profit was often described as being a need for superior production methods and management. (And if the users of a commons have no sense of control or ownership, a private owner may well do a better job of resource management.) Likewise, coastal fisheries, I learned in fishery school back in the 1970s, must be 'managed' by trained highly educated professionals usually based in a distant office, who know better than the local fishermen when the resource is being depleted.

It was certainly convenient for the land hungry gentry of England to be able to point to abuse and over grazing on the commons as a reason for taking them over and managing the land more 'efficiently' for private profit. However, many observers feel we have gone way too far in our recent privatization efforts. David Bollier, an author and scholar of the commons, writes *"One of the great unacknowledged problems of our time is the enclosure of the commons"*, something he defines as the expropriation and commercialization of shared resources, for private profit. Today, we are monetizing and privatizing just about everything from human genes, and cell lines, to copyrights, radio frequencies, and water. Some have argued that proposals to create a system of carbon trading credits in an effort to reduce greenhouse gas emissions is putting a price on the atmosphere, leading us down the slippery slope of privatization of the air we breathe.

A commons is shaped by the commoners, i.e. the population using it. The relationships between users the resource and among each other vary tremendously depending on the environment and the cultures using the commons. In the past 'commons' were generally physical resources such as water, grazing lands, or forests that produced vital food and fuel, or beach access essential to fishermen and other 'toilers of the sea'. And sometimes the cooperative management of these resources got pretty complicated.

Essential characteristics of successful relationships among the commoners included transparency, honesty, free collaboration, and communication. The commons were managed by people with a close connection to and great interest in them. These people generally had a detailed knowledge of the plants, animals, natural cycles and other aspects of the resource they were sharing. Frequently, resources were quite efficiently exploited. Sometimes a lottery was used to assure fairness as the grazing areas or fishing holes were assigned. Villagers often appointed 'police' or observers to enforce agreements. And various case studies of shared resources show it's not easy to do. People have disagreements and sometimes when outside forces (like Chinese factory trawlers or the World Bank) come in, the whole arrangement falls apart. Yet there is no doubt that history shows shared natural resources were managed sustainably for long periods in many different areas.(And are still being managed as commons in some places in the world today.)

In recent years the notion of the commons appears to be gaining some strength, and a number of books and lengthy legal and sociological papers have been published on the topic. Classes on the concept are now being taught in colleges and universities around the country. And here on Lake Ontario a small seed of an international movement has taken root in the Toronto area. Perhaps this is partly push back against the "commodification" of just about everything, actions that have resulted in price tags on some very questionable items. Should certain cell lines with unique genetic attributes for example be patented for profit? What about the rights of the person they originally came from? Many economists are now beginning to think that private property rights are not the solution to every social ill.

The collaborative approach essential to managing a commonly owned resource lends itself to grass roots democracy and local control, while the privatization for profit model works well with a top down management style from a distant authority. Possibly the rise of the Internet and open source programming is helping to revive the old idea of the Commons. Some of the practices of open source programming resemble management of the Commons.

Open source code refers to work shared by computer programmers to improve various programs. Wikipedia (itself an example of "open source knowledge") says open source code promotes learning and understanding. Having a crowd work on the problem or hunt down the bugs and errors also makes improvements in the computer code a lot faster and better than if the work is done by an insular group controlled from the top down. The free exchange of code through communication and collaboration by the developers using the Internet make the practice possible. There are some in the open source community that go so far as to consider proprietary software such as that created by Apple employees working under a 'dictator' CEO as "unethical" and "unjust" something akin to restrictions on free speech. (Disclaimer, this book was written using Open Office running on Linux Mint).

These days the shared collaboration that developed Linux based software is spilling over into all sorts of activities. Crowd sourced funding or direct lending and borrowing of money between individuals through websites are examples. The Creative Commons is another. Citizen science, also sometimes called crowd sourced science, has taken off with the advent of the Internet and good connections to same. According to a website called www.ostraining.com there's even an open source effort to develop a religion. The peer to peer collaboration made possible by the Internet seems to be spreading into many different areas. One observer wrote that 'open source' has become shorthand for transparent, collaborative and community minded. The open source movement also is highly compatible with the idea of the commons.

The commons, a broad social moral and sacred framework for human interaction with a resource and between the users of it, is related closely to a very old legal doctrine called the 'public trust'. This concept of lawful behavior, termed an "ancient duty" by environmental law scholar Mary Christina Wood, states that government must act as a trustee in controlling and managing crucial natural assets such as common property resources like water air or navigation rights. Government must "promote the interests of the citizen beneficiaries" over narrow exclusive ownership interests.[1]

The public trust has been upheld repeatedly in a multitude of decisions, cases, constitutions and courts around the world that refer directly back to the proclamations that a Roman emperor named Justinian made in 530 AD. He held that the sea, the shores of the sea, the air, and running water were common to everyone. These resources could not be appropriated for private use and must be open to all. Since Justinian's time the definition of public trust has been broadened to include wildlife and (at least in Vermont) groundwater, though at the same time property owners have been chipping away at beach access, stream fishing rights and anchoring rights that once were protected.

An often cited landmark case in U.S. public trust law involved the shoreline of Lake Michigan. Back in 1892 the U.S. Supreme Court ruled that the state of Illinois could not turn part of the Chicago harbor over to a railroad company. Today some environmental lawyers are seeking to use public trust doctrine to protect water and even to combat climate change.[2]

* * *

A few years ago a group of 'water warriors' teamed up with a number of U.S. Canadian and First Nations organizations and individuals and founded a non profit, Great Lakes Commons, to revive the notion of the commons and apply it to the Great Lakes. Maude Barlow of Canada and U.S. attorney James Olson among others, have promoted the concepts of the Great Lakes Commons and the doctrine of the public trust since then, presenting it to various groups and in late 2012 to the International Joint Commission (IJC). Barlow has worked on water issues for many years and is the Chairperson of the Council of Canadians, an influential public interest organization based in Ottawa. Olson is a legal scholar who established FLOW, a water policy think tank based in Michigan. The two of them have written articles, given webinars, made videos, and done the talk circuit promoting the idea as a game changer. They and others like David Dempsy and Alexa Bradley are also promoting specific ways to implement the concept of the commons to make it work.

With good reason. As we have seen, the piecemeal regulatory approach to Lake Ontario's problems has not done the job. We are not where we need to be. Modern environmental regulation, developed in the 1970s and 1980s, has attempted to limit damage from industry or nonpoint sources of pollution. The U.S. EPA or New York's DEC or some other body of experts determine how much bad stuff a landfill or city sewer or a nuke can put in the water. Various laws like the Clean Water Act, the Toxic Substances Control Act, and state and provincial statutes on hazardous waste still permit pollution (admittedly at lower levels than if there were no laws.) But they often fail to account for cumulative impacts and synergies between toxins and other factors like climate change or shifts in land use and agriculture. As Paul Baines, an advocate for Great Lakes Commons explains it, we need a system that creates incentives to do the right thing rather than one that attempts half heartedly to fix things after we've done the damage. Regulation has also failed to keep up with technology, and all too often the agencies charged with regulation have been underfunded and also subject to 'capture' by the very industries they seek to control.

A former director of a once successful bi-national advocacy organization called Great Lakes United, Jane Elder, explained the demise of that organization in a web post in 2013. In it she wrote that administrative changes resulting from legislation in the 1980s gave a larger direct role to each nation's lead environmental agency. This, she wrote, "would eventually neuter and subsume the gravitas of the formerly august IJC." Along with industry's efforts to "quiet the boisterous citizen advocacy at the biennial IJC meetings," this caused much of the broad binational framework to unravel in the 1990s. Today a bewildering array of organizations work, sometimes at cross purposes, on each side of the lake work to clean up and protect our waters. We need to bring back that broad international basin-wide perspective. Possibly, regarding Great Lakes water as a commons could do this.

Advocates of the commons and a stronger public trust doctrine believe the concepts would move the management of water, other resources, and the environment to a new, broader, and potentially simpler format. In a commons based approach the managers of the lakes would have to consider the daunting array of demands upon these waters in a more interactive and collaborative fashion than the current process allows. Robert David Steele emphasizes in his *The Open-Source Everything Manifesto,* the ability to aggregate informed and diverse views is essential to the model. Far too often water resource managers have operated in 'silos' separate from one another. When was the last time a farmer sat down in the same room with an engineer from the NRC, a soil scientist from the NRCS, a municipal water plant engineer, a yacht owner, and a fisheries biologist?

First Nations people including the several dozen tribes and clans that still live on the Great Lakes were commoners. They shared their resources and managed their commons with an eye to the welfare of humans, non human entities, and the unborn. Their legal traditions emphasized individual responsibilities and duties. Our U.S. and Canadian law is primarily based on rights. When we 'manage' water levels on the St. Lawrence, we attempt to balance the various interests and rights of the real estate industry, the home owners, boaters, fishermen, shipping, power producers and so on. As a result, the IJC has spent twenty years and millions of dollars trying to implement a new water level regulation plan that pleases every one. So far it pleases no one.

What would this situation look like if more of the various interests took on a greater responsibility and modified their behavior accordingly? My in-laws, for example, adapted their summer lake shore camp to comply with nature's relentless erosion of the shore. They demolished an old cottage that was about to slide over the bluff and built a new wood frame structure that in theory at least, could be jacked up and moved inland a hundred years from now if anyone still wanted to save it. They have not attempted to make the lake do what they want it to do. Other landowners in the area lobby Congress and the IJC for low lake levels and wide beaches so they can put a trophy house a hundred feet from an eroding shore with a three feet a year recession rate.

But as the last couple hundred pages have shown in a far from comprehensive account of Lake Ontario's troubles, there is a diverse and complex set of issues here to deal with. We must not only manage our own lake's watershed, but also deal with all the issues from the four upstream Great Lakes. As others have said, Lake Ontario contains the waters of all five Great Lakes. How could we possibly begin this task? We can't even get the various interests on one lake in a room to collaborate one issue, that of water levels. The commons is a time tested legal framework going back at least 2000 years in western tradition. If anything has the standing authority and breadth to do the job it would seem this does.

Of course, not everyone will go along with this game changer and the assumption of greater responsibilities. Perhaps one way to implement it is for lawyers to do what they're trained to do -litigate. Develop their arguments and take them to court. Over and over and over. And another way to make the change is through grassroots organizing and activism. And education. The concept of the commons and local control of same has largely been forgotten in modern lake shore society.

A friend suggested that my book would not provide all the answers. That's for sure. But there are some possible models out there that might be scaled up to a lake wide basis for dealing with the issues. And with the help of Internet based communications and data availability we just might be able to make it work. If you do nothing else please read the Great Lakes Compact in the back of the book and at least go visit the group's website at www.greatlakescommons.org. We are badly in need of a different approach than the one we've been using.

One idea floating around (if you'll pardon the pun) is the manage the lakes at the watershed level. This brings the issues back to the local people who are most concerned with them. A few years ago the people running the municipal water plants in New York City realized that the only way they could assure safe clean water for the city was to have a clean healthy watershed. That implied they had to get out of the city and go work with the land owners who lived in the eight counties of the Catskill region where the city draws its water from. So they did. The effort got kicked into high gear when the city learned they might be required by the EPA to build a filtration plant for their water supply at a cost of several billion dollars. Suddenly, there was serious motivation to work with the landowners and in some cases compensate them for protecting clean water.

Some of the land owners who were farmers did not welcome the idea of Gotham telling them how and when to spread their manure or otherwise manage their farms (which the water plant operators wisely did not attempt to do.) In the early stages of the program trust was decidedly lacking. But as David Moss in an account of the project wrote in a report posted at www.ourwatercommons.org, when urban areas realize they are dependent on rural land owners and the rural folk realize the city is inevitable and possibly even helpful to the regional economy, then you may begin to get somewhere.[3] Mutual interests were established.

However, better stewardship of the land must also help the rural standard of living. You aren't likely to progress to a goal of cleaner water unless the land owner benefits, too. That's one reason why some funding for research on how to grow perennials for space heating pellet stoves in the Catskills came from the Catskill Watershed Corporation, a local development corporation set up to protect water quality and strengthen communities throughout the watershed. A diversified steady income to land owners through sales of hay to the 'heat local' market could be a more sustainable alternative to row crops and bare soil. Perennial grasses or woody plants on the fields are far better for clean water than heavily fertilized acreage planted with Round Up Ready soybeans and Atrazine drenched cornfields.

Trying to compensate people to be better stewards on the land leads us into the thorny jungle of 'ecosystem services'. Should we compensate land owners for providing these services from their wetlands and uplands left in a natural state? Presently, we have a system of subsidies and price supports to encourage corn production with consequent nutrient and soil loss into our waterways. We don't compensate forest owners who simply want to keep trees on their land. Agricultural lands get a hefty property tax break from New York State to help keep food prices low. (At least I assume that was the original theory of the tax break.) Forest lands though, only get a break if they are managed for timber production, and then they must meet other criteria. A small woodlot of less than fifty acres managed simply for wildlife is considered 'wasted' under our current value system. It would be far better used to grow a subdivision of houses according to conventional market valuation. But the filtering and slow release of water that moves through tree canopies and woodland soils is an essential part of the general purification process that makes for a healthier lake, fewer blue green blooms in the bays, and higher waterfront property values downstream on Sodus Bay.

Pricing 'ecological services' and the 'external costs' of pollution is a controversial business. In some cases pollution's costs can be estimated in terms of increased medical bills or lost productivity. But in other cases it's impossible to put a value or a cost on a given ecosystem component. How much is an eel worth? How do you value the self sustaining infinite nature of a fishery in perpetuity if it's well managed? A forest is much more than a water purification plant. It provides a multitude of valuable 'services' and goods ranging from venison for the freezer and mushrooms for the dinner table to food for the soul. Many "services" are so intertwined you can't pick them apart and price each one. If it isn't done right unintended consequences may follow.

And by pricing everything the decisions are going to be made by Big Biz rather than the people. Some activists suggest putting a price on everything turns Nature into one more giant supermarket to be consumed by us. It fails to recognize nature is us. The whole scheme sounds suspiciously like another way to turn everything into a commodity. Are there better ways to preserve a watershed through collaboration and consensus and local control?

Possibly our hypothetical watershed councils of the Utopian future could be paid for by public funding. There has to be compensation to the members somehow. They must be knowledgeable, and a volunteer board no matter how committed, would soon be 'burned out'. The councils would need to be legally recognized and given meaningful authority and power unlike town planning boards whose often ignored recommendations are just that. As David Moss puts it in a report posted on www.ourwatercommons.org "An authentic participatory watershed governance structure is essential, with legally-recognized, publicly-funded watershed councils working in concert with public agencies and private interests".

Watershed health also depends on water 'stewards' to keep an eye on things. These informed 'water citizens' will keep restoration projects moving along even as local elected officials come and go. Like the villagers of old who patrolled the commons, they're needed to see that agreements are lived up to.

As part of an effort to build awareness of and support for the water commons at a grass roots level The Council of Canadians recently launched an international "Blue Community Initiative". The essentials are that the community government adopts a resolution stating water is a human right, the town or city water and sewage treatment plants remain under public control, and the municipality bans bottled water from city property. These first steps are designed to begin the slow but badly needed shift away from making a profit from water, perhaps the biggest single non-organizational obstacle to initiating the Commons on a practical basis.

Several Canadian towns and cities including St. Catherines and Niagara Falls on Lake Ontario have adopted the resolutions. Part of the Blue Communities effort seeks to establish a network of people who have an interest in their local water supply before the inevitable crisis comes to town. These people serve as the community's "water watch" commoners in training as it were, and, as we have seen many times in the past, community organization and opposition does impact policy (think Bloody Sunday at Selma, Alabama or the Stonewall Riots at Greenwich Village, New York that helped further civil rights). The Canadian Council, now promoting the Blue Communities concept cites a recent example of such influence. In one community, organized opposition who felt they had a connection to their local water prompted Ontario's regulators to rewrite conditions for the permit of the existing Nestle water bottling plant to mandate decreased withdrawals in the event that the Province came under drought conditions.

In 2012, after some prodding by activists, the Canadian Government officially declared water to be a human right following the lead of the

UN. To date, the USA has abstained from declaring water as a basic right. Lest you think such a declaration so obvious as to be unnecessary, consider the messy situation in the old Great Lakes city of Detroit where thousands of people abruptly had their water service shut off for over due bills as part of the city's bankruptcy re-organizing.[4]

Like it or not our rural lands and watersheds are shaped to a considerable extent by what city dwellers want. That includes water, second homes, recreation, and cheap food. But cheap food and clean water as we have seen in Chapter Three are not compatible. Huge industrial pig farms and dairy operations create huge pollution problems. For healthy water it is vital to encourage local high value food production of healthy fruits and vegetables over the corn-soy animal feed acreage we now see so much of in Lake Ontario's watershed. One way to do that is to encourage local food "hubs" or exchanges. And farmers markets where growers sell direct to consumers. If we must have 5000 cow dairies, we had better make sure each one has a digester! And in an ideal system, the residents would eat less meat and more home grown organic produce to help promote clean water.

The NYC water department through the Catskill Watershed Corporation the Watershed Agricultural Council and other programs has promoted small scale sustainable businesses and agriculture through efforts like on line market portals for producers to sell direct to consumers and microloans for small business. They have also promoted conservation easements to encourage natural landscapes and provide forestry management assistance.

Possibly some of the ideas used in the Catskills might be worth considering throughout the upstate landscape. Maybe individual watershed councils and Blue Communities on each lake could send reps to a top level binational council similar to the IJC that would report back to the Governments of Ottawa and DC. It would be helpful if not essential that the council members come from a diverse array of backgrounds and interests. They need the sense of 'ownership' that is essential for a Commons to work. It goes without saying our imaginary councilors also have to have a sense of responsibility- to the lake and to the unborn as well as to their fellow human lake users.

I would suspect we would want every council to have at least one First Nations rep familiar with the 'old ways' of his/her tribe or clan to help with that fairness item so essential to success. And there must be ample technology for easy communication and a sense of connection with each other. It does seem in this age of webinars and Google Hangouts, Zoom, and Skype that councilors could share and communicate without excessive amounts of travel.

Designating the Great Lakes and their watershed tributaries as Commons is not going to be easy. However, Vermont recently declared its groundwater to be a public trust not to be viewed in isolation from all other waters. State law there provided for detailed mapping for more oversight and regulation of uses and also began to put priorities on uses. Lake Ontario's commoners have to deal with eight states two Provinces and dozens First Nation tribes. I'm not sure how this is going to happen. But it won't be from the top down, I'm willing to bet. If it happens, it will be the way the Council of Canadians is trying to do it.

One grassroots community at a time.

From the website www.greatlakescommons.org:

The commons gives us something to be for—and until recently, that something has been missing from the debate. In a time of increasingly dire economic and environmental threats facing the region, the commons offers both a vision of a hopeful future and a viable approach to build one that is rooted in relationships, belonging, responsibility, and collaboration among communities, nations, citizens, and organizations.

Here's the text of the charter posted at the Great Lakes Commons website:

We, the people of the Great Lakes, love and depend upon our waters to sustain our lives, our communities and all life in our ecosystem. It is therefore with growing alarm that we confront a painful reality – that despite decades of effort the Lakes are more threatened than ever. As people from across the Great Lakes, we find this unacceptable. We cannot stand by while our waters are treated as an expendable and exploitable resource when we know they are a source of life.

Moved by a hope that we can yet create a thriving and life sustaining future for our Lakes, we step forward to take up our responsibility to care for and act on behalf of these waters, our Great Lakes Commons. Seeing that the health of our waters is intertwined with our own health and that of generations yet to come, we are called to assert a deeper connection and more powerful role in the future of our waters.

We hereby set forth the Great Lakes Commons Charter, a living document that affirms and empowers the wisdom and rightful role of the people of the Lakes as stewards of our waters. This Declaration and the First Principles emerge from the collaborative work of people and communities around the lakes. Together we reflect many walks of life, histories and cultures. At the same time, a single purpose unites us: to transition to a mode of Great Lakes governance by which the waters and all living beings can flourish. Towards this end, we affirm:

That the waters of the Great Lakes have sustained the lives of the people and communities in their basin since time immemorial and they should continue to do so in perpetuity.

That the waters, ecosystems, and communities of the Great Lakes are entwined and interdependent. Damage to any of these causes harm to the others.

That the Great Lakes are a gift and a responsibility held in common by the peoples and communities of the Lakes and must be treated as such as to ensure their preservation for coming generations.

That the boundaries of states, provinces and nations crisscross the Lakes but do not divide their natural integrity. All decision-making that impacts the Great Lakes must place the well-being of the bio-region and ecosystem as a whole at the center of consideration.

That the inherent sovereignty and rights of Indigenous peoples as codified in treaties and international agreements must be upheld as foundational to commons governance.

Therefore:

We join our voices in affirming the spirit and necessity of this declaration as the foundation for a renewed relationship and mode of governance for our Great Lakes Commons. We welcome the wisdom, standing and power that this document will accrue over time to shape the future of our Lakes. We invest it with our hopes and commitments to that future and to the future generations who will inherit the legacy of our actions.

In signing this Charter, we embrace our responsibility, individual and collective, to act on behalf of these waters and of future generations.

13. Last word; what can we all do to save our Great Lakes?

This voyage around Lake Ontario has come to an end. What course shall we set next? *Sara B's* beautiful island built ancestors were solar powered fishing boats, engaging in highly targeted fisheries that would likely have been sustainable if Tancook Islanders had been able to keep control over them. Her thrifty old engine was of a design originally intended for fuel derived from vegetable oils so farmers could operate self sufficient power equipment using renewable biofuels much as they had previously grown forage for their draft animals. Our boat's hull was built largely of local lumber from second growth forests.

Today she sails with a composite hull, the cedar and oak re-inforced and repaired with a petrochemical derived shell of resin and glass fiber. Sailed for fifty years by individual owners, today she sails as an operational and financial co-operative effort. The salt water world that existed when she was launched is no more. The lake she sails on will never be the lake of 1800. But perhaps can we work together with nature and each other in a much larger co-operative effort using modern tools to restore and repair the worst stressors here.

A founding member of Great Lakes United, Jane Elder, wrote of the group's demise, "Nature abhors a vacuum, and I hope that this unique niche will be filled again by a new generation of impassioned leaders who see the lakes as neither U.S. lakes, nor Canadian lakes, nor even as lakes of the First Nations or Tribes, but as the greatest freshwater treasure on the planet whose stewardship depends on our common vision and action." Will it be the commoners who rise up on behalf of our inland seas?

We appear to be at a fork in the road- we can go down the dirty fuels path and continue to privatize and consolidate power. Or we can listen to the call of open source everything- one that includes honesty transparency and integrity and collabortion. Can we collaborate our way down the road to sustainability? It's been said as individuals we're intelligent, but as a group we're brilliant.

The humming bird comes to mind. In a traditional African fable the animals watch the land burning up in a great fire and do nothing. But a tiny humming bird hurries back and forth between the fire and a water supply scooping up one drop at a time that he carries back to release on the fire. The watching animals tell him it's useless, and he snaps back, "Hey I'm doing the best I can!"

Here's a few ideas for Great Lakes "humming birds" and some drops to release on The Fire. As a wise old friend of mine observed- we'll never get it if we don't ask for it.

- Demand the Feds clean up the rest of their FUSRAP sites in the Great Lakes Watershed and also finish the job at West Valley -Digitup!
- Urge support for Federal legislative action on a comprehensive energy policy act to promote efficiency through uniform building codes and other regulations as well as truly sustainable renewable energy technology. While we're at it many believe a carbon tax would be the simplest cleanest way to fight climate

change.
- New York State's oil spill response fund very underfunded. Should a spill occur on land or water there would be little money available to clean it up.
- Let your state and federal officials know how you feel about barge transport of toxic dilbit on your drinking water supply. Say NO to freshwater transport of this material! The following quote is from the Great Lakes Commission 2014 report on Movement of Crude Oil Throughout The Great Lakes *"The U.S. Coast Guard, has stated that adequate response methods and techniques do not currently exist for spills of heavy oils to open bodies of freshwater such as the Great Lakes. Until adequate methods and techniques can be developed, current VRP (vessel response plans)requirements would likely preclude the shipping of heavy crude oil by tanker vessel on the Great Lakes;"*
- Ask your Congressperson and Senators to update the TSCA (Toxic Substances Control Act)- and put some teeth in it! Public health should be the primary goal of this legislation not cost benefit analysis to benefit industry and prevent implementation of regulation as has been done in the past. The new regulation should not prevent states from regulating dangerous toxins either. We should use the precautionary principle as Europe does when regulating chemicals.
- As far as individual actions to protect the lake go, try to eat local eat less meat and dairy products, and eat organic when possible.

- Conserve electricity wherever possible.
- Minimize or avoid lawn care chemicals and fertilizer use on your land.
- Reduce your carbon footprint as much as possible through money saving efficiency and other means

Notes on Sources Of Information

Chapter One: Adventures In Gasland

1 International Energy Agency fact sheet on the World Energy Investment Outlook 2014 says world- wide more than $1.6 *trillion* was invested in 2013 in the energy supply industry, a figure that has more than doubled in real terms since 2000. About two thirds of that total is spent on fossil fuel extraction, transport and refining. Sadly, the same report says in order to keep CO2 below 450 ppt in the atmosphere we could need to spend about 53 trillion dollars by 2035 on renewables. Might be time we got going!

2 *Well Casing leaks a presentation made by Dr. Antony Ingraffea to Physicians, Scientists and Engineers for Healthy Energy Oct 2012*
http://www.psehealthyenergy.org/data/PSE__CementFailureCausesRateAnalaysis_Oct_2012_Ingraffea.pdf

3 Cornell University College of Veterinary Medicine study IMPACTS OF GAS DRILLING ON HUMAN AND ANIMAL HEALTH by MICHELLE BAMBERGER and ROBERT E. OSWALD in New Solutions: A Journal of Environmental and Occupational Health Policy Vol. 22(1)51-77, 2012
The author's abstract stated; *Complete evidence regarding health impacts of gas drilling cannot be obtained due to incomplete testing and disclosure of chemicals, and nondisclosure agreements. Without rigorous scientific studies, the gas drilling boom sweeping the world will remain an uncontrolled health experiment on an enormous scale*

4 *Osborn, SG, A Vengosh, NR Warner, RB Jackson. 2011. Methane contamination of drinking water accompanying gas-well drilling and hydraulic fracturing. In* **Proceedings of the National Academy of Sciences** water wells within a kilometer of active gas extraction in some instances showed concentrations of methane at explosive levels. The authors wrote in the article abstract *"We conclude that greater stewardship, data, and— possibly—regulation are needed to ensure the sustainable future of shale-gas extraction and to improve public confidence in its use."*

5 Brown writes *"The Marcellus is known to have high uranium content", says U.S. Geological Survey research geologist Mark Engle. He says concentrations of radium-226—a decay product of uranium—can exceed 10,000 picocuries per liter (pCi/L) in the concentrated brine trapped in the shale's depths.*

To date the drilling industry and regulators have considered the risk posed to workers and the public by radioactive waste to be minor. However, her article points out that some public health officials see differently. She also pointed out in the report that at the federal level, radioactive oil and gas waste is exempt from nearly all the regulatory processes that the general public might expect would govern it. Neither the Low Level Radioactive Waste Policy Act or the Atomic Energy Act of 1954 covers NORM.

6 Mapping urban pipeline leaks: *Methane leaks across Boston Nathan G. Phillips et al in Environmental Pollution Nov 2012*

The team covered 785 road miles within Boston and found among others, six leaks where methane concentrations exceeded the explosion threshold of 4%. In a later study the researchers drove 1500 miles around Washington and found twelve locations where methane reached potentially explosive concentrations while one leak was big enough to supply seven households at typical user levels.

7 EarthWorks report 2012 New York Oil & Gas Enforcement – Inspections on line at

http://www.earthworksaction.org/issues/detail/new_york_oil_gas_enforcement_inspections#.VJCQDXsYGJw

Chapter Two: Some Sustainable Solutions

1 According to the Energy Information Administration website New Yorkers state wide spend $2,374 per capita on energy (less than half of the $5,719 the folks in North Dakota had to put out.) About half of that went for residential heat and power. Energy efficiency can save everyone a lot of money while cutting green house gas emissions. California began implementing energy-efficiency measures in the mid-1970s, including building code and appliance standards with strict efficiency requirements. Since then California's energy consumption

has remained nearly flat on a per capita basis while national U.S. consumption doubled.

2 Wood pellet companies are currently either expanding or building plants in various locations near the coast in the south and southeast. Pellets are then shipped to European markets. One article contains a quote "Wood waste is a good source for power and heat, which can be used to power homes or facilities, said Terry Walker, a Clemson University biosystems engineering professor."

To an engineer those tops, brush, bark and slabs are waste. But to an ecologist dead wood is the capital of the forest and is vital to its well being. The forest is an intricate efficient recycling system. There is no "waste" in a forest. Removing "wasted" material and making it into pellets without renewing the lost materials is not a sustainable practice.

Biomass production must be a closed cycle of nutrient replenishment and renewal. Dairy digesters keep the nutrients on the farm instead of sending them off to Lake Ontario via ditches and streams. If hybrid willow or other woody material can be grown in a buffer strip to capture nutrients in runoff that otherwise would enter the lake, then pellet production from woody perennials might be at least somewhat sustainable.

3 Regarding corn ethanol and water;

http://www.worldpolicy.org/sites/default/files/policy_papers/THE%20WATER-ENERGY%20NEXUS_0.pdf by Diana Glassman et al 2011

This report from a non partisan global think tank has a comparison of the amounts of water used to produce energy required for a round trip between NYC and Washington DC. Ethanol from irrigated corn would require 35,616 gallons of water versus gasoline from conventionally produced oil that would require 35 gallons of water to extract and refine.

Chapter Three: Dead Birds and Cheap Food

1 On the subject of BMAA and blue greens there is some debate in what causes the deadly neurological disorder known as ALS (Lou Gehrig's Disease). Millions of dollars have been spent on genetic research, but some scientists hold that environmental factors, such as exposure to BMAA, a substance produced by a number of different cyanobacteria, are the main causes of the disease. This understandably might not go over well with the waterfront real estate interests located on lakes subject to blue green blooms.

The cause of ALS is not unlike the situation with cancer. Many feel we should be looking harder at all the chemicals and increasing levels of "background" radiation in our world as contributing to the rise in cancer.

In the article *The Emerging Science of BMAA: Do Cyanobacteria Contribute to Neurodegenerative Disease?* Published on line in *Environmental Health Perspectives 120(3): a110–a116.*
Published online 2012 March Dr. Walter Bradly says only 5–10% of ALS, AD, and Parkinson disease cases are due to inherited genetic mutations. Dr. Bradley, an ALS expert and former chairman of neurology at the University of Miami Miller School of Medicine wrote "Hundreds of millions of dollars have been spent looking for predisposing genes, but . . . there is really a need to concentrate much more on environmental toxicants,".

As has often been said proximity does not always mean causality. The jury is still out on this one. But play it safe and don't drink the water if there's a blue green bloom going on!

2 The website www.farmaid.org has some scary statistics on corporate consolidation in the American food supply sytem such as "In the seed industry, four companies control 50% of the proprietary seed market and 43% of the commercial seed market *worldwide.*" I first became aware of the issue when a neighbor growing grass fed beef told me there was an acute shortage of small butcher shops within a forty mile radius of his farm. The meat processing business was and continues to be a bottleneck for local meat production so much so that Cornell and others have helped develop mobile abattoirs for on farm processing that are often owned cooperatively by several farmers .

3 Adult humans convert about 5 % of the nitrates ingested with their food to nitrites. Babies convert them at a higher rate and can suffer from a blood disorder "blue baby syndrome". Nitrite is believed to be converted to carcinogenic nitrosamines in the body, but as is so often the case the epidemiology is not conclusive enough to link nitrates in water to cancer in water drinkers.

4 CAFO regulation of non point runoff – About half the pollution entering our nation's waters is estimated to be from non point sources. Yet the federal government still can't regulate CAFO's and so must rely on incentives and voluntary compliance to Best Management Practices. As of this writing there are carrots but no sticks it seems in the regulation of runoff. In 2013 a federal appeals court ruled that the EPA could not regulate CAFO runoff under the Clean Water Act.

"This court declares that the litter and manure which is washed from the farmyard to navigable waters by a precipitation event is an agricultural stormwater discharge and therefore not a point source discharge," Bailey wrote, "thereby rendering it exempt."

Chapter Four: Cow Power

1 *Indiana residents question Ohio manure imports By RICK CALLAHAN Associated Press November 26, 2010,*

2 from CVPS Cow Power FAQ report on line at
http://www.bluesprucefarmvt.com/elbo/assets/pdf/Cow-Power-QA.pdf
Central Vermont Power Service

3 Cornell study of bioreactors in Susquehanna preliminary study; Although nutrient concentrations and bioreactor performance results have varied from site to site, the average concentration for all six of the bioreactors for the past year of sampling data shows that the nitrate concentration was reduced by 50 to 60 percent, from around 9 to 3-4 mg/L (ppm). Phosphorous reductions were much less conclusive.

Chapter Five: Water and Power

1 The establishment of a park for the public good would seem to be an area precedent and early example of the concept of land held in public trust as a Commons.

2 Toxic waste sites around Niagara Falls Hooker and Love Canal.

An interesting article on the chronology of land transfers and responsibility for the subsequent construction on the Love Canal site is "The Truth Seeps Out" by Eric Zuesse published in *Reason* magazine in 1981. Zuesse looked up the deed of transfer between the Hooker Chemical Company and the school board and quotes the liability warning to the purchasers contained in the deed. *"the grantee* (that's the buyer)*herein has been advised by the grantor that the premises above described have been filled, in whole or in part, to the present grade level thereof with waste products resulting from the manufacturing of chemicals by the grantor at its plant in the City of Niagara Falls, New York, and the grantee assumes all risk and liability incident to the use thereof.* Zuesse also printed the last sentence of the deed "*It is further agreed as a condition hereof that* **each subsequent conveyance of the aforesaid lands shall be made subject to the foregoing provisions and conditions.**" explaining that this was to assure any future owner would also know about the buried toxins. It seems that somehow, unfortunately, this did not happen.

3 LOOW and present Chem Waste landfill portion of same; from a petition to DEC on behalf of several municipal entities re permits and approvals for the Chem Waste RMU 2 project expansion by attorney Gary Abrahamson posted on line at;
http://www.dec.ny.gov/docs/legal_protection_pdf/cwm00112petition.pdf

Chapter Six: Pipelines and Unconventional Oil Plays and the Lake

1 CCIW staff cuts; In remarks posted at the Council of Canadians website water rights activist Maude Barlow wrote that these deep cuts "threaten science education and the public health" and called the Canada Centre for Inland Waters "the most important scientific monitoring agency for the imperilled Great Lakes..."

2
http://www.ijc.org/php/publications/html/hamhar/hamharsa.html#hhaoc
In the late 1990s the harbor was in sad shape being highly eutrophic often deficient in oxygen and supporting an unhealthy and limited array of plants and animals. By 2006 the harbor was said to be half way towards its goals of 'remediation' by 2015 at a total cost of 1.4 billion. However, the second half of the clean up may take a little longer than

the first, and may well cost more than projected as it tackles more diffuse non point sources of pollution such as urban storm water runoff.

3 Corrosive impacts of dilbit; A 2013 study of pipeline safety done by the National Academy of Sciences for the government which critics said was little more than a literature review, concluded dilbit was no more corrosive than any other type of crude oil. However, a small study of heavy crude transport in California by the California State Fire Marshall's office completed in 1993 concluded otherwise. That study looked at the track record of pipelines moving heavy crude in California over a ten year period. It showed that pipelines operating in the range of 130°F to 159°F were nearly 24 times more likely to leak due to external corrosion and six times more likely to leak from any cause than pipelines operating under 70°F. The California study took into account other factors and found that regardless of pipeline age, coating, or pipeline materials, pipelines with higher temperatures had more spills due to external corrosion. The chemical reactions that corrode metal occur at a faster rate at higher temperatures. This is the temperature range used to transport dilbit.

4 Pipelines failures; The process of repurposing and or replacement of existing lines involves much less regulatory oversight than new construction. Existing pipelines that cross national borders like Line 3, can be repurposed to carry tar sands crude without any presidential or state department intervention. Enbridge has two massive lines that run parallel to the much publicized Keystone that it is re-purposing to carry Bakken Shale oil and dilbit. With little media coverage and far less regulatory red tape Seaway and Flanagan South will be able to move over two million barrels a day of either light or heavy crude from the western fields to the Gulf Coast when completed. Another line is being repurposed by Enbridge to connect to 6B, the infamous line that dumped dilbit into the Kalamazoo River, and then on to Line 9 sending Tar Sands dilbit oozing eastward with almost no environmental review or regulation.

However, the 'engineering' of doing such repurposing is not well understood. The dense heavy dilbit could subject lines to little studied issues associated with cavitation or possible harmonic vibrations. Some scary weld failures due to low frequency vibrations have been documented in high pressure natural gas lines. Given the lack of oversight of pipelines, this is not comforting.

5 Pipeline spill incidents information taken from *Leak Detection Study U. S. Transportation Dept by independent consultants Kiefner & Associates, Inc. Dec 2012 done for the Pipeline and Hazardous Materials Safety Administration (PHMSA)*
The study states; *there was a 57% probability of a spill costing a million dollars or more to clean up within a ten year period for a given pipeline based on the number of spills between 2001 and 2011.*

6 For more on the subject check out *Liquid Pipeline: Extreme Energy's Threat to the Great Lakes and St. Lawrence River by Maude Barlow http://www.canadians.org/sites/default/files/publications/GL-Pipelines-Final-web.pdf*
She calls the transport of heavy crude dilbit and volatile Bakken Shale Oil along with hydrofracking a *"threat to the Great Lakes that has not received anywhere near the attention or concern it deserves."*

Chapter Seven: Plastic Is Fantastic But Not In Food and Water

1 The toxins associated with bioaccumulation in fish that have resulted in consumption advisories on Lake Ontario today include dioxins, mirex, mercury, toxaphene and PCBs. Some of the persistent organic pollutants in lake sediments may take 15 years or more to break down. Bioaccumulation results in concentrations of toxins in higher levels of the food chain. While a diatom or algae cell might contain .02 ppm of a given contaminant each step up the food chain concentrates it ten fold. By the time the material passes to a top level predator it may have been concentrated a thousand or ten thousand times.

Some of the endocrine disruptors can cross the placental barrier and affect the developing fetus even at very low levels. While the concentration of many toxins that caused deformities and mortalities in fish eating birds in the 1960s have dropped off, 'new' pollutants of emerging concern like the flame retardants and pharmaceuticals, some of which may be toxic or have estrogenic activity, continue to contaminate the lake's food chains. Some of these contaminants are not completely removed by municipal drinking water plants.

2 Theo Colborn virtually created a whole new field of scientific study with her ground breaking work *Our Stolen Future* co-authored with Diane Dumanoski and John Myers and with her other publications. After she wrote a report for the World Wildlife Fund "Great Lakes Great Legacy" in 1988 the concept that chemicals like radiation, could impact the unborn became increasingly accepted. It was her Great Lakes research that first brought endocrine disuptors into the popular view. A Wikipedia article states *"Colborn's work has prompted the enactment of new laws around the world and redirected the research of academicians, governments, and the private sector."* The book *Our Stolen Future* has been called a logical sequel to *Silent Spring*.

The big idea that Colborn helped reveal is that very low levels of exposure to a chemical and the timing of that exposure during an individual's pre and post natal development could result in profound and lasting health effects even impacting the next generation. Before her work, the science of toxicology was (and is) focused on acute exposures and the rule was that as the dose increased the response would also increase. It turns out to be just a wee bit more complex than that. (Find lucid and detailed information on how chemical exposures in the womb and to the newly born may alter growth and development at The Endocrine Disruption Exchange website *http://endocrinedisruption.org)*

Colborn started her work career as a pharmacist. Later in life she went back to school and got an masters degree in aquatic ecology. She put her pharmacy background to work studying effects of cadmium and molybdenum exposures on aquatic insect nymphs. At age 58 she earned a doctorate with specialties in chemistry, toxicology and epidemiology. With a varied and interdisciplinary scientific background and work experience she was able to connect dots that others failed to see with her subsequent work. Long after she had written the Great Lakes report in 1988, she remarked on how the catalog of health effects of chemicals in that work "changed the world".

In addition to being a ground breaking scientist Colborn was also a tireless networker and advocate on behalf of the environment and the unborn. She worked hard to get the scientists out of the lab and talking to each other and founded a non profit The Endocrine Disruption Exchange (TEDX) to ensure that the area of study she began would live on after her death. And in her 80's she began investigations on the environmental impacts of hydrofracking that was then booming in her home area of Colorado. She continued to give lectures, media interviews, and to mentor younger scientists until her last days. She died in December 2014 when I was writing the first draft of this chapter. The formal obituary posted at The Endocrine Exchange website, states she died peacefully at her home with her family by her side.

3 *Why The Toxic Substances Control Act Needs An Overhaul, And How To Strengthen Oversight Of Chemicals In The Interim* by Sarah A. Vogel[1], and Jody A Roberts published May 2011

4 For a few ideas to reduce plastic trash try these places. *http://www.lifewithoutplastic.com/store/, myplasticfreelife.com* or do a search for others to find some good ideas. Nearly all the trash that goes "away" in our household is made up of packaging, a lot of it being mixed material stuff that uses more than one kind of plastic in the package. The mix makes it very hard to recycle. It has changed the way I shop.

Chapter Eight: The Great Atomic Lake Down In The Dumps

1 SEC special exposure cohort update; Additional Linde Plant workers were added in 2012 by the government in recognition of their right to compensation as a "special exposure cohort".

From a law office newsletter issued by the firm Lipsitz and Ponterio LLC *"the U.S. Department of Health and Human Services recommended to Congress, in April 2011, that the government establish a SEC[special exposure cohort] for Linde plant claimants who worked at the plant between 1954 and 1969. (In 2005, Linde Ceramics workers received SEC status for the period from October 1, 1942 to October 31, 1947. During this time period, the facility actively processed uranium ore for the Atomic Energy Commission.)*

We now have the pleasure to report that SEC status has also been recommended for men and women who worked at Linde between 1947 and 1954. Once this recommendation becomes final later this year, it will close the gap between the SEC for 1942 to 1947 and the SEC for 1954 to 1969, and establish SEC coverage from 1942 through 1969.

the above was posted at the law firm website in a 2012 newsletter http://www.lipsitzponterio.com/Publications/Newsletter/2012Winter/EEOICPAProgramExpandedforWorkersatLindeCeramics

2 For more information on the West Valley mess visit the archives of the West Valley Coalition at
http://www.fredonia.edu/library/pdfs/WestValleyguide.pdf
The library website states; "The Coalition on West Valley Nuclear Wastes (CWVNW) is a true coalition of concerned people from western New York and local, state and national organizations. The Coalition was formed in 1974 to study the reprocessing operation of the nuclear fuel and buried waste practices at the West Valley nuclear site. Their group presumes that concerned citizens can learn, communicate, and participate effectively in the nuclear and environmental decisions to be made for the West Valley nuclear site. The Coalition's monitoring, advocating, lobbying, litigating, and acquiring of scientific, federal and state government information on West Valley has been met with modest success over the years. The Coalition's efforts helped implement the West Valley Demonstration Project of 1980."

3 *Human Health Implications of the Nuclear Energy Industry*
find it at the website for Canadian Association of Physicians for the Environment (CAPE)
http://cape.ca/human-health-implications-of-the-nuclear-energy-industry-2/

Chapter Nine: Great Atomic Lake Power and Light and Heavy Water

1 U.S. Plant financial analysis; Alliance For A Green Economy did an analysis of the Ginna plant's financials after its owner Excelon asked for a hefty rate increase to cover the costs of operating the plant. They figured the subsidy would run about 216$ per customer for the duration of the contract. They also questioned Excelon's assertion that Ginna was essential to grid reliability because of a rising demand for electricity in the area. The Alliance notes that PSC documents show a drop of peak demand from 1752MW in 2011 to 1508MW in 2014. If the trend were to continue a couple more years (admittedly a decided IF) there would be sufficient electrical generation to meet peak demand without Ginna.

Alliance For A Green Economy ran their own set of numbers for an alternative to propping up Ginna that showed how a refit of homes with energy efficient appliances and a modest investment in increased wind and solar generation could create almost four times as many jobs over a ten year period than would be 'saved' by operating the nuke at less cost to the customers.(Home efficiency refits come in at a cost per MW saved of HALF that of the power plant production cost.) And perhaps the biggest plus for some of us who think about the future of humanity and the water it drinks is the fact that we would stop making rad waste and eliminate one more ticking time bomb on the lake shore.

Find the analysis here:

http://allianceforagreeneconomy.org/sites/default/files/Ginna_Economic_Impacts_January_2015.pdf

2 double standard for radiation risk vs toxic chemical risk=group letter to the EPA, August 2014

http://www.nirs.org/radiation/radstds/groupletter40cfr190f.pdf

The letter criticizes proposed changes to relax further regulation of radiation risks.

The EPA uses risk standards for carcinogenic chemicals typically set at a risk of an additional cancer in the population as between one in a million and one in ten thousand. However it derives a different risk analysis for radiation exposure called an "effective dose equivelent". Critics say this derived exposure is based on "subjective committee-defined numbers" and is "opaque" and is based on 'questionable science'.

And, critics say, radiation risk is underestimated because it is measured by cancer that results in deaths. Other EPA standards use the more 'sensitive' risk indicator of an induced cancer (which may result in plenty of misery and medical costs to the patient, but not outright death.)

A further criticism is that the EPA uses a standard 'reference man' (young male) for setting radiation dose limits. Most other toxin standards take into account gender and age (women and children are less tolerant of radiation)

3 tritium from a report prepared for Greenpeace posted at
www.greenpeace.org/canada/Global/canada/report/2007/6/tritium-report-canadian-facilities.pdf

Tritium Hazard Report: Pollution and Radiation Risk From

Canadian Nuclear Facilities by Dr. Ian Fairlie from the report summary; "Those Great Lakes with nuclear reactors on their shores have tritium levels 2 to 5 times greater than those of Lake Superior, which has no reactors. The tritium level in Lake Ontario is increasing each year, due to discharges and to major tritium leaks in past years from Candu stations. Tritium concentrations in drinking water, in air, and in vegetation and food near Candu stations are all significantly increased. These result in high tritium intakes in residents living within 5 to 10 km of Candu reactors and very high tritium intakes in residents who live within 1 to 2 km. However, because of tritium's very low dose factors, the radiation "doses" to those exposed are considered insignificant and are declared "within safety limits" by nuclear regulators. "

4 http://www.rachel.org/lib/cerrie_report.041015.pdf a report on the risks of "internal emitters" radioactive materials that are taken up and incorporated in the body's tissues from the government appointed CERRI that Fairlie served on.

5 alternatives to nuclear power; Dr. Mark Diesendorf author of the book "Sustainable Energy Solutions For Climate Change" in a presentation on line assumes that electricity will play a larger role in heating and transport than at present in a sustainable economy. He presents a model that uses heat pumps, biofuels for rural land transport and some air transport, and electricity for urban and inter-city transport. He also assumes a large role for high efficiency building construction like the net zero house I visited. Possible renewable sources of power generation might include geothermal and coastal wave generators, and key to the role of 'intermittent' solar and wind would be a smart grid. Dr Diesendorf and others have modeled hourly power demand scenarios using actual data and a 'smart grid' and conclude that on the rare occasions some additional power was needed it could be supplied by bio diesel fueled compression engine generators or gas fueled turbines.

The Smart Grid allows "demand management' where customers cut their usage when demand is high and supplies are limited. And Diesendorf proposes some of the cost of upgrading the grid could be paid for by dropping the many subsidies now paid to fossil fuel producers and users.

A number of other advocates have also pointed out that the old model of lots of excess power production sitting around on 'standby' is not only inefficient, but very costly. Even "base load" generators like nukes are off line about 10 % of the time. (Dairy digesters manage to hit 'design peak ' 75 to 80% of the time with absolutely no rad waste by product).

Chapter Ten: Reweaving The Lake's Web of Life

1 Back in 1998 some charter boat operators decided to reduce the cormorant competition for fish in the Henderson Harbor area. They went to the rookery island and blasted birds out of the trees stomped on eggs and killed over 800 'devil birds'. They believed the cormorants were eating juvenile smallmouth bass and other valuable game fish. The men were eventually caught and fined for their misdeeds. Many anglers supported the action and viewed the bird slaughter as an act of "civil disobedience" (the cormorant is a protected species under the Migratory Bird Treaty Act).

An article in the Smithsonian magazine from 2003 reported baseball caps printed with "First Annual Little Galloo Shootout" in Henderson Harbor. The birds are widely viewed as a scapegoat for the lake's decline in game fish abundance caused by many factors.

They do eat fish especially, in recent years, round gobies. Science suggests they eat what's available in the three to five inch size range. If the DEC has just dumped a lot of small trout in the shallows, then some of them get eaten by cormorants. Gobies are a mixed blessing for the game fish population. They are eaten by bass, but they in turn eat bass eggs. The true impact of the cormorant on the lake's game fishes is unclear at this point.

2 In one 2008 study published in *Canadian Journal of Fisheries and Aquatic Science* by Leslie B. Knoll et al inland lakes in Michigan that had zebra or quagga mussel populations had more that triple the amount of harmful microcysin toxins present. Other studies on Green Bay off Lake Michigan and elsewhere have also documented increases in cyanobacteria where large numbers of mussels are present.

3 Dekker W. and J. M. Cassalman (coordinators) 2014 The 2003 Quebec Declaration of Concern About Eel Declines Eleven Years Later-Are Eels Climbing Back Up The Slippery Slope? Fisheries

Chapter Eleven: The Lake and Climate Change

1 2015 *Unprecedented 21st Century Drought Risk in the American Southwest and Central Plains Drought Risk in Western North America."* A study on pending climate change impacts in the southwest and central plains from Science Advances, a peer reviewed online publication of the American Association for the Advancement of Science. Co-author Toby Ault is quoted in a Cornell University press release that the data indicate a high risk of an extended drought of decades duration in the south- west and midwestern plains (well within range of a Great Lakes water diversion via Mississippi).

2 Great Lakes water level predictions; Many of the past efforts to estimate future lake levels have used the Large Basin Runoff Models developed by Croley (1983); or Croley and Hartman (1984). Commonly cited projections that employed this runoff model indicated that, on average, future lake level are likely to decline on the order of 0.15m (0.5ft) up to 0.61m (2ft.)by 2050. But recent data after a couple of cold winters shows higher water in the upper lakes than has been seen in fifteen years. The great climate change experiment continues. A good guess is that water levels may possibly become even more variable in years to come on all the lakes.

3 *http://www.cias.wisc.edu/wp-content/uploads/2008/07/energyuse.pdf*
EPA's website on climate change and electricity production states that some areas in the Southeast and southwest are already putting plans for new power plant construction on hold partly because of water constraints.

Hydroelectric power plants are sensitive to the volume and timing of stream flows. Along the Colorado River, a 1% reduction in stream flow can reduce electricity output by roughly 3%, since water flows through multiple power plants in the river basin.

Chapter Twelve: Commons Comeback Could It Be Our Last Chance?

1 Mary Christina Wood -article on her work here

http://billmoyers.com/guest/mary-christina-wood/

2 Professor Wood states that regulatory agencies have failed us. They all too often have been "captured" by the industries. She writes, *"Humanity cannot hope for a livable planet if government agencies continue to license industries to pollute and destroy the remaining natural resources. Environmental law becomes profoundly relevant to the daily life and future wellbeing of every citizen alive today."*

3 David Moss Urban Water Utilities and Upstream Communities Working Together report posted at *www.watercommons.org*

4 Basic Right to Water- Detroit shut offs

In the fall of 2014 thousands of people had their water shut off in Detroit. For various reasons water rates had gone up to about twice the national average (aged leaky pipes being part of the problem, the city's bankruptcy agreement being another). According to news reports posted on line the shut off brought UN scrutiny to the city and a public hearing at which one resident (who had been paying her bills) said her monthly charge went to 600 dollars after neighbors started using her outside faucet. The UN declaration does not say water must be free or that it be used unwisely and indiscriminately. But it would seem to be a good effort to achieve some sort of balance in a world badly skewed towards profit. As of this writing the situation was as yet unresolved. And America does not recognize water as a basic human right.